HV
5293
M67
A35
1985

Moran, Meg——

Lost years

D1006730

	DATE DUE		

LOST YEARS

17⁰⁰

LOST YEARS

Confessions of a Woman Alcoholic

Megan Moran

DISCARDED

EL CAMINO COLLEGE LIBRARY

DOUBLEDAY & COMPANY, INC.
GARDEN CITY, NEW YORK
1985

HV
5293
M67
A35
1985

Library of Congress Cataloging in Publication Data
Moran, Megan.
    Lost years.
        1. Moran, Megan.   2. Alcoholics—United States—
Biography.   I. Title.
HV5293.M67A35   1985   362.2'92'0924 [B]
    ISBN: 0-385-19293-2
    Library of Congress Card Catalog Number 84–18850

Copyright © 1985 by Megan Moran
ALL RIGHTS RESERVED
PRINTED IN THE UNITED STATES OF AMERICA
FIRST EDITION

6-16-86 — MW—36129

In memory of the founders of Alcoholics Anonymous,
with deepest gratitude.

In memory of my father, with love, understanding and peace.

For my husband, with all my love.

Author's Note

In upholding the tradition of anonymity of the program of Alcoholics Anonymous, *Lost Years: Confessions of a Woman Alcoholic* has been written under a pseudonym. The author owes a great debt of gratitude to Alcoholics Anonymous and has tried to remain true to the principles of that program in writing this book. All ideas and opinions presented in *Lost Years* are the author's and they have not been sanctioned or authorized by Alcoholics Anonymous. The author has attempted to present an honest picture of Alcoholics Anonymous and sobriety in the hope that this book might help a suffering alcoholic.

LOST YEARS

PROLOGUE

I love this beautiful old crystal wineglass. It was part of a set—a birthday present from college friends some years ago. Now there's only one left. I just don't know how the others broke. I've tried to take especially good care of them. At least I still have one, and one is all I need.

I'm glad to have this full half gallon of wine. I don't want to go out tonight. I want to relax, have a few quiet drinks and curl up with a good book. Thank God for my wine. It's so delicious.

I think that I used to have lots of friends. I did things. I went out. I never got very many phone calls in an evening, but I certainly had more than I've had in the last two months. The phone hasn't rung. Nobody has called me. Not even my mother. I haven't even had the luxury of not answering a ringing phone. Where have they all gone? Do they think I've moved away?

They don't care. I've known that since the very beginning. That's why I'm happiest home, alone, on nights like tonight with my crystal glass and chilled white wine. This really is much nicer and more private than getting dressed and sitting in some bar or restaurant. I just wish I had some scotch tonight. Sometimes the wine lacks punch.

I've made lots of wishes in my life, many more important than wishing for a bottle of scotch, although scotch, at times, can be an important wish. I always wish for a man, and whenever I get one he's the wrong kind. I really wish I had that warm, soft, loved feeling in my heart.

My secret fantasy is to contract a terrible, fatal illness and have thousands of visitors come to my hospital bed to apologize for not loving me enough. It would be worth it even if I had to die after-ward. I just want one moment of feeling loved.

Please, bottle, last for the rest of the night. I don't want to get dressed and go out again. I'll measure what's left and see if I can make it . . . Three full glasses. That's probably just enough—but what if I don't fall asleep right away? What if I wake up in the middle of the night scared and shaking? I always need a drink then to calm down. All this back and forth to the liquor store is tiring and annoying. But I don't dare order a case of wine because then the liquor store people would know that I drink too much. They know I live alone. They'd put two and two together.

O.K. I've got my boots on and a belt around my nightgown, holding it up under my trench coat. I'll have to go to that liquor store over on First Avenue because I haven't been there in a few days. I'd better hurry, only ten minutes till closing. Walk faster. Oh no, they're putting the gate down. Run. Run.

"Wait! Wait!"

"Sorry, lady, we're closed."

"Listen, my watch says there are three minutes until closing. Just give me a bottle of white wine. That's all. I don't even have to come in."

"But lady, the cash register is empty."

"Well, here's five dollars, keep the change."

"O.K., lady, wait here."

Thank God. Thank God. Thank God. I should have told him I was having a party and we ran out, or something like that. Well, I'm sure he didn't think it was just for me alone. I'm a little hungry. I think I'll get a slice of pizza for the walk home.

Goddamn pizza. Always makes me vomit. Bad stomach. Always throwing up. I never get to eat dinner anymore. So who cares?

Where is my love? Where are my friends? Where's Mommy? Daddy, don't be dead anymore. Come back. Nobody loves me. I miss you. There's a hole in my heart. It's goodnight time. Sleep is coming. Goodnight, damn world. I hate you and I'll show you all someday.

Good. The room is spinning. It won't be long now . . .

THE BOTTOM

Eight A.M. Another day. Another damn day. I'm late again and I can't get out of bed. I can't lift my head off the pillow, my eyes burn, my mouth is parched and the taste in it is making me sick. The nausea overwhelms me and I lurch for the bathroom, two long rooms away. My head is pounding and my stomach is retching. I make it to the toilet and vomit up my guts.

It feels as if my insides are being ripped out of me. Not just the vile contents of my stomach, but my stomach itself. And my heart—and worst of all, my soul. There's nothing left inside other than last night's half gallon of wine. There's no life anymore. No feelings. No spirit. No person. I am a container for my booze. Without my booze I don't exist, but because of it I'm dying, and I'm only twenty-seven years old.

How can it be all over for me, my parents' lovely, perfect little daughter—career woman, with a promising future as an editor with one of New York's most prestigious publishing houses? I'm achieving everything I've always wanted but it's not enough. It's never enough. Never enough booze, never enough love, never enough recognition, and certainly never, never enough happiness. I'm alone, I'm lonely, I'm unhappy and sick and my life just isn't worth it anymore. Clutching the toilet bowl at 8 A.M. on June 10, 1980, I know that I can't deliver anymore. There's not going to be a future for me because I can't fake it. The jig is up. I have no reason to keep living. All that I look forward to is my next drink—and my next drink always makes me sick.

After making love to the toilet bowl, I'm starting to come to life. Next, it's into the shower to stand under the hot spray for as long as possible, soaking my parched body inside and out. It's never long enough. I can still feel the dehydrated tissues of my brain cracking. Before brushing my teeth, which is too great a shock to this mouth under siege, first I'll drink some chocolate milk and take some aspirin. Then I'll brush. Now some more liquid. More milk, never coffee. Coffee is deadly on a hangover as bad as this one.

Every morning for the past year has been this way and I know if I didn't drink until I passed out every night, I wouldn't feel this bad. But I need to drink, to relax from the pressures of my job, to fill my empty evenings, to help myself feel better and less lonely and unloved. It doesn't work—and today is the beginning of another uphill battle. It's an eternity from now until lunchtime but I have to keep moving and pull myself together. Somehow I have to make it to the office, hide my bloodshot eyes and hang on until I can leave the horrors of the morning behind and pick up that first redeeming drink of the day. That cool, glorious drink that goes straight to my head and takes all my pain and fear away.

I don't know when it all went wrong. I can't point to a day, an incident, a time, when my life started falling apart—when dreams turned into nightmares. It seems as if it's been forever that mornings have been full of sickness, fear and despondency. I never wanted to die. I've never considered suicide. I've always wanted a happy life; in fact, happiness has been too important to me. I've searched too hard for the perfect feeling and I've become more and more convinced that I'll never find it. I'm lost, desperately lost. I don't want to die, yet I can't bear living this life.

I remember one perfect moment at age eighteen when I was

deciding about college and anticipating my freedom as an adult. It was a crystal-clear spring evening, stars were shining in New York City and I was looking out to my future. I couldn't see anything; the future was vast and wide open and, at that moment, I was sure that life was going to be a glorious adventure with endless possibilities. And now, less than ten years later, it's just about over for me. I feel cheated because it's all so ugly now. Am I fated to die young and lonely and desperate?

When I was young, my father told me that I was blessed when I was born. "Your Irish freckles are angels' kisses," he said, "and you are going to have a special life."

I always believed that, and when I was told that I had a guardian angel sitting on my right shoulder to take care of me, that angel became my friend all through childhood. I talked to my angel and he protected me at night from the dark. Why do guardian angels leave us when we grow up, just when we need them most?

Last night there was no angel to protect me. When I closed my eyes to go to sleep, the ugly voices came, yelling at me, telling me bad stories. Even with the light on, they came to torture me, so I had to get up again and have some more wine to get rid of them.

Last night was like so many other nights of this past year. About twice a week and then again on weekends, I meet my friend Barbara for a drink. Barbara is the only person I can drink with now. She is as unhappy as I am and she drinks the way I do. I've known Barbara all my life. Barbara is tall, thin, blond and beautiful. I'm average height, brunette, freckled and overweight but I've always felt shorter and dumpier than I really am when I'm around her. When we're in a bar together someone is always trying to pick Barbara up and, of course, it makes me feel worse than I already feel.

But Barbara and I stick together. In some strange way we need each other although we hardly enjoy being together. Last night's ritual in our local East Side hangout began with Barbara explaining why she was only having one martini.

"Just one martini tonight because the taste is so exquisite. One tonight as a treat, then I'll switch to white wine."

This is part of our ritual, explaining our drinking. My explanation followed: "I'm off scotch, except for very special occasions, so I'm starting with white wine."

If she sounds ridiculous then I must sound just as bad. Lately, Barbara has begun counting her drinks. It's so goddamn annoying, her telling me she only had two glasses of wine last night with dinner and then insisting that all she's having tonight is two glasses. She's trying to make me feel that I drink more and that she drinks this much only when she's with me. I can't handle it so I tell her how little I'm drinking. It's boring, depressing conversation. In between counting our drinks, we recite our current woes. We need these drinks to wind down, we tell each other, after the shitty day we had. Because of the shitty lives we're having. Five drinks later, we say goodbye—kisses and hugs. Home to have dinner, write letters, do our nails and into bed early. We both know we're lying; I haven't written a letter in two years. I'm getting away from her so I can finish my drinking in peace.

Safely in my apartment, door locked, into the fridge and there's the wine. But not enough for the rest of the night, so out I go again, across the street to the liquor store.

"Hi, Megan, how's the publishing business today? Another half gallon of cold Folonari?"

I realize that I bought the last one just last night, so I need a story to go with this trip.

"Oh, no, thanks, Jim. I have plenty of Folonari, but it's a colleague's birthday tomorrow and I thought I'd get him a good bottle of wine. What do you suggest?"

"This year's Beaujolais. How about a bottle of that?"

"Beaujolais, terrific! Could you do me a big favor and gift wrap it? Thanks."

"That'll be six thirty-five."

"Here's a check for twenty dollars. I'm low on cash."

I'm always low on cash. I had twenty dollars tonight and now it's almost gone. Somehow I'll have to cover this check tomorrow.

That was close. I locked myself back in the apartment and opened my gift-wrapped bottle of Beaujolais. Drink slowly, Megan, this is it for tonight. I put a frozen dinner in the oven, then forgot about it. I started reading some book proposals, sipping my wine, then I decided to make a few phone calls. That's when my real trouble began.

Why is it that whenever I have a few drinks I decide that I need a big sister to confide in when all I have is a younger sister who doesn't have a clue about me? I call Peggy anyway. I call her too much. She's beginning to bug me, telling me I'm drunk and preaching to me. Maybe I need the preaching, maybe I want some help, but why turn to Peggy? She's a housewife, uneducated, hooked on the soaps, and she spends the day clipping coupons and doing laundry. She doesn't know me or understand me, drunk or sober. Calling her is a big mistake. We've never agreed on anything in our entire lives. We can't talk to each other for more than five minutes without fighting. But she's the only sister I have and sometimes I just need to fight with her.

"Peggy, this is Megan. What's new? Oh, I had a miserable day, then I met Barbara for a drink and you know how depressing she is. I feel rotten. No, I'm not drinking. I told you, I just had *A* drink with Barbara. Dammit! I'm not drunk. I don't know why I bothered to call you. Just forget it!"

As usual, a friendly chat with my sister became World War III in thirty seconds. I don't need her anyway. I'm going to call Mark and tell him what I think of him and his new slut girlfriend. . . .

I woke up later, it could have been ten minutes or two hours, and the phone was off the hook. Oh, God, who else did I call? Who did I beg to help me? Why can't I just stay off the telephone? Nobody ever calls me, so I should stop calling them. They must all hate me.

I'll put the TV on and have some more wine to help me sleep. That's it. Time for sleep. But the voices are back, they're torturing me. I need to put the lights on and have another sip. It's O.K. now, Megan, go to sleep. I finished the bottle and passed out. And I woke up to another damn day.

"Joan, please order me up a roll and chocolate egg cream and hold my calls until I finish my breakfast." I breeze by my secretary trying to assume a harried and extremely busy air when all I'm really doing is making a mad dash for the office so I can close the door. Joan is quicker than I and she catches me.

"Megan, the chief is looking for you. He's been here three times since nine-thirty and he wants you to call the minute you get in. Something about joint strategy for today's publishing meeting."

"O.K., I'll call Charlie, but please don't let any other calls through. I've got to get this publishing proposal finished." I shut the door.

What I've got to do is try to get some makeup on and pull my hair into a braid. I look like hell. I always look like hell and my mother still lies to me. She insists I'm beautiful. If that's the case, why weren't the men on Park Avenue doing double takes to catch a glimpse of me instead of mowing me down to steal my cab? They weren't looking at me because there's not much to see. I abandoned my contact lenses today, the contact lenses that my mother bought me a year ago to make me even more beautiful! I only wear them for her now because I can't get them on in the morning. My eyes are too red and raw and burning. They need Visine and sunglasses instead. I know that Mom's partially right and I do have some good features, but I can't feel beautiful. I can't even attempt to look attractive. I feel so disgustingly ugly and as I fought for that cab on Park Avenue, I knew I looked as bad as I felt. My clothes are expensive but the black linen pants suit with the elastic waist was purchased to hide my swollen body. I can't lose weight because I can't diet. I can't diet because I can't stop drinking.

I'm safe now. I'm locked in my office and the worst part of the day is over. Only two hours left until lunch. If only I didn't have to take the damn elevator up these nineteen floors. I don't understand why my heart stops and panic sets in when the doors close and the car shoots up. From now on, I won't ride it alone. It's bad enough that I had to give up the subway, but I just can't see myself running up and down nineteen flights twice a day. Sometimes I feel like a frightened little animal.

"Charlie, it's Megan. Listen—I worked at home all morning finishing the proposal. I'm just tying up the loose ends now and we can get together in about an hour to go over it. Don't worry, Charlie, it's perfect as usual. And yes, good morning to you, boss."

Thank God I finished the publishing proposal yesterday because I can't even focus on the words in front of me. In an hour, after my breakfast and my morning Coke disguised in my coffee cup, I'll be able to handle Charlie and even the art director.

If I make it through today then I'll make sure that tonight is different from last night. I'll go home after work and pamper myself. I'll take a bubble bath and do my nails and set my hair and watch TV. I'll drink tea and eat dinner—and I won't drink.

The intercom interrupted my evening planning.

"Megan, John Weldon is on the phone. I told him you weren't taking calls but he insists that it's urgent. Can you talk?"

"Oh God . . . Yes, Joan, I'll take it."

"Hello, John."

"Hi, Megan. How about drinks and dinner with your favorite former boyfriend tonight?"

"Well, tonight I really need a quiet night at home. Can we do it tomorrow night?"

"This is my only night in town, babe, and I'd love to see you."

"I just can't tonight."

"Please, Meg, I won't keep you out too late."

"Well . . . O.K. I'll meet you at the Oak Bar at six-thirty."

"Great! See you later, Megan."

Oh God, I can't believe he called. This has to mean that he wants to try again. Look at me! I can't meet him looking like this. I'll have to run home later and change and try to get those lenses in. This could be my lucky day. Maybe John Weldon is going to save my life after all.

"Megan, it's eleven, time for your meeting with Charlie," the ever-efficient Joan, my protector, is on the intercom, "and don't forget your twelve-thirty lunch at Nippon."

I'm living for my twelve-thirty lunch. How could I possibly forget it? It's lunch that keeps me going through the morning and sets me up to make it through the rest of the day. It's not the food at lunch, it's those wonderful first drinks of the day. I have a large stable of lunchtime foils and my calendar for lunch is booked three months in advance. Sometimes my lunches are friendly, but mostly they're business with the occasional friendly business combination. I've managed to find all the big drinkers in publishing and cultivated relationships with them. Lunch has kept me going in my profession. I'm good at it because I need it, and after a few drinks I've been lucky enough to do some smart business. I'm always early for my lunch dates, so that I can have my first one in peace and stop my hands from shaking.

On the rare occasion that I find myself without a lunch date, I go "shopping." Sneaky women can get drunk at lunchtime in Bloomingdale's, and that's one of my great discoveries. I can't drink alone in a bar in broad daylight because I can feel my desperation showing. It says I need that drink. So I go "shopping" instead and stop for a "bite." I don't want to face the truth. I must keep it at bay as long as I can.

Lunch today is with one of my favorite book review editors, a friend from my days as a publicist. It certainly doesn't hurt an editor to keep in touch with reviewers, so lunch with Ralph is business as well as pleasure. Ralph fills me in on all the hot gossip at "the rag," his name for the country's most prestigious book review. I plug a few of my current books and get some tips on who's going to be the critics' next literary darling. And to top it all off, Ralph loves to drink. In fact, he's the only person I've ever had lunch with who drinks more than I do. I try to keep up and I stay at a good fighting pace, but he always manages to beat me by one. I love Ralph. He enjoys lunch and doesn't pretend that he's got a two-drink limit. His lunchtime motto is "No bullshit, more booze." What luck that I found Ralph in my early days in publishing because now I can always count on him for a delightful lunch.

But today's lunch was a trifle too delightful. I'm drunk and I have a publishing meeting in half an hour. Time for the cold water, coffee and mouthwash.

Into the bathroom with my repair kit, I just hope I can have five minutes in peace. I hope Martha, the dragon lady and sales director, is finished with her after-lunch pee. She's the only person I can't face right now. Well, I'm safe. The bathroom is empty and with a little work I can at least look sober. The coffee will help me to act sober and might keep me from telling all the sales executives in the meeting to go to hell.

"Yes, Charlie, I'm all ready. Pick me up and we'll go in together, and together we'll introduce this decade's most important new novelist, whatshisname! Just kidding, darling."

It's true that God takes care of drunks and little children. They loved me this afternoon. I was brilliant. They all want to read the manuscript, even the dragon lady. And Charlie was beaming at me with those eyes he reserves for senior editors. I can feel the promotion. After lunch everything looks 100 percent better than in the morning. I'm O.K. I don't have to stop because I'm brilliant when I'm drunk.

It's almost five and I just have time to fly home, change and meet John at the Oak Bar. I feel good today and I bet I'm going to have good luck tonight.

John Weldon is a masochist's dream. He's handsome, well bred and a perfect gentleman—otherwise known as a real heartthrob. Trouble is, he knows it, likes it and uses it. And I fell for it all in a very big way. John and I worked for the same company but we didn't start seeing each other until after I started working elsewhere. One of John's big lies was "I don't date women I work with." While we were going out, he was sleeping with two women he worked with; maybe "sleeping with" and "dating" are two different things in his mind. He was dating me and sleeping with them.

My first date with John was not really a date at all. I had been working on a dance book before leaving the company and the author invited me to bring some friends to a disco party at Regine's. His editor, Carla, was a friend of mine and she was interested in Dave, another co-worker, so I invited them both and was planning on making a big match. Unfortunately, Dave had the hots for me and I had to dodge him all night. John was invited to make it a foursome. I hadn't really paid any attention to John and that night I was just looking for a dancing partner. For some reason I was on a hiatus from romance, and John found that very attractive. We danced and drank the night away. The more I drank, the more interested I became. We wound up carrying each other home and falling into bed. I was surprised when the next day I decided that I wanted to see him again. He wasn't my typical drunken one-night stand. John was different. John had real potential. And that was my first major mistake.

John should have been born a Kennedy. I know that secretly he wished he had. He was from Massachusetts but he was only half Irish and half Catholic. He went to the right prep schools and college but he doesn't have a pedigree, and I think that's his greatest disappointment in life. I was attractive because I was Irish and Catholic, I went to the right schools, but unfortunately, I didn't have a pedigree either. Part of John loved the romance of the working class and the other part was a total snob. Thus began our love-hate relationship that was a lot more working-class than upper-crust. Once I figured all this out on date number two, I should have made a run for it, but I wanted to be good enough, I wanted to make the grade. Needless to say, I never did. Drunken screaming brawls on Third Avenue didn't help me to get any extra points either.

Our evenings ended in two ways. Either we were drunk enough to jump into bed and have extremely fast sex or we were drunk enough to have a loud, wild fight about why we were not spending the night together. I should explain. When I say we were drunk, I mean I was drunk. After our first night together, when John matched me drink for drink, he told me that as a rule, he didn't get drunk with women —and from then on he didn't get drunk with me. He would only have two or three drinks in an evening, which didn't put a damper on my drinking, but I was less than ecstatic about it. I was looking for a drinking partner as well as a lover, and as time went on I realized that I'd gotten neither. John would tell me that he got drunk with the guys but I was suspicious of him and didn't believe that he was a real drinker. Since John would only drink two to my four, I got smart quick and started drinking before we went out. So I was always buzzed when the night began and blitzed when it ended.

I decided it was love. Why? Because on the outside he had everything I thought I wanted in a man, but the inside was, of course, a different story. John wanted no part of love, no commitment, no relationship, he didn't want anything other than an occasional dinner date and very occasional sex. I didn't know that he had other sexual outlets, as they are politely called. After two months of bad times, too many drunks and too many tears, it was almost over. Then my father died and John became the man I had to marry.

Marriage hadn't entered my mind until my father's death, but in my enormous pain I believed I could never be left alone again. I was so afraid of being alone that I decided I had to get married. Poor John. Now he was really in trouble but he stuck by me and saw me through months of grieving. No matter what has happened between us, I will always love him for what he did. He showed his true colors as a human being and he didn't leave me until I was strong enough to take it. That he left was inevitable. He'd been leaving me since our second date, and once I made him my lifesaver he had to go or be smothered by my neediness. But I begged and I screamed and I cried and I threatened and I fought and I drank and I drank and I drank. There was so much high drama all the time that I had no idea how I really felt. I needed to act out. I needed to be the center of attention. I felt I was having a nervous breakdown. The only thing that seemed to calm me down and take care of me was my white wine and I started drinking it every day.

So I don't need to see John tonight. My troubles started with him and they haven't yet disappeared. And I'd still change my entire life for John Weldon. I'd marry him in a second even though I know we'll always be bad for each other. He keeps coming back, messing up my life and leaving when I start needing him again. The real problem is that I let him. I continue to hope that this time it will be different.

Well, drinks seem to be going well. John is happy to see me and he lets me know it. "Megan, every time I see you, I wonder why I'm not seeing you. It's so good to spend an evening together."

This is it. This sounds as if he's coming back. This sounds like commitment and a move to Boston. Stay cool, Megan, and for God's sake don't get drunk tonight.

"Megan, let's go downtown and eat at Mary's to celebrate the reunion."

John leans over in the cab and puts his arm around me. I don't make a move, not yet. I need to hear him tell me how much he wants me.

"Megan, I'm so comfortable with you. I love having you in my arms."

That's not "I can't live without you," but it's close enough. I soften, I melt and the kisses begin.

The rest of the evening was a warm haze of red wine, holding hands and acting like lovers. After dinner, John suggested brandy and soda at a nearby jazz club. I was disappointed and then afraid. If he's keeping me out it's because he's not coming home with me. Oh God. The horror of it struck me so hard, I felt physical pain.

We had our nightcap and got into the cab. I couldn't bear the pain knowing that I wasn't ever going to get another chance to make him fall in love with me. I was drowning in the silence, so I confronted him.

"I've had a wonderful evening and I don't want it to end at my doorstep. Please tell me you're coming in with me."

"Megan, let's not ruin the evening. I have an early business meeting tomorrow and then I'm flying back to Boston. It would be a mistake to start something we couldn't finish."

"Boston isn't very far and, anyway, I know a beautiful finish for our relationship—"

"Stop, Megan. Please don't. Here we are. Just kiss me goodbye."

I struck him as hard as I could across the face and with a piercing drunken moan I walked away. I staggered past my building down to the corner bar and drank Martell's and soda until I couldn't remember where I was or why I was crying.

It can't be morning. I just went to bed. Oh, I'm sick. Why am I so sick? Think, Megan, what happened last night? It was John—he came and he left, again. And I wouldn't come home. I was afraid to come home with my broken heart. I went to Ryan's and I think I remember someone carrying me home. I'm a mess. I threw up on myself. I can't go to work today. How can anyone go to work with a broken heart? I need to stay in bed and try to exorcise John Weldon from my heart. I'm in too much pain to allow the rest of the world to exist. I'll call in sick and I'm sure it will be no problem after my terrific showing yesterday. Everybody gets a twenty-four-hour bug once in a while. Anyway, I am sick. I feel sicker than I've ever felt. I'm not sure I can talk into the telephone and I'm afraid I won't be able to get out of bed. Oh God, my stomach is cramping. I'm having a colitis attack. I need Maalox, I need aspirin, I need hot chocolate and a heating pad, I need clean sheets. I can't move. I need someone to take care of me.

The day was interminable. It was hours before I could move just to take off my dirty clothes. Now, at 7 P.M., I can take a bath, drink some tea and eat some soup for dinner. Tonight, I'm finally having a quiet night at home, and tonight I know that I can't handle a drop of alcohol. Because I'm so sick, I don't feel torn by the strong need for a drink. My body is fighting back and today, in a certain way, it's stronger than my mind.

I'm drinking too much and hurting myself. But I need to drink because the people I love always leave, and my bottle has stayed for the whole ride. It's all that's waiting for me on the blackest nights. The bottle takes its share too. For a very bad night, I pay with a very bad hangover. I wonder how many other twenty-seven-year-old women are ever chained to their beds for an entire day with a hangover that goes beyond being a hangover but becomes a sickness and a pain so devastating that movement is impossible. I think very few women. In fact, I think very few people ever have hangovers this bad, not even after New Year's Eve. So what's wrong with me? Why can't I stop? Why am I killing myself? Is it because of John, because of my newly broken heart? I don't think so. I think John is an excuse, just as being single in New York City is an excuse, just as a demanding job is an excuse. I have so many excuses, one for every night of the week, 365 days of the year. Nobody hears them but me. I don't have to answer to anybody but myself, yet I feel that I'm in a constant state of hiding out. I don't want *them* to find me. I don't want *them* to know. I don't want *them* to see what's inside. *They* are all out to get me—but *they* don't exist. It's just *me*. I know that I'm hurting myself very badly. I can't stop. I can't stop. It's all I've got.

"Yes, darling, it's a wonder what a day in bed and a good night's sleep can do. I thought I had a terrible flu bug but I woke up this morning feeling terrific. I'm so glad you called, and let's have lunch soon." I'm glad I got rid of that bitch. I don't need her first thing in the morning. Where is that secretary of mine and why isn't she answering the intercom?

". . . Yes, Megan."

"Joan, we have to get to work on my speech for the conference this weekend. Please block out an hour this afternoon when we can work without any interruptions. In the meantime, continue with the callbacks from yesterday and bring me up to date on submissions.

We're going to have to read a little faster around here, soon there's not going to be room in this office for my desk. Thanks, kiddo. I'm sorry to be pushing so hard today, but I have to catch up before I leave town for the conference. Oh, Joan, why don't you order us some lunch. That is, if you don't mind staying in . . ."

I feel like myself again. I've got energy and putting in a hard day's work is very refreshing after the days of trying to slide by. Since I feel so good, I'm not going to drink tonight. I want to get my health back so that I'm in terrific shape to go to the writers' conference in Boston. It's amazing, I'm in the mood to buy a book today. I'm even in the mood to talk to an author and, miracle of all miracles, go over galley corrections. I'm damn good on the good days. Trouble is there are too many bad days.

Buzz. "Yes, Joan."

"Megan, Charlie is on the phone."

"Megan, it's Charlie. Listen, I need your help this evening. I have a dinner planned with these two top cookbook writers. I'm trying to sign them and I know nothing about cooking. Will you please come along so there can be some intelligent food conversation as well as a pretty face? Dinner's at Lutèce so you'll be well fed."

"Oh, Charlie. I'm just getting back on my feet. But if you really need me . . . I have to go home and change first, so I'll meet you at the restaurant."

"Thanks, Megan. You're an angel."

Well, I'll just have one cocktail and one glass of wine with dinner. If we have champagne after, then I'll have just a taste. Just a little taste and I'll be O.K. . . .

What a superb night! What food and what extraordinary company! I hope that Charlie is planning on making me the editor on this cookbook project. I know I put on a terrific show tonight, and no matter how tough it was, I only had two drinks. Now I deserve a few at Ryan's with Maxie. I'll give him a call.

"Hi, Max, it's Megan. Do you feel like meeting me at Ryan's for a quick one? It's only ten o'clock and I want to tell you about the fabulous dinner I just had with my boss and the country's two culinary kings. Great! I'm on my way uptown now. I should be there in fifteen. See ya!" Good old Maxie. He'd come out at 2 A.M. on a Wednesday night for a shot.

Ryan's is my hangout. It was my father's hangout before me, but in the old days it was an old-fashioned male Irish bar. These days it's still a dive but the clientele is young and, for the most part, single. I feel at home walking into Ryan's, almost more at home than walking into my apartment. Ryan's has helped me to grow up. Since age sixteen, it's seen me through a lot of boyfriends and a lot of good times. When the times haven't been so good, the bartenders and the waiters watch out for me. They take me home when I've had one too many and they keep the creeps away when I'm sending out my "let's play" signals. I feel good at Ryan's. I belong there, they care about me and half of the time I drink for free. So there's no better way to end an evening than stopping at Ryan's and meeting Maxie.

Maxie is gay. Once he decided that he wanted to go straight just for me, but I talked him out of it. He's eternally grateful and we've been best friends ever since.

I like to drink with Maxie because he laughs a lot. Sure, he loves a good cry as much as I do, but for the most part he believes in having fun in bars. He also makes friends very easily and we're always being swept away by some "divinely rich fag" for a bite of late supper. Maxie also takes care of me. When I'm with him, I'm not allowed to be depressed and morbid, and I'm not allowed to pick up guys unless Maxie approves. Since all Maxie approves of is gays, I can't get into much trouble.

"Megan, darling, I'm over here." Maxie, of course, has commandeered two stools in the center of the bar and now he's jumping up and down, waving madly. As if I could miss him. No chance.

"Hi, love, that's very sexy leather but I doubt that anybody will notice here at Ryan's."

"Megan, you look divine. Black is fabulous on you! And your hair is billowing!"

"Oh, Maxie, you always make me feel like a million dollars. I guess that's why I never get tired of being with you."

"So let's drink, darling. I'm in a scotch mood, how about you?"

"Scotch would be terrific. I just sat through three hours of drinks and dinner and I nursed two drinks. Can you believe it! I'm so thirsty I think I need two quick ones to wet my whistle."

"My dear Megan, why did you suffer so through dinner? Why abstain, you can be a charming drunk. But then again, you can also get a teensy bit sloppy. So you were smart since you were with your boss and two luminaries. Tell me all about it. I have hours before the sandman arrives."

In telling Maxie all about my dinner, I was struck by how glamorous it really was. I joke about being in the glamorous world of publishing and still being unable to pay rent on my rent-controlled apartment, but tonight I really was enjoying the glamour. I had dinner at Lutèce, New York's finest restaurant, with two celebrities and the editor in chief of a major publishing house. That's impressive. And Maxie is such a perfect audience for the blow-by-blow. The food was divine and the company stimulating but it was such a struggle for me. This is the part that I refrained from telling Maxie. All I could think about for the entire evening was sticking to my two-drink limit, and when I finished my second drink all I wanted to do was get to Ryan's. I spent an hour and a half waiting to leave. I wanted a drink much more than the food and I would have bolted before touching my main course if I had been allowed to leave. It was very difficult remaining calm and charming and keeping the conversation going. I kept fading in and out. I was perspiring and my hands were shaking and I was afraid that I was going to burst into tears at any moment. I think I was feeling all of this because I needed a drink. As soon as I settled into Ryan's and began telling my story, it sounded infinitely more pleasurable than it really was. Something is wrong with me. I think my nerves are going.

Six drinks and two hours later, Maxie and I said good night. I promised myself that I would make it an early night, and I did. I was only pleasantly high when I fell into bed alone at twelve-thirty and my last thoughts before I went to sleep were how proud I was of myself for not getting drunk tonight.

This morning I'm not hung over! A little foggy with a bit of a headache, but I'm not sick. I don't have to throw up and I'm not angry that the sun is shining. I think I'll even walk to work. This is my last day before my conference in Boston and I don't want my nerves to start acting up. A brisk walk will do me good and I'm going to call Laurie for lunch first thing when I get to the office. She'll have some good advice for the weekend.

Why do I need everyone to tell me how great I am when I never believe them anyway? Where is my own inner confidence? I always have to measure my own success through someone else's eyes.

I read my speech to Laurie over lunch and, since she's a Dorothy Sarnoff graduate, she gave me some great pointers on delivery and poise. Now, on the train, I'm more excited than scared and I'm looking forward to a smashing expense-account weekend. I'm traveling by train because I'm a romantic and I love trains. It is so sophisticated sitting in the bar car sipping cocktails and sharing stories with my fellow travelers. Tonight my fellow travelers aren't doing much talking, except for the bartender who keeps threatening to proof me, so I'm keeping myself company with *Savvy* and *Vogue*. What a pleasant and civilized way to travel.

My hotel is the Ritz-Carlton and I certainly felt pampered upon checking into my room when I found a bottle of champagne and a basket of fruit from Charlie, my editor in chief, wishing me luck. The room is luxurious and I put the champagne on ice, ordered hors d'oeuvre from room service and drew a bubble bath. Now this is the life of a glamorous New York editor! Soaking in my bubble bath, sipping my champagne, I fantasized about the interesting men I'm bound to meet this weekend. Writers can be so sexy! And an editor is certainly going to be in demand.

I dressed carefully for dinner—in black silk to hide the extra pounds and accentuate the dramatic auburn hair; it's surely my best feature. After my makeup and sparkling fake jewels are on, I feel pretty attractive and ready to take the plunge.

The dining room is large and upon entering there's a long check-in table with agendas and name badges for all conference attendees. Once I checked in, I was delivered to the director of the conference, a fat unattractive male whose claim to fame was authoring twenty-

odd grade-B men's adventure books. My party shimmer started to
fade when it looked as if he was to be my escort for the evening, but
before long I was deposited at a table with a whole group of writers
and editors and the director disappeared. Luckily, on my left was
Mike Reed, a bestselling author and one whose last book I desperately wanted to buy. I was in the auction bidding for it until the last
moments when the price took a great leap upward and knocked me
out of the ball game. I was delighted to meet Mike and immediately
began plotting my strategy to get an early look at his next book.

Since I started the evening with a bottle of champagne in my
room, when I sat down to dinner I decided that it would be wise to
slow down and be careful, so I ordered club soda. After dinner I
decided enough time had passed since the champagne, so I began
drinking scotch and water. I timed my drinks because I wanted to
remain perfectly in control. The dancing began and Mike Reed and
I had a couple of pleasant twirls around the floor.

As the night progressed, Mr. Reed wandered off and found a new
and prettier dance partner and I became more and more wild on the
dance floor. If only they would all clear the floor and watch me
perform, was my secret wish. I stopped counting my drinks, having
lost my resolve somewhere in the scotch bottle, and I made a pass at
Mike. When he politely refused me, I got angry and became abusive. Mr. Reed was a perfect gentleman, so he led me from the
dance floor as quickly as possible and deposited me in my room. I
didn't remember anything else the next morning when I woke up
with a very big head and an equally large feeling of dread. It was two
hours before I was due to make my speech and I wanted to die. I
couldn't possibly face any of those people who saw me drunk last
night!

The phone started ringing, and out of self-defense for my hangover, I picked it up.

"Megan, this is Mike Reed. I thought you might not be feeling
terribly well and I just wanted to reassure you that all is O.K. You
were pretty drunk last night but I'm really the only person who
knows. I got you to your room before anyone else had the chance to
notice. So please don't worry, have some breakfast and knock 'em
dead this afternoon. I'm looking forward to hearing you. Bye."

"Mike, wait, Mike—" He hung up.

This wasn't the first time I'd made an ass of myself in my professional capacity. A few years earlier I had a hysterical crying jag at a publicity party for a football book when a leading NFL quarterback didn't fall madly in love with me over two drinks. I left that job and publicity a few months later. Too many parties and too much drinking in P.R. work. It was too dangerous for me. Now it looks as though editing is becoming just as dangerous.

I gave my speech that afternoon—sick, sweating and shaking. I skipped the evening cocktail party, opting to sleep off my hangover instead. I made a brief appearance at dinner, left very early and retired to my room and my bottle. The weekend had turned into a disaster. I was my usual self, either drunk or sick. Why couldn't I just be normal like everyone else?

Sunday morning I decided I couldn't take another minute of the torture so I packed up and left. I flew home instead of taking the train, and that was a mistake. In my state of hangover anxiety, I was paralyzed with fear that the plane was going to crash. I drank during the entire flight but the liquor wasn't working. It didn't help ease the anxiety. I couldn't relax and I couldn't get high. All I could visualize was my own death and, in a way, I wanted to die. It was getting harder and harder to face the mess I was creating every single day.

Needless to say, the plane landed safely and I ran for a cab to take me home where I could safely hide out. Then I realized it was Sunday and I had no booze left in my suitcase. Did I have any at home? I prayed and prayed that there would be a bottle waiting for me, but just in case, I stopped at the corner deli for two sixpacks of Heineken. Luckily, there was a bottle of white wine and a half bottle of scotch in the apartment. I started to relax, ran a bath and poured myself a tall one. The anxiety was diminishing but every five minutes or so I would run through the disastrous weekend. It was as if a movie was playing in my head. I couldn't stop it so I made my way through the scotch bottle, through the wine, and finally I passed out while I was working on the Heineken.

My life had become a series of escapes. I wasn't living, I was escaping. I escaped with booze, in the bars, in my apartment, behind my office door. I was involved in such complicated maneuvers to get my booze, to hide my booze, to get high, to hide myself from my co-workers, my family, my friends, the world. It was taking so much energy just putting the pieces back together every day. All I wanted to do was lock my door, stay in my apartment and drink. After this terrible weekend, I decided that weekends were going to be all mine—no commitments, no people, no bother, no controls. On weekends I was going to drink all that I wanted.

I approached the next weekend—my first free weekend—with the kind of excitement one reserves for a great vacation or a big New Year's Eve blast. I planned my drinking and all during the week I bought my supply at various liquor stores. I had to stock up yet protect myself from being discovered by the local merchants. Naturally, I was drinking all week so I wasn't putting aside as much as I planned. It was like filling a bucket with a hole in the bottom. By Friday, I managed to have three half gallons of wine and a quart of scotch. I was purposely going light on the scotch because sometimes it makes me very crazy. I bought another half gallon of wine and a couple of sixpacks on my way home from work, then I closed the door, locked it, took the phone off the hook and the party began. "Freedom!" I shouted as I danced around the apartment mixing my first few scotches and blasting the stereo. "Megan Moran is free at last from all those bothersome assholes who stare and stare and stare. Nobody can see me now. Nobody can give me that sickening concerned look. I can do whatever I want." So I stripped off all my clothes and paraded around naked—drinking, dancing and talking to myself. Friday night I finished off the scotch (bad planning) so that when I awoke sometime on Saturday I had to start drinking wine. I skipped dinner on Friday, so Saturday I decided to make myself some eggs and toast. I had some coffee and a glass of wine before tackling the breakfast, then dutifully I swallowed the eggs. They came right back up so I decided, "What's the use? I'm not going to bother eating anymore this weekend."

The rest of the weekend is a blur. I woke up periodically, not knowing if it was day or night, I'd drink some more and pass out again. On Sunday, with only half a gallon of wine and some beer left, I tried to taper off in order to prepare myself for the Monday morning blues. I set the alarm for eight Sunday night. I woke myself, showered, drank hot chocolate and ate toast until I began to feel slightly alive. Then I ate some soup and drank tea to try to sober up before going back to sleep. It was painful and I was so sick that all I wanted to do was pass out and not wake up again. I didn't drink for the rest of Sunday night and I fell back asleep at 1 A.M. Was there a chance that I'd be sober enough on Monday morning to put it all back together for another five days?

Not only was I struggling to keep it together after a weekend of round-the-clock drinking, now I also had to glue myself back together every morning of the week. Occasionally, I would keep myself from drinking for one day but that was the absolute longest I could go without booze. I would take that test on days when I was severely ill with a hangover and I knew it would be harder to get it down than to stay away. With all of this effort being expended to get my booze and hide my hangovers, I had very little energy remaining for anything else, especially work. I wasn't working, I was sliding by. Occasionally, I'd get lucky and sign a terrific book during one of my liquid lunches, and that would be good for six months' worth of effort. I'd gotten smart and because of my "heavy work load," I freelanced most of my manuscripts to outside editors. I could barely read, never mind edit. I knew it was only a matter of time before my work façade would crumble.

In all other areas, I had given up the façades. I decided it was time my life was my own and that meant no intrusions from the outside. I stopped practically all socializing. I would only occasionally meet a friend for drinks or dinner. I wouldn't go the movies or to the theater or spend Saturday afternoon bicycle-riding in Central Park. My college friends were, for the most part, wealthy and very social and I received many invitations to events and weekends away at summer homes or winter cabins. I turned all of these invitations down for one reason only: I needed to drink and I couldn't be in any situation that separated me from my supply of booze or easy access to it. So I accepted a few dinner dates and fortified myself liberally before facing anyone. I should have stopped socializing entirely because there was always trouble.

My last social event of the 1980 season was a dinner party of approximately ten college friends celebrating one close friend's visit to New York. The party was in a restaurant on the West Side and I had four or five cocktails on the East Side before venturing across the park. Everyone was happy and elated to be together and I couldn't stand being there—and I was in the midst of my closest college friends.

"Oh, Megan, it's so good to see you. I must hear all about publishing. It sounds so fascinating."

"Not really, Sally. I'm bored with it. Excuse me." So much for small talk.

I made my way to the bar, ordered a scotch and took it to the ladies' room. I sat there for ten minutes plotting to disappear from the party, but my pride wouldn't let me. I returned to the insufferable sight of smiling faces and warm hugs.

"James, I'm so glad to see you. It's been too long and I believe we have some unfinished business." I was impressed with my line. It was a straightforward aggressive come-on. James didn't buy it.

"No, Megan, that was finished a long time ago. Can I get you a drink?" With that, James the guest of honor left my side and we didn't speak another word all evening.

Finally we were seated and I ordered carafes of wine for the table. Nobody objected, so every time one emptied, I ordered a replacement. I kept one carafe of wine in front of me at all times and didn't let my glass empty. I heard nothing of the conversation. I was in charge of the wine and didn't have time to pay attention to anything else. The carafe in front of me started growing until it filled the entire table. I could see my friends' reflections in the carafe and they were laughing and talking and hadn't noticed what happened. I didn't say anything but I became terribly afraid that I wouldn't be able to lift the huge carafe when I needed to refill my glass. I grabbed hold of the person next to me.

"Greg, darling, would you please pour me a drink?"

"Sure. Here you go, Megan." Well, he didn't seem to have any problem lifting it. I'll have to try next time. Since I had Greg's attention he tried to be sociable.

"So tell me all about yourself, Megan. It's been four years since I've seen you. How's life?"

"Boring, Greg. Very boring." That shut him up.

I wanted to be invisible and at moments I felt that way. The rest of the table was very involved in conversation. Nobody paid any attention to the amount of wine on the table yet I couldn't focus on anything else. I felt invisible until each time I reached for a refill. Then I was sure that all eyes were on me and at least one person was keeping count of my drinks. "Why am I here?" I kept asking myself. "Why am I wasting my time with this vacuous group?"

The "vacuous group" used to mean a lot to me. They are warm, loving people who care about one another. I am an outsider only because I'm putting myself there. I'm shutting them out just as I'm shutting the rest of the world out. Why? Because I know there isn't anybody who can understand my pain and who can share my secret.

Ten minutes before the party broke up, after coffee and dessert, the last carafe was empty. I emptied it and as soon as I realized that the supply was gone, I panicked. I announced that we needed more wine—a toast for the road—and everybody disagreed with me.

"Megan, we're just about to leave. I don't think anybody wants more wine."

That's fine for you, Chris, you strait-laced shithead, but I'm not the only one. I can't be.

"Chris, darling, Sam wants to have a toast with me, right, Sam?"

"Of course, Megan. Waiter . . ."

Thank God for Sam. He always stands by me and takes me home when I'm too drunk to hail my own cab. It looks like tonight he'll have his hands full. I hope his stupid little blond girlfriend doesn't mind.

The carafe came. Sam helped me drink it very quickly as we said good night to the group. We were the last to leave and Susie, the blond, was a bit perturbed. Sam and I had our arms around each other, singing on our way to the car. Susie walked behind us. I decided this wasn't the night to take Sam to bed with me. After all, it had been our running joke for six years and I was enjoying the flirtation immensely. We kissed good night. Susie snarled.

I stumbled through the door. What else happened? Hopefully, I passed out immediately because I don't remember one more minute of the evening. I can't imagine that I had it in me to go out again or to start making phone calls. Whatever happened, I woke the next morning, half undressed, lying on the living room floor. The phone was ringing.

"Megan, this is Sally. How are you today?"

"Oh, I'm just great, how are you?" The ringing of the telephone had almost blown my head off but I wasn't going to reveal that to Sally.

"I'm surprised you're O.K., Megan. I thought you might be feeling the effects of last night."

Who does she think she is, calling me to check on my hangover?

"Oh, poor Sally. Are you feeling badly? I've heard that a raw egg in some tomato juice can help, but I've never really had to try those silly remedies."

"Cut it out, Megan. I'm calling as a friend. I watched you last night. You drank an enormous amount and still it wasn't enough. You insisted on that extra carafe and Sam helped you out because he felt sorry for you and was embarrassed for you. I'm worried about you, Megan, and I'm not the only one. You're drinking too much and you seem terribly unhappy—"

"Listen, Sally, nobody asked you to count my drinks and nobody asked you to call. Mind your own business and don't bother me again. Friends like you I can certainly do without!"

I slammed down the phone on my college roommate. "Damn her! Miss Perfect—plenty of money, the perfect man, job, clothes, summer vacation—and she has the nerve to tell me what's wrong with me. Damn her to hell! Damn them all! That's my last stupid dinner party. I should have stayed in by myself like last weekend."

Well, Megan, you always knew it was just you. Start accepting that fact and living with it. You don't need them. You have your own apartment—your hideaway from all the craziness out there. It's bad enough to be among them from nine to five, five days a week. The rest of the time you can stay home and have some peace and quiet. Home. I read somewhere that the condition of one's home is an outward manifestation of one's mental health. Help! Maybe I am sick.

But I'm working on it. I've been redecorating and painting my apartment for two years. I haven't made much progress. I really haven't had the time. Now if I stay at home more, I'll be able to finish the job.

I inherited a rent-controlled apartment on the Upper East Side from a great-aunt of mine. Most of my friends assume that a New York family apartment is a co-op on Park Avenue. Not so in my family. I inherited a tenement. I have three rooms—one bedroom, a living room, a kitchen and a bathroom I'm afraid to spend much time in.

My aunt believed in wall-to-wall carpet and flocked wallpaper. I've stripped the wallpaper and taken up the carpet. Under the carpet were ten layers of linoleum. I've ripped it all up and I'm left with wood floors coated with layer upon layer of old paint. They're an ugly dirty brown.

The walls have cracks and holes all over. White paint isn't going to make it. I now realize, a little late in the game, that my aunt knew what she was doing with the wallpaper.

My plan is to paint the entire apartment white. There's very little light so I want to give the illusion of light. I'm also going to sand the floors down to the natural wood. Everybody thinks that is a crazy idea, but that doesn't matter.

In the meantime, the apartment is a mess. I haven't washed the floors because it seems silly to wash them when they're going to be sanded. But two years have passed since I moved in and they're very dirty. I've painted half of the ceiling in my living room and one window. I'm trying to get the painting done but I can really only work for about two hours on Saturday and then I'm bushed. It's really too much work for a person my size. I don't have any curtains yet so I've hung sheets on the living room windows and an old bedspread across the window in the bedroom. I haven't built my bookcases so I have ten cartons of books lining the living room. It's dark and dreary and dirty. I don't have the energy to fix it. I know how I want it to look but I can't start the process and move from point A to B to C. I want to snap my fingers and have it all finished. I want a man in my life to finish the plastering and painting. That's the bottom line. Without a man, what's the use?

Obviously, my apartment *is* a true reflection of my inner self. My apartment is depressing and I'm depressed. My apartment is gray and I'm gray. There's no light in my apartment and there's no light in my life. Which has to come first, my overhaul or the apartment's?

If I fix my apartment, will I be fixing myself? Will I be making myself healthy and happy and whole? I don't think it's going to work that way. I get all geared up on Saturday morning to put in a long day of painting. I get all of the paraphernalia out, put on my favorite painting clothes, pop open my first cold beer and climb the ladder. Two hours later, when the first sixpack is finished, I'm finished. Somewhere during those two hours, drinking the beer became the main priority. It's so predictable and yet I refuse to see that Saturday after Saturday after Saturday it's sixpack after sixpack after sixpack.

Nothing changes. Life is standing still. The thought of fifty more years of this dreariness is frightening. It feels as though life is nothing more than a very slow death. It certainly isn't what I expected. I'm thoroughly disappointed but I see no way out. Love probably makes a difference in some lives, but love has escaped me. Instead of love, I've gotten pain and loneliness. What else is important? Work? Well, that's losing its sparkle for me. I don't have the energy to make the effort any more than I have to. I've lost the desire to go the distance for the book I believe in. The reason? There's not much I believe in anymore.

It's only slightly amusing that I've become a cynic. I once believed in it all—peace, love, flowers, friendship, dreams, beauty, marijuana . . . No more marijuana, no more dreaming. With the scotch comes the sophistication and the cynicism. I'm beginning to see that my feelings are coming from outside of me—first from the joints, now from the booze. That could be the problem but I think it's a lot more complicated than that.

Enough of this nonsense going out with old college friends. I know where I belong. Tonight, I have a date with a drunk. I mean a *real* drunk—the kind even I'm embarrassed to be with. But embarrassed or not, I'm going out with him. Why? He's a boor. He's ignorant, uneducated, has read nothing in his life other than the *Racing Form*, and he drinks more than I do. That's my only reason for having a relationship with Brian Murphy. I can't bear him when I'm sober and I hate him when he's drunk. He's disgusting. His whole body twitches, he drools, he falls in the gutter, he smells. I'm not like him when I'm drunk. He's a real alcoholic, I'm not. I only stay with Brian, whom I really despise, for two reasons: I can drink as much as I want and it's never as much as he drinks, and his behavior reinforces the lie that I've chosen to adopt: I'm not an alcoholic.

Luckily for me, Brian is not a violent drunk. He's mainly an isolated drunk. He goes on binges for two or three days and disappears. I don't mind his disappearances at all. The longer he's gone the happier I am. But still I sometimes receive the middle-of-the-night phone call to go and retrieve him from some joint—and I do it. I suppose I do it because it's more reinforcement for me. I will never reach his degree of alcoholism. I know this relationship is insane and only creates more chaos in my life, but for some sick reason I need it. I need to feel better than somebody. Sometimes I just stand back and watch myself go through the motions. Those are the times that I'm most afraid of my destructive behavior.

"Brian, let's go to that little Italian place on York Avenue for dinner."

"Anywhere you want, Megan. Just as long as I don't have to walk too far." Brian doesn't move unless he really has to.

I chose the Italian restaurant the same way that I choose all of the places where we dine. It's out of the way and chances are very good that we won't be spotted. I'm so ashamed of this relationship that I would never dream of introducing Brian to any of my friends and I'd die before I'd let him near any publishing colleagues. He doesn't seem to notice and he certainly doesn't care. He'd prefer staying in his apartment eating TV dinners and watching TV. We do that often enough.

"Megan, what are you doing spending time with me? I know you'd never consider marrying me, would you?"

"God forbid! What an awful thought! Strike it right away! I'm only hanging out with you, Brian, because you pay for dinner."

And that's a great deal of the truth. Brian is ten years older than I, from another generation where men paid for their dates. Although I'm a totally liberated woman, my finances are tight and I could use a free ride. Brian is the only man I've ever dated who has consistently paid for every meal. I'm using him for that as much as he's using me for companionship. I can't say he's using me for sex because most of the time that's impossible. I've discovered it's true that drunks are impotent.

While we're having our cheesecake and espresso with anisette, Brian lets me know his plans for the rest of the evening.

"Megan, I'm going to drop you at your place tonight. I'm not feeling well and I need to be alone."

"That's fine with me, Brian. I'd much prefer being alone tonight myself. In fact, I think it's time we ended this stupid charade . . . And listen, I know where you're going and I know your plans for the next two days. When the drinking is over and you need someone to drag you home, don't bother calling me. I've had it with that scene —and I've had it with you. There's no sense to this ridiculous drunken arrangement. I think I'll be better off drinking alone. So goodbye, Brian, and don't bother calling. I've never had anything to say to you anyway."

What a relief! I only hope this is the last time I make that speech. If only there were some way I could program myself *not* to call Brian when I'm drunk and desperate. Brian left and I jumped in a cab and headed for the West Side. Tonight's a night to drink out of the neighborhood, someplace where he can't find me. I wound up at Teacher's and found Barbara holding court over her martini.

"Martinis are just for weekends," she'll tell me, but tonight Barbara is a welcome sight.

She seems glad to see me but I wonder how she'll react when she hears I'm spending the night.

"Megan! You're on the West Side! I don't believe it! What happened? Did the East Side burn down? George, did you hear that, the East Side is up in flames, so Megan is here with us tonight to cool off. Bring my friend a Dewar's with a splash."

"Hi, Babs, you're in a very cheerful mood this evening. Or did I just luck out and arrive in time for the cheerful mood swing of tonight's drunk? I hope you already passed angry and depressed and cheerful is tonight's final stage because I'm looking for some light-hearted fun."

"Well, you've come to the right place. Megan sweetie, meet my friends George, Fred and Sammy. Isn't Sammy adorable! We've just been laughing the night away."

We continued to laugh and drink and drink and laugh. By the time I went home with Barbara she was beyond being interested in a male escort for the night, so my presence was welcome, especially since I was able to fit the keys in the lock.

We took ourselves to brunch Sunday afternoon, feeling hung over, of course, but pleased with ourselves that we'd had a "normal" evening. We hadn't wound up in bed with some strangers and we hadn't spent part of the evening drinking downtown in some waterfront bar. Last night we simply hung out in the neighborhood. We drank too much but that's O.K. because we didn't make asses out of ourselves. So naturally, brunch began with a toast to our good behavior.

Sunday brunch never lasts long enough. All too soon it's 6 P.M. and Sunday night is beginning. I have a long history of bad Sunday nights. In college it meant studying, and today it means the end of my round-the-clock drinking for another five days. One reason I hate to stop drinking on Sunday nights is that it feels so bad on Monday. Sometimes the best answer seems to be not to stop drinking. Don't let the hangover begin. Push it away with a little drink every couple of hours. I'm afraid to do that because I don't want them to find out at work and when I'm drinking, I can never tell if it's showing. My friend Jackie told me she has the same problem so she overcompensates. As a result, her husband always knows when she's drunk because she speaks veee-ry slowly. It's a funny story, but what's not so funny is that her husband left her. She says she's glad now because she can drink the way she wants without having to hide it, but Jackie looks terrible these days. She wants her husband back. She cries about him into her vodka. I wish she had him back too, because she was a lot more fun when she was sneaking a few on the side. Thank God I'm not married and I don't have to go through losing a husband and crying in my scotch. I have enough to cry about. The only thing good about being dumped is that it's a perfect reason for drinking. People drinking their way through divorces get away with a lot more than regular drinkers such as myself. Well, maybe someday I'll have the same opportunity. Right now it's time to wash and iron and do some reading for tomorrow's editorial meeting. What could be worse than a Monday morning editorial meeting? Having a hangover for the Monday morning editorial meeting. I'll stop drinking and start reading and if the fates are with me, this will be a promising manuscript, possibly a first novel destined to win the National Book Award. I need a little luck soon. Lately, my stars haven't been shining all that brightly.

They used to shine, didn't they, Megan? What happened? Why am I always asking what happened? Have I had such an awful life? When I feel alone and lonely most of the time, when the men I've tried to love never loved me back, when my only friend in the world is a bitch I know I can't trust, then the answer to that question is yes. What am I going to do about it? What can I do? I can comfort myself. I can find strength in my solitude. I can do without the rest of the world. I can have another drink.

I have to get away from the city for a while. Alone. I want to put the pieces back together. I want to feel strong and independent and self-sufficient. I want a week alone at the beach to read Jane Austen and Virginia Woolf, and thank God next week I'm going to have it. I didn't give Charlie much notice but I got such a deal on a beach house and I couldn't bear one more miserable weekend in the city.

This vacation is going to solve all my problems.

It's going to be a week of peaceful solitude, of reading and writing and contemplation. I'm going away alone for two reasons: I want to and I have to. I'm a woman alone with no lover, no protector and hardly any friends. I don't want friends. I don't need friends. I don't want anybody to see inside of me. Nobody has ever been able to fill my void. Nobody can care about me enough, nobody can love me enough—and nobody wants to.

The weather is perfect—hot and sunny—and I step off the ferry eager to begin my adventure. Maybe it would be different. Over and over I keep telling myself, "Megan, you're alone but you're not lonely. You're going to have a wonderful week. You're going to be renewed, you're going to find yourself and finally be happy." I believe this.

After settling into the big old comfortable house, I set out in search of supplies. A trip to the market for dinner and some staples and a trip to the liquor store for refreshments. I've figured out my drinking schedule perfectly: chilled white wine for the afternoon, gin and tonics for sunset cocktails, wine again with dinner and good warm cognac as a before-bedtime relaxer. It's so exciting planning my days, my beach time, my meals and my drinking.

I returned to the house just in time for the sunset cocktail. It all feels perfect and I'm happy. I have a chance. First I'll have two crisp and elegant gin and tonics, then I'll fix dinner and eat by candlelight. I'll chill a bottle of white wine to accompany my meal of broiled fish, fresh asparagus and warm French bread. It's darkening very quickly so I think I'll forgo my planned evening walk on the beach under the stars. After all, it's my first night and I'm a bit nervous of the surrounding darkness.

Tomorrow I'll get my bearings and the island will be mine. Tonight, I'll curl up and read until it's time for sleep. A couple of hours and a bottle of wine later, I head upstairs to get ready for bed. But the house squeaked and all the doors and windows make me uneasy and I wound up listening for the bogeyman. This won't do. I brought some cognac to bed and decided to sleep with the light on. After a while I passed out.

My first day on the beach, I feel white and fat, so I hide away from the crowds and watch the waves. I'm afraid to go swimming alone. I hadn't thought of this, but when I take off my glasses I can't see and I'm afraid that a shark will sneak up on me. So I take little dips at the water's edge with my glasses on. What a relief to get back to the house for lunch and gin and tonics on the deck. I wasn't comfortable at the beach, it felt as if everybody was staring at me. Nobody said hello or even smiled. I didn't belong.

By the third day, the ocean is no longer peaceful. It's too big and threatening. I'm afraid to go in and I feel conspicuous lying on the sand. I've retreated to my deck and my gin and tonics. I'm trying to feel peaceful and content, instead I feel sunburned and fat and lonely. Tonight I must talk to another human being so I'm headed for the local bar. A few drinks and dinner out is just what I need to perk myself up. It didn't happen. I sat alone on a barstool for an hour watching all the friendly people being friendly to each other. I was too embarrassed to sit and eat at a table by myself, so I left and returned to my dark empty house. Forget dinner, I drowned my sorrows.

For the next two days, I was drunk around the clock. I couldn't stand the torture any longer, so I left the island two days early. Back to New York, back to my favorite bar where people talk to me.

I didn't find myself during my summer vacation. I didn't have a moment of inner peace. But I'll tell some terrific stories about the benefits of a week alone in the perfect beach house, at the perfect ocean, on the perfect vacation.

I've barely been home for a week and tomorrow my brother Joe is coming down from Boston for the weekend. I haven't yet recovered from my fiasco at the beach and I just can't bear a weekend of people and partying. But I'll have to because I can't say no. It's not very often that Joe has a "free" weekend, free from family and business responsibilities, and he loves getting together with the old gang and hanging out at Ryan's. On second thought, maybe a visit from Joe will lift my spirits.

Sometimes Fridays feel as though they'll never end and this is one of those Fridays. I swear the clock's been stuck on three o'clock for the last hour. I want to get out of here. I can't bear another phone call.

Buzz. Somebody's reading my mind. "Megan, your brother Joe is in the reception area. Should I go get him?"

"No, thanks, Joan, I'll go." Well, at least Joe will get me out of here early, after I give him a tour.

"Hi, little sis!"

"Joe, have some respect for a working woman!"

"Come here and give me a hug. It's great to see you. You look fine but you could drop ten pounds and look even better."

"Listen, Joe. Let's not discuss my weight in the office. Wait until we get home and then you can pick me apart."

"Sorry, Megan. How about giving me the grand tour? I want to meet this editor in chief of yours. I've never met an editor in chief before."

"O.K., but promise you'll behave and not tell any amusing stories about me."

"I think you've got the wrong brother, Megan. Lead on."

When we arrived at Charlie's office, he wasn't on the phone. It was the first time ever that I'd caught him without the receiver stuck to his ear. Just my luck.

"Hi, Megan, come on in."

"Hi, Charlie. I'd like you to meet my brother, Joe Moran, from Boston."

"What a pleasure! Welcome Joe. Have a seat."

We bullshitted with the boss for half an hour. Joe was funny and charming and Charlie wouldn't stop singing my praises. At the end, he insisted that I take Joe to Rockefeller Center for a drink on him and he sent us on our way. Joe was very impressed, by Charlie and by me, so the weekend was off to a good start.

Drinks at Rockefeller Center led to dinner at P. J. Clarke's, then uptown to Ryan's to meet Joe's buddies. I could have begged off at this point but I was pretty high and I didn't want to stop drinking. We partied until 2 A.M. and Joe was up at eight this morning, out for a run in the park before his 9 A.M. baseball game. I was out of it, in bed until noon, and now I'm nursing my hangover for an hour before I have my first glass of wine.

It's Saturday. It's the weekend and I believe in brunch on Saturday and Sunday. If I don't go out for brunch, I have my own at home—coffee, a piece of toast and a glass of wine. If brunch in a bar is perfectly acceptable behavior then brunch at home is too.

After two glasses of wine, my hangover is gone. I've found the secret of the morning drink.

There is a big street fair in the neighborhood and I've spent the afternoon roaming through it, drinking beer. Joe came home from the park in the late afternoon and my sister Peggy and her husband, Tom, met us at the fair. Everybody was drinking beer, but they were just getting started. By six o'clock, I was already very drunk but I headed for the bar along with everybody else. I don't remember much of what happened during the evening but I became morose and decided to leave and spend the night with my ex-boyfriend, Brian the alcoholic.

I forgot to tell my brother that I was leaving and since he didn't have keys to my apartment, he was locked out for the night. This wasn't so terrible because he just went home with my sister, but today I'm embarrassed. Joe said, "No problem, I'm cool," and he was. But I'm a mess. I've been drunk for too many days in succession and I spent the night with a man I hate and swore I'd never see again. I'm in a great deal of pain. My brother saw this.

About half an hour before he was leaving on Sunday afternoon, Joe and I had our first and only heart-to-heart talk. Joe and I are not very close, there are years of sibling rivalry between us, but when he said, "Megan, you seem deeply unhappy. Is there anything I can do to help you?" I broke down and cried. How could he see through me? I thought I was keeping up a good front, but at that moment, I opened up to him and let him know that, yes, I was hurting. All I could tell him was that I didn't know who I was anymore, that I had lost touch. He never mentioned my drinking and neither did I—because at that point I still didn't know that drinking was my problem. We talked for a while and Joe suggested that I go to someone for counseling. Joe had been through a hard time recently and said he got a great deal of help from a priest in Boston.

After he left, I decided to go to a priest I admired—a very spiritual man who did more than preach Catholic jargon. His was the only mass I ever went to, when I went at all. I don't consider myself much of a Catholic, but I knew I needed some heavy-duty guidance.

This was at the end of my summer. It felt more like the end of my life. Talking to Joe made me realize two things: First, that I wasn't hiding it anymore. Second, that I needed help and I'd try to find it, but I wouldn't reveal my secret. I knew that drinking was the glue that was holding me together and no matter what, I couldn't let another human being (and certainly not a priest) know about that. If he could help me sort out the reasons why I was so unhappy, then I knew I wouldn't have to drink so much. But nobody could ever understand my relationship to my bottle and I was too ashamed and too frightened to risk anyone's finding out.

The bar is packed. It's Saturday night again. I'm alone because I'm trying to stay away from Brian. Every time I'm with him, there's trouble. I can't stand him, but I keep going back for more. Since I've talked to Joe and I'm trying to pick up the pieces and put my life back together, I know I have to stay away from Brian. He's a drunk and he's an embarrassment. No more. I'm on my own and that's why I'm here at Ryan's alone.

The real question is, why the hell am I here at all? After last weekend I should have quit drinking forever but that thought sends shivers up my spine. I've been better all this week. I didn't drink at lunch and waited until I got home after work to have some wine. It's eight o'clock Saturday night and I'm about to have my first drink of the day. I don't know why I'm playing this control game. I have no intention of quitting drinking. It's not my problem. Brian is my problem. I'm my problem. But white wine isn't my problem.

"Good evenin', Megan me darlin'. Will ya be havin' your wine or your scotch tonight, sweetheart?"

"Hi, Johnny, I'll have a glass of wine, thanks."

"I haven't seen ya all week, Megan, but I don't blame ya after last Saturday night." Johnny's laugh echoed through the bar and I could feel it mocking me.

"Listen, Johnny, don't laugh at me. I don't need you to laugh at me."

"Oh, Megan, I'm sorry. I didn't mean to hurt ya feelin's. Forgive me and you drink tonight for free."

"Well, I guess that's an offer I can't refuse. You're forgiven. By the way, it's over with Brian."

"Good. I'm glad you're ridda that bum. Ya can do much better. As a matter of fact, let me introduce ya to me friend Thomas. He's a college man—"

"Hold it, Johnny. I'd like to be single again for at least a week. I'll let you know when I want a matchmaker."

Ryan's is certainly not an official singles bar, but there is an unofficial scene going on here. Too many preppies are infiltrating the place and I feel like booting them all out. Ryan's should really be reserved for serious drinkers; that way we wouldn't have to line up four deep at the bar. Mr. Ryan likes the new clientele and he caters to them. They're rich and they travel in large groups so they're welcome at Ryan's. I, on the other hand, am not a very desirable patron. It's true I'll drink all night, but it usually only costs me five bucks. Ryan believes that sometimes the regulars have to get booted out. They expect too many free drinks. But Ryan likes me. He liked my father. I'm always welcome.

"Megan, you're drinking too slowly. Are you in mourning? Put a smile on that face and have a real drink with me." Ryan spotted me and now the scotch is being poured. What a relief! I'm getting so tired from so much white wine.

"Thank you, Mr. Ryan. It's always a pleasure to have a drink with you. To your health and happiness."

"Cheers and down the hatch. So tell me why the long face, little Megan. Is it your mother, money or a man?"

"All of the above and none of the above. I'm just not feeling good about life these days. I'm depressed and I'm bored and I'd like to trade myself in for another model."

"Forget all that nonsense and get yourself loaded. If you act happy, you'll be happy. So let me tell you a joke to get that smile working again . . ."

I guess that's why I'm here, to have somebody make me smile. Mr. Ryan is a sweetheart, but after two drinks I'm no longer laughing at his silly jokes. He doesn't mind. A cute blonde has just taken the stool on his other side—an ideal moment for me to "go mingle." Before I've said goodbye, Ryan is buying a drink for his new companion. The interesting thing about the man is that he always seems happy and perfectly content with his life. He loves the bar, he loves the clientele and he loves to drink. I've never seen him out of control or heard him utter an unpleasant word. I just don't understand how the man does it. He's been drinking in this bar twenty years longer than I have and he's still happy and healthy. I feel like shit, physically and emotionally, and "fun" just no longer exists. But I keep trying, so I move down to the other end of the bar to find the good times there.

"Hey, Megan, come on over and have a drink with me." Paul, my high school sweetheart's best friend, is waving me over. I guess I'll say hello but I won't spend much time with him or I'll start crying into my scotch over Ben, my lost high school love.

"Hi, Paul. I should have known you'd be here on the lookout for new arrivals. Did you see Ryan's new companion? She hasn't been here before so you might be able to convince her to have a drink with you! But for now, you're stuck with me."

"Listen, you little wise-ass. I am not on the prowl twenty-four hours a day, seven days a week—"

"That's right. A person has to sleep sometime!"

"Cute, Megan. Cute. End of picking on poor Paulie. What's your pleasure and how the hell are you?"

Johnny, the bartender, brought the refills and I ordered a hamburger and Paul and I started catching up. He's a terrific guy, very handsome, athletic and funny, but also very shy with strangers. As a result, one of the Upper East Side's best catches rarely has a girlfriend. I tease him and he teases me and, underneath it all, we're old and dear friends.

"Paul, it's so good to relax with you and talk about old times."

"I feel the same way, Megan. In fact, I may feel just a little different—like, I'd like to take you home for a nightcap."

"Oh, Paul, that will ruin a perfectly good friendship. Let's have a few more drinks before I say good night."

"Forget it, Megan. I don't want a few more drinks. I've had

plenty and so have you. I'm leaving and I suggest you do the same before somebody else *has* to take you home."

"Goodbye, Paul. I take care of myself. I don't need your suggestions."

Paul left and I had one more for the road. But what happened to the road? Johnny said he'd walk me home on his break. Did he? Did he take my clothes off and put me to bed? Did he come to bed with me? Come on, I know that's impossible. Johnny walked me to the door and I did the rest. I just don't remember because I had one too many. I wonder if everyone at Ryan's last night forgot how they got to bed.

I hurt. It's Sunday and I feel like such a sinner. I wish I had the comfort of God. Maybe I'll get up and go to church. I'll go to Father Brennan's mass and maybe it will help. I doubt it, but I'll try. I'll try if my legs are working and if I have enough time to get sick and clean up.

It's awful being out at ten-thirty on Sunday morning. I feel very unsteady and I'm sure all these perfect-looking families on their way to church are all talking about me. It's not very cold out, but I'm shivering anyway. I guess I didn't dress warmly enough. Who am I kidding going to mass? I don't belong there. I doubt everything that goes on there. If they knew about me, I bet they wouldn't even let me in. Just because I show up at mass today doesn't mean that the hand of God is going to come down and pick me up and fix this mess. That's a nine-year-old's prayer to a nine-year-old's God.

I wish I believed. I wish I had some comfort. Well, it's too late now for wishing. I'm here and I'll sit in the back so that I can leave if I have to. Father Brennan is celebrating the mass. That's a break. Now, at least, I don't have to listen to some priest from the old school tell me what a sinner I am. Father Brennan talks about life, not death; about peace of mind, not sin. He's the only priest I've heard in the last ten years I can listen to. Maybe I could talk to him. Maybe he could help me.

Before I even knew what I was doing, I found myself in the sacristy after the mass, looking for Father Brennan . . .

"My name is Megan Moran," was all I could get out before I burst into tears. Father Brennan wrapped me in his arms and said, "Now, now, Megan, it can't be as bad as all that. Just relax a bit and we'll go have a talk in my office after I get out of these vestments."

When he spoke to me, I began to feel safe. If anybody could help me, I knew this priest would be the one. When we got to his office, Father Brennan sat me down and said, "Megan, tell me what the problem is. You seem frightened and very upset but if you can talk to me, I'm sure we can work things out."

"Father, I didn't know where to go or who to talk to and although you don't know me, I've been coming to your mass off and on for years. Your sermons are always about the real world and real problems so you were the only person I thought of who could help me."

I started to cry again and it was a couple of minutes before I could continue.

"I don't know what's wrong. It's not one specific thing. My world feels very dark. I'm so unhappy. Every day is awful. I can't face it, I'm alone, I have no friends. Nobody loves me. I hate my life. I'm not living. It hurts inside and I can feel my spirit dying. I know I'm dying inside."

"Well, we certainly can't sit by and let your spirit die, Megan. It sounds as if you're going through a dark night of the soul and I can promise you that I'll help you get through it, and once you do, you'll find the sun shining on the other side. I promise you. Now you just have to have faith in me and in God."

I had no faith but I wanted to believe him. More tears. Father Brennan comforted me, brought me a cup of coffee and told me to hang on. He gave me advice on how to get through the next few days until he would see me again. He told me not to spend too much time alone, to make sure I ate properly, to get rest and to try to relax. He gave me his number in case I needed to talk to someone. In case I was feeling worse. I knew he was afraid that I might commit suicide, so before I left I said, "I just want to know how to live. I just want to be happy."

I left the parish house with the tiniest ray of hope trusting that this wonderful man would help me. I hung on for three days until my next appointment.

When I was back in his office after three days of trying to find a way to explain myself, all I could say was the same words, "Life is dark. There's no joy. I'm not even living." He listened and comforted me but after the first week these explanations were not enough for Father Brennan. He probed. He made me describe all the events of the last week to try and find the cause of my troubles. This made me very uncomfortable because I was lying when I gave him day-to-day reports and left out all of my drinking. A couple of times I said "I went out" when I really should have said, "I got drunk."

After two weeks, Father Brennan asked me if I drank. How dare he? I thought. That's it, I have to get away from this man. I quickly responded that I sometimes drank wine "socially" and in moderate amounts. So there.

But then he shocked me by saying, "I asked because I am an alcoholic and I once went through the terrible anguish that you're describing." With that introduction, he told me his whole life story with booze and he told me that it was only when alcohol almost killed him that he gave up, went to A.A. and stopped drinking. I sat there for an hour, mesmerized by his story. He described so much of what I felt. But still, I wouldn't reveal my secret because I still couldn't believe that alcohol was my problem, not my cure.

I left that night and said to myself, "Poor man. What a life he has led! What horror he has gone through!" I was so caught up in my own self-deception that I couldn't see that he knew my terrible secret—and he was trying to make me see the truth.

At the next session, I was able to admit that I got drunk one night during the past week and, as a result, some terrible things happened. I was beginning to tell the truth and because I was telling it I was beginning to see it.

The truth. The truth. The truth. I have always prided myself as being a truth teller and I've always scorned liars. I've never paid attention to the phrase "lying by omission" but now I have to face it. If I don't tell Father Brennan the truth then I'm lying. I hear this little voice inside of me that says I have a drinking problem. But then right away comes a much bigger voice that eats the little voice and helps me pour another drink. I *need* to drink and as long as I go to work almost every day and pay some of my bills, then I'm entitled to drink. I have nothing and no one else filling up my life. I need companionship. White wine keeps me company during the cocktail hour, the dinner hour, the prime-time TV hour and the hour for love before bedtime. By that time, my wine has taken good care of me and I don't have to think about the caresses I'm missing. I don't care anymore. I'm alone and I can take care of myself, as long as I can drink.

I need to drink. I'm sure that Father Brennan doesn't understand that. He stopped because his liver was very bad and he could have died if he continued drinking. If I was really an alcoholic and I was that sick, then of course I'd stop drinking. Right now, all I have to do is cut down and maybe try not to drink every day. Father Brennan probably told me his story just to scare me and to show me what could happen to me if I didn't slow down.

I'm going to make a chart and I'm going to drink only every other day, and when I do, I'm not going to get drunk. That way, I can prove to myself and to Father Brennan that I'm not an alcoholic and maybe he can find out what's really wrong with me. Since I already had drinks today at lunch, I'll start tomorrow. Tomorrow I won't drink. What a thought! I'll fortify myself tonight so that I'll be able to face tomorrow.

I don't usually think about a drink first thing when I open my eyes in the morning, so why am I thinking about one right now? I'm not terribly hung over, just vaguely foggy with a wake-up headache, nothing a long shower and some aspirin won't cure. I don't want a drink this morning, so why am I thinking of one? . . . Now I remember! This is my first day of nondrinking according to my new plan. Oh, damn, I have a lunch date today. I can't get through a lunch date without a few. Damn. Damn . . . Well, I'll have to try. As soon as I get to the office, I'll check my calendar and see who's on for lunch. If it's someone who drives me crazy, then I cancel or I drink. There's no other choice. I've been playing this lunch game long enough and I'm not going to start changing the rules now.

"Good morning, Joan. Who's on for lunch today?"

"Publishing's favorite, Harry Walters. You'll have to make nice to him if you want his star author."

"Dammit, couldn't I cancel just this once?"

"Megan, Charlie is the one who introduced you to Walters and set this thing up. It wouldn't be wise to cancel under those circumstances. Instead, why not treat yourself to a really great lunch—how about La Côte Basque? That would be something to look forward to."

Usually I spend my mornings waiting for lunchtime the way I used to wait for the bell ending classes in high school. Today, I'm dreading it and not because I don't like Harry Walters. He's a fascinating man with one of the most impressive client lists in the business. He's funny, he's charming and he's great friends with Charlie so he'll be especially nice to me. Trouble is, he drinks. And if he drinks, I'm going to have to drink. Otherwise, I'll be nervous and shaky and I'll blow the deal. I need this deal. It will help me slide through another six months.

I arrived at La Côte Basque five minutes early, which was early enough to be seated and waiting at the table, but not early enough for my usual sneak drink before the lunch date arrives. I timed it perfectly because I still haven't decided to drink or not to drink. I'm leaving my decision in the hands of Fate and Harry Walters. My date arrived promptly and presented me with a manuscript and a nosegay of violets.

"Good afternoon, my dear Ms. Moran. Don't be alarmed or too excited. This is not the manuscript you planned on charming out of me over lunch. You still have the opportunity to be charming. Before we discuss my million-dollar author, I want to convince you to read my most favorite new novelist. Hence the manuscript, *Green Mornings,* and the violets."

"Why, thank you, Harry. They're both welcome. Tell me a bit about this novel."

"Certainly, my dear, but we must order a drink first. Waiter— What will you have, Megan?"

"A gin and tonic, please."

"Yes, and I'll have the same. So, I'm delighted to be lunching with you. Charlie is full of praise for your work and I'm always happy to get to know the new blood."

We got through all the formalities over two gin and tonics and then settled down to a superb lunch accompanied by a bottle of wine. Harry insisted on dessert and brandy and I, naturally, said "What the hell" and went all the way. Not only did I drink my way through lunch, I ate my way through lunch, up to and including Sacher torte for dessert. We kissed and hugged as if we were dear dear friends saying goodbye and my last words were a promise to read *Green Mornings* overnight.

I think I've been suckered. It's almost three so I'm going to call Charlie, report in and head home with my manuscript.

"Charlie, your friend Walters tried to get me drunk so I'd tell him all your secrets. He didn't succeed but he came close and he stuck me with an overnight read, promising to return the favor by giving us an early exclusive on Ruth Simon's book."

"I knew you could do it, Megan!"

"I'm going home, Charlie. I'll call you tonight when I finish this thing. Let's both keep our fingers crossed that it's a first novel we'll want to publish. I hate doing it any other way. Ciao."

"I'll talk to you later—and Megan, thanks for the good work."

Well, I broke my promise but at least I earned my salary today. As soon as I get home, I'll brew a pot of coffee and start reading. I should be finished by eight so the night won't be a total loss. I know I'm out of wine at home but I'll wait until I finish reading before I buy a bottle. I really have to get this work done and then I can have a few.

After reading fifty pages, I knew the novel was for me. Beautifully but simply written, it's the story of a single New York woman who goes to the mountains of Vermont to teach for a year. She falls in love, with her students, with the country and with a man. She sheds all her urban anxiety and settles down to a simple country life. What a dream! I'm so jealous of this character I can't put the manuscript down. When I'm on the last twenty pages, at 8:25 P.M., the phone rings. Damn it.

"Yes, who is it?"

"Megan, it's Charlie. How is it?"

"I can't put it down. I'm on the last twenty pages and I'll call you back."

I hung up on the boss. When I finished, after I stopped crying, I dialed Charlie.

"Harry Walters has made us a gift, Charlie. This is a beautiful novel and I *have* to publish it."

"Thank God. This has certainly been a lucky day, Megan. Let's just play it cool at first with Harry. We don't want him taking us to the cleaners."

"Of course. I'll do what you'd do: tell him I hate it but I'll publish it if he pays me, right?"

"Watch it, Megan! I'm the boss. Now go make yourself some dinner and buy a bottle of champagne on me. I'll see you in the morning."

"What a great idea! Night, boss."

Some days are better than others, Megan. On some days you can't do anything wrong. On some days, it doesn't matter that you drink and on some days, the world brightens up again, doesn't it, Megan? It's not all over for me. I won't worry. I couldn't possibly be an alcoholic. Now, I'm going to buy that champagne.

I think I'll go to a different liquor store tonight. I'm tired of having to explain myself and my purchases to my regular liquor store man. It's a beautiful night and I'd like to walk a few blocks anyway. I'll also stop into that French bakery that stays open late and choose some appropriate accompaniments to a bottle of Mumm's. Mumm's was my first champagne and has remained my favorite for sentimental reasons. Of course, I drink some of the cheaper stuff when I'm paying and my pocketbook is slim, but I refuse to stoop to the cheap New York state champagnes. It's better to have a simple bottle of wine. Champagne must be as beautiful as it is delicious, and to my romantic head, it must also be French. I adore the fact that I discovered that I could drink and enjoy a bottle of champagne alone. I wonder if there's another person in New York City tonight drinking champagne alone in a beautiful fluted glass by candlelight, with croissants and chocolate and Brie. I wonder if Charlie realizes that I took him up on his offer immediately and that I'm not sharing this celebration with anyone. In fact, champagne may be the best solitary drink. Everything about it sings and sparkles. Champagne is an event and a bottle of one's own should certainly chase any blues away and fill the moment with light and laughter—even if it's only the sound of one's own voice. I'm having a very special celebration tonight. I'm celebrating two discoveries: one, a fabulous new novelist; and, two, I'm not an alcoholic. I can drink and I do my job brilliantly. That's what my life is devoted to right now—drinking and working—so why give up half of it when there's no need? I'm O.K. Tonight I'm better than O.K. and I'm going to keep myself there. No more dark nights of the soul, Father Brennan, and no more frightening mornings. I'm almost on top of the world—no more falling off.

It's 1 A.M., way past bedtime. There's just one more glass of champagne left and it's coming to bed with me. Lock the door, blow out the candles, turn on the light for the bogeyman and crawl into bed. I'm exhausted. I want to finish this last sip before I fall asleep . . .

This morning I'm a little less brilliant because I have a very heavy champagne head. But today my spirits are undaunted and I can brave this hangover; after all, it was achieved in a good cause. I've got to try very hard to get to work on time, no matter what it takes. So I'll give the head three extra-strength aspirin and a very short hair of the dog. Just today because I have to get rid of this hangover.

"Good morn— Oh, look at these! Aren't they beautiful! And they're from the boss! Joan, do you think Charlie has a crush on me? What a wonderful treat!"

"Megan, what's going on? Charlie keeps running down the hall looking for you. I arrived at eight-thirty and he was already at it—and you're early today. It's not even nine-fifteen. If you don't stop him, he's going to be exhausted by 10 A.M."

I flew down the hall. Charlie had two authors in his office and since I had already barged in, he invited me to stay. It was a very crazy fifteen minutes. I could hardly sit still while they were doing everything but standing on their heads trying to sell their next proposal. Finally, Charlie got rid of them, promising to get back to them by the end of the week.

"Megan, Megan, Megan. You're acting like you've been drinking champagne for breakfast!"

"Damn. I should have thought of that! I'm just so excited, Charlie. I know you're going to love this book. Promise me you'll give it an hour this morning so I can call Harry and make an offer?"

"Well, where is it? I have exactly one hour before the board meeting."

"Joan is xeroxing it. I'll get you the first fifty pages right away. Do you want some breakfast? I have some danish on the way."

"Yes, yes, yes. Just get moving."

"Oh, Charlie—"

"Um."

"Thanks for the roses. It's my first dozen."

"I'm glad."

"Joan, did Charlie call while I was on the phone?"

"No, Megan."

"It's been an hour, hasn't it? He'd better not go to that meeting without calling."

"It's been forty-seven minutes. Calm down, Megan. Wait a minute; here he comes."

"So tell me, boss, can I buy it?"

"Not only can you buy it, but I want the deal settled before lunch. Here's the strategy: tell him you like it but I'm wary because the author's an unknown. Also, first novels don't sell. Offer three thousand and pay five. If he screams and carries on tell him you'll go to seventy-five hundred but you're risking your job to do it. That's high enough, and I bet you'll hold him at five. Make the deal before lunch and send a messenger for Ruth Simon's manuscript. Make copies of the first novel for everyone, and make three stat copies of the Simon book before five. See you later. Also, get that young writer lined up for lunch with both of us."

"Right, boss. Thanks. Joan, did you hear all of that? I think it would be best if you picked up the Ruth Simon book. Is that O.K.? We'll order lunch in and then you can grab a cab downtown to Harry's office and back. Right now, I need a contract proposal and then get Walters on the phone—and, Joan, sit in here with me and write down everything you hear (except, of course, the cursing). That way, we'll have no contract foul-ups—at this stage, at least."

I succeeded in buying *Green Mornings* before lunch and I got it for five thousand. I probably could have gotten it for thirty-five hundred but I never follow Charlie's instructions to the letter. I didn't want to cheat the author. After all, she put her heart and soul in that book and she deserved the five grand. If Charlie knew I felt this way and paid a penny more than I had to, he might laugh but he would probably fire me on the spot. Nevertheless, I felt the five thousand was fair. The afternoon was insane. Poor Joan spent hours at the Xerox and then I had to chase around to all the execs and make sure that they went home with Ruth Simon's latest.

By the time I was ready to leave, it was six-thirty and I was exhausted. The thought of spending another night with a manuscript, no matter how good, was not appealing. I stopped at Ryan's on the way home for a couple to pep me up. It seems that work always comes in waves and this is one of those eighteen-hour-a-day weeks when there's no room for anything else. Well, tonight I'm making room for an hour at Ryan's. I need a break from the world of publishing madness.

"Good evening, Johnny. I'd like a scotch mist before dinner, and maybe another one with dinner, and maybe a third after dinner . . ."

"Good to see you, Megan. Your friend Paul has been asking about you."

"Well, don't tell him a thing, Johnny. Now, please, I'm dying of thirst."

The night slipped away and I went right along with it. The manuscript sat at my side and occasionally, I turned and toasted it and the great world of publishing. Somehow, the night turned into morning as it has a habit of doing, and I was still on that barstool. But I wasn't alone. Some guy was listening to me being happy, sad, sexy, sultry, nasty, bitchy, angry, noisy, quiet, sweet, sickening. When I get this way, my life is out of my hands, and I'm out of control. I can see and hear myself but it's all through a veil and I can't change my behavior. It went on and I don't know how he got back home with me, sitting on my bed, naked . . .

I hate myself. I'm a slut and a whore. I'll go home with anybody at the bar who spends ten minutes flattering me and who buys my drinks. I can't imagine where all this self-hatred comes from. I suffered no sexual abuse as a child, yet that's how I act out all this hatred. I get drunk, sleep with another drunk and wake up in the morning not knowing his name. Nothing could be worse than this degradation. I don't think I do it for the sex because I can never remember the sex. I pass out almost immediately and the next thing I know, it's morning and I have to wake up to a foul-smelling, dirty drunk. Sometimes I can't make them leave fast enough. They get insulted and want to be treated respectfully. Of course, I'm frightened of what could happen to me so I play the game, eat breakfast, give them the wrong telephone number and kiss them goodbye. It's the worst part. It's enough to make me want to die. I think part of me wants to die, that's why I put my life in jeopardy bringing strangers home. Somehow I think it's safer if I bring them to my house instead of going someplace strange with them. But it's no safer. I could be mutilated and murdered in my own bed just as easily as anywhere else. I don't know what I'm doing when I'm drunk. I'm out of my mind and out of control and can't take responsibility for my actions. If this is what happens to me then I should stop getting drunk. Isn't this shame awful enough to make me stop drinking?

Last night it was a guy who claimed to be a doctor. I grilled him for hours to be assured that he was telling the truth because I felt it would be more respectable if I brought a doctor to my bed. He talked medicine but I'm sure I just fell for a well-rehearsed jive act. He knew where I was coming from and decided to beat me at my own game. Sometime after we got back to my apartment, I had a moment of clarity and knew I had to make him leave. I knew if I reneged on my promise and tried to throw him out there might be trouble, so I made myself sick. I went into the bathroom and stuck my finger down my throat. It didn't take much at that point to make me vomit. I went back to him without washing up, with vomit all over me. Then I pretended to have an attack of diarrhea, and after running to the bathroom I returned a few minutes later and described the terrible attack. Needless to say, I turned him off fast and he was practically whimpering as he ran out the door. I thought it was hilarious and even though it was 4 A.M., I wanted to call someone and tell my amusing story. I was proud of myself. I thought I was hot shit.

This morning I'm not so proud. I'm not such hot shit. I feel lower than low. I don't even deserve to be alive. I am ashamed and I don't understand how I became so morally bankrupt. From now on, I'm going to drink at home, alone. I can't take any more risks that I'll bring home another man—and he might be the last. The one I've been looking for. The one who'll put me out of my misery. Permanently.

So, Megan, the good news lasted for a day. Once again, I was happy, successful and in control of my life. Once again, and for one more day. Now it's in pieces again—and why? It's because of booze. It's because I'm an alcoholic. If only I could stop fighting. If only I could give up. If only I could tell Father Brennan the truth . . .

THE BEGINNING

My father was an alcoholic, although nobody would ever mention that word. He was a wonderful man and a terrible drunk. When I think of how it all went wrong for me, I think of him. When did I stop living and begin dying? Maybe it was two years ago when my father died. I was left with a hole inside. I picked up my bottle of wine one night, cradled it in my arms and said, "You're all I've got now," and I meant it. From that moment until this I haven't gone for more than one day without a drink.

There will never be a more devastating moment in my life than when I was told my father was dead. I screamed for so long that the neighbors called the police and six policemen with guns drawn appeared at the door. It was a living nightmare. Nothing could take the pain away and nobody could ever know how I felt. I had to numb the pain with alcohol. After the funeral, when I was left alone again, I had to drink.

My father's funeral was our Park Avenue church's best. Our old family friends include many priests and they all came to stand on the altar and honor my father. The Jesuit who spoke the eulogy spoke of a man with a joyful spirit, a warm heart and the light of God in his eyes. It was the saddest and proudest moment of all our lives. Yet I cannot forget that this exceptional human being, my father, was a drunk. I cannot forget it because I, too, am a drunk.

His death shouldn't have been such a terrible shock to me because my mother was preparing me for it for years. She succeeded in making me afraid of death from an early age—afraid that my father would die when he didn't come home at night, and then afraid in my child's mind that he would kill my mother and maybe all of us during his horrifying drunken rages. How could I have loved him so much when he frightened me so?

I have two sets of childhood memories—the happy ones and the secret ones. The secret ones are so bad that I repressed them for most of my life and only recently have accepted them, embraced them and, finally, understood them. I didn't ever believe that my father was a drunk. I knew he was sick and I knew he didn't mean to hurt us. He never physically abused any of his children but now I know I was mentally abused. He was two different people. I have memories of sleigh-riding with Daddy in the winter and going for ice cream sodas in the summer. When he worked nights, I would come home from school for lunch with my sister Peggy and he would make special treats. He was also the Sunday morning chef for the family. It was always a show when Daddy was in the kitchen cooking the bacon and flipping the pancakes, singing Irish ballads.

But then there were the Sunday mornings when we had to tiptoe around his snoring body on the living room floor afraid to wake him. His drunken smell used to sicken me and make me ashamed for him. I knew how embarrassed my father would be when he woke up and saw the condition he was in. I always felt such sadness for him on these mornings. How could I understand his remorse at ten years old? Maybe I understood because even then I was an alcoholic, before I picked up my first drink.

I stayed close to my father on these mornings after a drunk. I knew he would need me to bring him beer and ginger ale and toast.

I also knew that he needed my love on these days when Mommy and the rest of the family wouldn't talk to him. I felt whatever pity a ten-year-old can feel for a parent. I knew it was wrong to ignore my father's presence, to act as if he didn't exist, to walk around him not looking at him or speaking to him. This action seemed just as bad as what my father had done the night before. But sometimes when it was really bad, even I had to abandon him and give him the silent treatment.

My father did his serious drinking in the neighborhood bars. The only drinking that was done at home was social drinking. My parents were too working-class to partake of a cocktail hour at home or wine with dinner, and when people came to visit tea and cake were usually served. When there was a family party—a christening or graduation or birthday—the whiskey flowed and the good times rolled. My father loved parties and he was always the life of them. He never ran out of jokes and witty conversation and when the witching hour came, he was always happily crooning an Irish ballad.

At family parties and Sunday dinners, there was always at least one Jesuit sharing dinner with us. Growing up surrounded by priests brought a sense of grace to our home. We were always bowing our heads to receive a blessing. The priests would arrive laden with gifts and expensive scotch and they'd remove their Roman collars and proceed to get sloshed with my father. But these evenings were fun; they were warm and loving, and owing to the presence of God's men I felt very safe. We went to the beach with priests, where we called them "uncle." We went away for weekends to Jesuit retreat houses, where we swam and played softball and did very little praying. We went to the priests when there was trouble and they would take care of my father. He would take the "pledge" and be "on the wagon" for a few weeks or months. However long it was, it was never long enough.

I knew too much as a ten-year-old. I knew about complete personality changes, I knew drunken rages, violence, verbal abuse, hangovers, fear, shame and sorrow. These are not the normal feelings associated with childhood.

I also felt that I had grave responsibilities as a child. I had to protect my mother from my father, and I had to comfort my father in his remorse. I also had to stay awake nights praying for his safety. Every night he didn't come home I was sure was the night when we would never see him again. My mother always said that Daddy was going to kill himself. I lie in bed and waited for the moment to come.

As I grew older, my feelings changed as my responsibilities changed. I became more understanding of my mother and took on a lot of her attitudes, which included self-righteous anger. Then I picked up my first drink and my sympathies immediately swung back to my father.

My father's favorite bar was only two blocks from home, and as each child grew up we took turns going to the bar and bringing him home. This responsibility humiliated and shamed me, but it had to be done. If we succeeded in getting him home before the point of no return, then we could forgo the rage and violence and have the much easier job of getting a "happy" drunk to go to sleep. My cover, when I went to retrieve my father from the bar, was to take the dog for a walk. For some reason, I felt less obvious and more protected with the dog. I would pass by the bar window a couple of times to make sure he was there, then very quickly slip in, before any people on the street could see me. Once inside, the hard part began. I had to discern the degree of my father's drunkenness before I decided on my approach. I could be stern and reproachful, or tempt him with mouth-watering descriptions of the dinner awaiting him, or sit down and have a Coke or two until he decided he was ready to leave. I succeeded in getting him home only half of the time.

It was an old Irish bar, the kind with the separate entrance for wives and children, who were relegated to booths in the back. The bar was reserved for the men. Occasionally I would see a woman at the bar and I knew it was wrong. Before I ever knew about whores and loose women, I knew that women on barstools were not like my mother. Proper ladies didn't sit at the bar and drink alone. The bar was always dark, which made it difficult finding my father when I peered in the window, and that made entering all the more frightening.

"Oh, Megan, me darlin', come and meet my good friend Paddy."

He always took on a brogue when he was drunk. From his welcome I could tell we were still in the happy stages. His good friend Paddy the bartender had known me since I was a baby so formal introductions weren't really necessary.

"Hi, Dad. Tipper and I are here to escort you home to a delicious steak dinner."

"Have a seat, toots, and I'll get you a Coke."

"But, Dad—"

"Never mind. One Coke will only take a minute."

I had one Coke while he had three more beers and shots and then he was willing to go home for supper. There was no steak for supper. Macaroni and cheese was on the menu because the man of the family hadn't yet brought home the remainder of his paycheck. My mother's second biggest fear, right behind expecting her husband to die from the drink, was that she wouldn't be able to salvage most of the weekly paycheck before Ryan's Bar got it. If I failed in my mission tonight, more troops would have to be sent out. It was payday and getting him home was crucial.

Oh, how I hated leaving the bar with a drunk, holding him up and weaving up Second Avenue, invariably past most of the neighbors and some of my classmates. These were the moments when I hated him for shaming me so. I wanted to pretend I didn't know him and leave him falling down in the gutter. This drunk man was not the father I loved. This drunk was a monster who frightened me and wrought havoc in a basically happy family. My loyalties lay with a healthy father and not a sick drunk. But I had to hold him up and get him home, for my mother's sake.

But Mom wasn't very pleased to see us fall through the front door. She immediately got to work picking his pockets.

"Michael, you're fifty dollars short here and we have to pay two months' rent, tuition, the monthly bill at the market, and Brendan needs new sneakers for basketball. There's never enough money and we practically starve to keep you in drink. Don't you care about your family? Is drinking all you care about?"

Mother was yelling at him and he was drunk, and we all knew that the slightest provocation would start a full-fledged blowout.

Megan Moran

"Mom, please don't start fighting with him now. Please wait until tomorrow," I pleaded, but Eileen Moran's Irish anger could be as deadly as her husband's.

"You children leave us alone and go watch TV," was her response.

"Eileen, I'm sick and tired of your ungrateful bitching. I work hard all week and I'm entitled to a few beers on Friday night. If there was any reason to come to my wife, maybe I wouldn't stay out all night. But you're a coldhearted piece of wood with no room in your bed for me, so just keep your mouth shut and be glad you're getting what you're getting."

Daddy was fired up and from the sound of it the shouting would go on for hours. Then he'd go out again and come home at 4 A.M. ready for a knock-down, drag-out fight.

I sat with one ear cocked to the television and one to the kitchen waiting for the moment I'd have to jump up and place myself between them, warding off blows. My brothers and sister were on the same alert. I wasn't the only child in the family who believed that she'd saved lives and who took on the responsibility of protecting Mommy from attacks. No other children grow up this way. The rest of the world is "Ozzie and Harriet," "Leave It to Beaver" and "The Donna Reed Show." If they made a TV show of my family, they'd have to call it "Drunk Daddy."

". . . No wonder I spend as little time here as possible. I can't get a decent meal or a moment's peace in this place. I've had it!" The door slammed and Daddy was gone. Peace for a few hours, but the price to be paid at 4 A.M. won't be worth it. We all watched TV until bedtime, then we fought sleep, somehow feeling that if we could stay awake we could prevent the nightmare.

Children don't understand adults arguing, fighting, crying. They are frightened by these things because adults are all that children have to protect them, take care of them and make their lives happy. The first time I saw my mother cry, I didn't think she would be able to stop because she didn't have her mother to fix it. I knew I couldn't fix it and I was terrified. I don't remember why she was crying, I just remember my panic. The first time I heard my parents fighting, I was sure that my father would kill my mother. Though he rarely struck her, the horrible yelling was enough to convince me.

That night we all knew they would fight when my father came home drunk. I became so afraid of these fights that I would sneak into my mother's bed to protect her.

"Mommy, please let me sleep with you. It's too dark in my room and I'm scared."

"O.K., Megan, crawl in."

"Mommy, is Daddy home yet?"

"No, don't worry. Just go to sleep."

I lie there trying not to sleep, forcing myself to stay awake until he comes home. Sometime later, I was wide awake after hearing the apartment door slam shut. I could also feel my mother wake with a start. We both lie very quietly, afraid to move. I prayed, "Please, God, make Daddy go to sleep. Please, God, don't let him come in here."

There was a loud crash in the living room and my father's swearing began. "Eileen, get out here. Do you hear me, get out here right now or I'm going to come in there and drag you out."

"Don't go, Mommy. Please stay here. He'll fall asleep."

"O.K., I'll stay, Megan."

But he wouldn't stop. "Eileen, if you're not out here in two minutes, I'm going to drag you by the hair on your head."

"Megan, I'm going out and I'm just going to talk to him and get him to go to sleep. Don't worry, I'll be right back. Go back to sleep."

I prayed so hard when my mother went into the living room. Then I heard my father's curses, "You bitch, you lousy bitch." When I heard Mommy cry, "Michael, let go! You're hurting me," I jumped from the bed, ran into my brothers' room and woke Joe and Brendan.

"We have to go help Mommy. He's hurting her!"

The three of us ran out to the living room and saw our drunken father holding our mother down by her hair. We climbed on top of him and beat at him until he let go. We were screaming and crying, "We hate you. We hate you." All of a sudden he let go, and with a stunned look on his face he yelled at all of us to get out of his sight.

I took my mother back to bed. I knew she was safe. I held on to her under the covers and waited for my father's drunken snores to shake the apartment before I let myself fall back to sleep.

I knew he was sick and I knew he was drunk. I knew these things from the time I was six years old and I kept them hidden inside of me. I loved my father more than anyone and the truth was that he loved all of us and he showed it enormously. We all forgave him his drunkenness because most of the time he was loving us, making us laugh and keeping us happy. He was always so sorry about the bad times it was almost as if he couldn't believe that he said and did those awful things. He tried so hard—and succeeded—in making it up to us. My mother would be back loving him after two days, but he could make his four children love him the next morning.

This was a long time ago and I believe that the worst of times occurred when I was very young, but maybe they just seemed so much worse to my child's mind. In many ways these are memories worth forgetting and I'm sure it was good for me to pack them away years ago and only take them out now when I have the means to understand them. On the other hand, repressing these memories didn't help me to understand my own personality.

Growing up in an alcoholic family was a schizophrenic experience and there was no way for me to sort through all the mixed messages I received as a child. One day would be full of happiness and love and the next would be disaster. I grew up in an emotional war zone.

When my father wasn't drunk, he was affectionate and loving. We never had much money but we knew that we were being given as much as was possible. I never went hungry but I remember eating lots of macaroni and cheese casseroles. If I needed a new party dress, my mother made sure I had one. Although we were poor, my parents refused to think and act poor, so we were given much more than the bare essentials.

Having an alcoholic father was like having two fathers. My "real" father was a very moral and idealistic man—decency, respect and love were extremely important to him and these are the values that he taught his children. Education was also very important. My father was basically self-educated. He grew up during the Depression, the child of two alcoholic parents, and he had to quit school and help support the family from age fifteen. I was always surprised by his intelligence because I didn't think that a person who didn't graduate from high school could be intelligent. Yet my father read Shakespeare and Dickens and Tolstoy and he was familiar with every author I studied in my fancy liberal arts college.

Because of his lack of education, Dad insisted that all his children receive good educations and three out of four of us went to college and became professionals. Bringing home a bad report card, even if it was from the second grade, was not tolerated. My brother Brendan was a C-average student and he, more than any of the children, experienced my father's wrath. My father would study with him and keep him up half the night until he mastered his homework. I was always a straight-A student, and although I was praised for it I knew that anything less was unacceptable.

My father was also a very funny man. He used humor to combat any difficult situation. He believed in it and knew that if you looked hard enough, there was always a bright side. Because of his wit and his great storytelling ability, he had many friends and was in the spotlight at every party. When Dad drank socially at family gatherings or friends' parties, he almost never got drunk. He got happier and funnier and he drank and drank but he didn't go over the edge. In my drinking career, I haven't been able to accomplish that but I've tried and tried and tried.

Eileen and Michael Moran loved their children and also loved each other enormously. Even with all of the bad times, my mother couldn't bring herself to leave my father. It was a great love, she told me, the once-in-a-lifetime kind, complete with bells, fireworks—and tragedy. One of my best childhood memories is sitting at the breakfast table witnessing the grand kiss that my father gave my mother each morning. It was a family game.

We would all be sitting at the breakfast table eating our assortment of Chex, Kix and Wheaties and Daddy would come out to say goodbye as he left for work.

" 'Bye, kids, I'm off to keep you in shoes."

"Wait a minute, Daddy, you're forgetting something."

"Oh, sure I am, that's right," and he would come around the

table and kiss all of us, saying, " 'Bye, Megan, 'bye, Peggy, 'bye, Joe, 'bye, Brendan. Now that's it. I'm late and I really have to run."

"No wait!" we would all scream. "You forgot to kiss Mommy!"

"Oh, I did, didn't I. Do I have to? I'm really late."

"Yes, you have to."

Daddy would reach around, take Mommy in his arms, lean over, then turn to us, "Are you sure I have to?"

"Yes, yes, yes. A long one, with a dip." By now we were all laughing wildly. He wrapped her in his arms, dipped her over as far back as she could go and then, with one last remark like "Oh, this hurts!" or "Watch out for your nose," he'd plant a loud, long smooch on my mother's lips. We all cheered and clapped. "Now you can go. Goodbye, Daddy!"

Sometimes, even after those wonderful mornings, he wouldn't come home from work. The black undercurrent of my father's alcoholism was always running through our lives even when the days began happy and full of love. I never knew when it would strike but sooner or later it always did. Sometimes it took two weeks or three or even a month, but the night came when he wasn't home for dinner and we prepared ourselves for the horror. As a child, I found it impossible to reconcile the two sides of my life. When my father came through the door falling-down drunk, he was a monster.

As I got older, my father's alcoholism seemed to tone down. He didn't get drunk as often, and when he did he just came home in the middle of the night and fell asleep. By the time I was a teenager, there were no more screaming, hitting fights in the middle of the night. This helped me to black out the early years and pretend that the horrors from early childhood didn't exist. Wishing them away took them away for a while and probably helped me to grow up fairly well adjusted.

When your father is a drunk, you have to learn how to live with secrets and with shame. Although most of the neighbors were awakened at one time or another and saw the police taking Daddy away for the night, the first rule of the family was, keep it from the neighbors. My best friend lived in the same small building and her father was an alcoholic. She grew up with the same rules, and as a result we never told each other our most painful secret until we were teenagers. From age five, we shared absolutely everything except the most important thing.

Dealing with "the secret" as an adult helps to put it all in perspective. What doesn't help is that my family still refuses to look at the past. They have good memories of my father, as do I, and they don't want the truth to tarnish those memories. For me, the truth hasn't tarnished the good memories but polished them. I now understand how sick my father was and how he fought his alcoholism, and sometimes he succeeded in keeping it down for a long time. At the end of his life, he rarely drank, and only about half of the time when he did he got drunk. It was a very tough battle he was fighting with booze and eventually he lost. My father didn't die a drunk. He didn't have cirrhosis of the liver and he'd hardly been drinking for the last year of his life. But alcoholism killed him. It killed him because years earlier it damaged his heart and when he was first told to stop drinking, he couldn't. Over the years, his heart worsened and at the age of fifty-three it gave out. He was a beautiful man and in so many ways a strong man. Even when his heart was terribly weak, he gave the impression of strength, and that's one of the reasons why I never could see that he was close to death.

When I was a teenager and began to drink and drug, my attitude toward my father's drinking changed. I never let him see me drunk because that would have been totally unacceptable, but I loved to drink with him. I was no longer ashamed to go to the bars to bring him home because I could sit and have a couple with him. I began to understand the attraction and desire for alcohol. I fell in love with it immediately and from the moment I had my first drink I wanted another to back it up, to make the good feeling even better.

When I started drinking my relationship with my father changed. I looked for opportunities to drink with him because it was a chance for me both to drink and to communicate with my father on a more equal level. It worked. We had many wonderful times drinking together and, for the most part, my father didn't get drunk with me, just pleasantly high. After I went away to college, we began a tradition of going out to dinner alone when I was home on vacation. I loved this because I wanted to learn from my father, I wanted to hear his life experiences and his wisdom. I sought his advice and, most importantly, his approval. We had many dinners together with my mother, but for me she was an intrusion. She counted his drinks and she counted mine. She tried to limit my drinking and made me feel like a child. So I always managed to arrange a father-daughter dinner, usually on an evening when my mother had another commitment and we had to fend for ourselves.

A favorite spot for these dinners was Porter's, a neighborhood bar-restaurant that claimed to be the oldest bar in Yorkville. My father corroborated this statement as fact and told me that when he was young they had held Nazi meetings in this old bar.

I vividly remember one specific dinner at Porter's when my father was fifty, three years before his death. As usual, we had cocktails before dinner, wine during dinner and cognac afterward. We ate wonderful treats: stuffed mushrooms, escargots, filet mignon and chocolate mousse pie. The best stories came with the cognac, but this evening Dad shocked me.

"Megan, I'm not going to live forever. There's a lot I couldn't do with my life, a lot of opportunities missed. I've made the best life I could and I've been given great joy through my children. I'm proud of all of you. I suppose over the years, I've forgotten to tell you the most important things—my hopes, my dreams, my love for all of you . . ."

"You've told us a lot, Dad. We all know how much you love us so I wish you'd stop getting so morbid. You've only turned fifty! You're in the height of your middle age."

"Now, just listen to me, Megan. I won't argue with you about my longevity, I just want to give you my hope for the future.

"For many years I was bitter about lost opportunities. I had to quit school to support my parents during the Depression. I dreamed of someday going to college. Then I fell in love with your mother and then came the war; college was slipping away. You know that I was a pilot in the Marines. What you don't know is that I was offered a job as a commercial pilot with TWA, but because of an ear injury during the war, I couldn't pass their physical. For years, I felt I was dealt the wrong cards. I drank too much. Then I started seeing all my terrific kids growing up into fine adults and now I'm filled with gratitude for my life.

"I know you can fulfill my dreams by fulfilling your own. Reach as high as you can, don't let go and don't give up. You can do anything and be anything. If you want to write the Great American Novel, you can write it.

"This is all I have to pass on to you. I tease you about what I'll leave you in my will when you know there won't be a will. All you can inherit from me are some basic principles to live by: Be honest, laugh instead of crying, give love and you'll get it—and don't stop trying for the pot of gold . . ."

By now there were tears in both our eyes and my embarrassed father laughed and said, "You see what happens when you give me a couple of drinks!"

We laughed the rest of the night as I listened to endless stories of my father's family and my own. After that night, I knew I had been given a gift. I knew that my father was an exceptional human being and all at once I forgave him his alcoholism and banished the bad memories of his drunkenness from my mind forever. He deserved all my respect and my love.

I'm not alone in my attitude toward my father. Everyone in the family chose to forget the bad times. The good times were too good. The man was too good.

At this time, I felt that drinking brought us closer together. We were able to share an elegant meal with cocktails and wine, and we were relaxed enough to open up and talk about the most important things. I gave alcohol the credit for that, it made me feel; whether good or bad, it heightened my senses and made me sensitive to my feelings. Alcohol was a vehicle for relating to my father and for getting in touch with my own feelings. I loved the way it made me feel. The giggles and tears were all so delicious when induced by alcohol.

As a result of experiencing my father's alcoholism, I saw that there were two ways to drink—the happy, social way and the angry, sick, violent way. Getting drunk the happy way was perfectly acceptable, but the other way was unspeakable. I was certain that I would never drink like that, but I am my father's daughter. I look like him,

I have some of his sense of humor, and I wound up drinking like him. In my family, alcoholism has been passed down for generations.

My grandfather died on the Bowery and I never knew it. I never knew him either because he died when I was six and I don't remember ever seeing him when I went to visit my grandmother. Now I know why he wasn't there.

So many secrets surround alcoholism. My father's past was a secret that he kept from his children because it would bring us shame. We kept my father's alcoholism a secret for the same reason. The stigma probably hurts the alcoholic and the family as much as the disease. People die rather than accept the facts. My father died rather than admit his alcoholism and I could have died for the same reason.

Since few people understand and are knowledgeable about alcoholism, the alcoholic is defined as a Bowery bum or a person with advanced physical symptoms such as cirrhosis of the liver. An alcoholic in the earlier stages of the disease is called a heavy drinker and the disease is left untreated until, for many, it's too late. That's why alcoholics don't get to a program like A.A. until they have reached their bottom, until there's no place left to go. Most alcoholics must be completely destitute and hopeless before reaching out for help. For some it is too late for A.A. It was too late for my grandfather and my father. Still, I hoped it would be different for me. I was young and I was a woman—and women can't be alcoholics.

THE FIRST DRINK

"**Y**ou trust me, don't you, Megan?"

"Of course I trust you, Ben."

"Well, since you trust me, you know I wouldn't suggest anything dangerous or anything that would make you feel bad—"

"*Ben,* what *are* you talking about?"

"See this, Megan. It's not a cigarette. It's called a joint. It's grass —marijuana—and when you smoke it, it makes you feel high and happy and almost as if you can fly. It's the most wonderful feeling in the world! I want to get high with you, Megan. You're the only person I ever want to get high with. You'll love it. Trust me."

"Oh, God, Ben. Can't we go to jail for having this stuff? What if we get caught? I'm too scared to do this. What if I get too high and can't come down? I've heard that can happen."

"No, Megan. That could only happen if you smoked a lot of marijuana cigarettes. It won't happen by just sharing one. I promise."

"Are you sure I'll like this?"

"Megan, you know how much I love you. You know I just want to make you happy. *This* is going to make you happy. O.K., I'm lighting it. Now watch how I inhale. You have to hold the smoke in your lungs for as long as you can. O.K., watch . . ."

"Aagh. Aagh. It burns. I don't like how it tastes."

"You're doing fine, Megan. Just relax and have a few more puffs."

"Oh, Ben, I feel funny. Do I look funny? Is my face getting big? Are you tickling me? Oh, look at the clouds. Let's go sit on one. You're right, I feel as though I can fly."

"Careful, Megan, we're on the roof. Come on, let's go to the park."

"O.K. But we should be careful of the giant grass blades and the miniature monster people hiding behind the rocks. Ben, I'm so funny, aren't I?"

I loved being high. We laughed and played all day. Ben called it a spiritual experience and I decided I wanted to be high all the time.

There is so much going on at my house that my parents don't notice I'm changing, except in external ways. My mother bugs me because I won't wear dresses anymore, and my father made me remove the American-flag patch from the seat of my pants, but that's as far as their awareness goes. I'm still in the top 10 percent of my high school class, my grades are almost always A's, so I'm considered a good kid. Being a good kid is the perfect cover for being a bad kid.

On weekends, Ben takes me to the East Village, where we get high with our friends and the rest of the hip world at the Fillmore East. The Fillmore was the first rock concert hall in New York, built by hippies for hippies. Our music is so important and our pot is so important. We're sending a message. We're out to fuck the establishment, legalize marijuana and end the war. There is nothing else worth believing in or talking about. Getting high and making love, not war, is all I believe in. I haven't yet made love, but I believe in it.

"We are Volunteers of America, Volunteers of America, Volunteers of America . . . !" the Jefferson Airplane is singing in their annual free concert in Central Park. Ben and I are here with the rest of our friends. I'm high on pot and I feel united with every other

person at the concert. We all have a common purpose, we all trust and love each other. The stranger next to me is holding out his wine bottle. I accept it and offer him my joint. Now we are one.

Ben and I want to go to an island. We have a dream to find a utopia—Atlantis—a special place full of flowers and fruit and marijuana. We are going to spend our lives there. We vow to always be together and always stay high. Staying high is more than a physical state of drugged euphoria, it is a political statement and that statement is at the core of us. We must stay high to show the world who we are. But for now, I'm not breaking the news to my parents.

The weekends are the best time because we can be together almost all the time with our friends. My father is drinking too much lately and I can't bear to be home. During the week, I escape for a few hours with Ben. We just walk around the city and talk about how our lives will never be that way—no drunks and no unhappiness. I resent my father's drinking because he's making my life unhappy. So it's such a relief to break out for the weekend, even if I do have to be home at midnight.

This Friday, the party begins at Andy's house where we're all getting high and listening to music before we leave for the Jethro Tull concert at the Fillmore East.

"Andy, somebody is at the door."

"Police! Open up!"

Oh, God, what am I going to do? I can't move. Where is everybody going? Somebody's run out on the terrace.

"Ben, get Alex off the terrace. He's so high he might jump."

"Flush the pot down the toilet. Everybody cool out, the drugs are gone. I have to let the cops in. Megan! Megan! Ben, take her to the bedroom."

When I awoke from my faint, I was told that the cops turned out to be two ex-friends playing a little trick. They made a big mistake. They were sent away to play cops and robbers someplace else. Alex didn't jump off the terrace but he left to go "uptown" and cop some more dope. Alex was into the hard stuff and Ben was trying to help him. Alex would hang out for a while but he always split. Sometimes when he parted, he took his friends' money with him—without asking for it. Alex scared me. I was afraid of him and hard drugs and sometimes I was afraid of pot. Ben said that part of the side effects from smoking a lot of pot was getting the heebie-jeebies and he had a cure for them.

"Drink a little wine, Megan, with every few tokes and it will take the edge off," he suggested.

I followed his lead and soon I was taking fewer tokes off the joint and more sips from the bottle. The heebie-jeebies were kept down.

I can be a new person when I get high. I can be anybody. Being high is freedom. Freedom from my family, from my Catholic girls' school education, freedom from all the rules. I'm part of the new generation and I believe in marijuana, free love, no bras. I've been sent home from high school numerous times for not having a bra on. The principal now waits on the steps for my arrival. We've both gotten smart: she doesn't chase around looking for me all day, and I wear a bra for my trips coming and going. It's a game because I know I'm the principal's favorite student. I have some of the highest marks in the school, I'm active in extracurricular activities and I'm going places. She knows it and in her way, she supports my cause. But rules are rules. I'm here to break them, Sister is here to enforce them.

Last Sunday, I was a guest on some Catholic priest's 6 A.M. radio talk show. Luckily, the show was taped during two afternoons the previous week, so all I had to crawl out of bed for on Sunday morning was to listen. I was chosen, along with a boy from our "brother" Catholic school to discuss Christianity and youth. The priest liked what I had to say and called me "provocative." It was a very funny scene at my house. The family woke to the alarm and climbed on or around my parents' bed to hear the program. It was still dark outside but I was making my debut on the airwaves! The only other people who heard the show were all the family and friends required by my mother to listen under pain of death, and the religious community of New York City. That included my principal and I'm sure she had a good chuckle. Naturally, I kept it all quiet on the outside and didn't tell my friends the good news. The good news was that I believed what I had to say about Jesus. My only problem was that it was becoming more and more difficult integrating the two sides of my life. My parents were proud and knew they could rest easy as far as I was concerned. What they didn't know was that I spent all day and night yesterday getting high and trying to be a radical. It is taking a lot of practice but I'm getting better at it and shedding much of my schoolgirl persona.

There is nothing really subversive about Ben either. He's the boy next door. He's captain of the basketball team—a clean-cut all-American boy with a slight variation on the theme. That is, his hair is long, he smokes dope and he's a conscientious objector to the Vietnam War. What's changed is what has happened to our generation. In order to be a part of it, we have to be a part of the radical teenage scene. Ben is the same way I am but he's more secure. He doesn't have to get involved in every cause, from civil rights to boycotting grapes, but I do.

Ben was my first teenage love. We've been together since I turned thirteen. For four years, he's been my life, my love, my escape from my family. Ben taught me how to smoke cigarettes, smoke dope, drink, French-kiss. I love Ben and he loves me—so much that sometimes it frightens me. He's too serious, too ready to make a lifetime commitment. I can't do it. So Ben and I are coming apart. I'm meeting new "freaks" in the park, at the marches, and I don't want Ben to tie me down. I'm only seventeen and it's time for dating lots of guys. The only trouble is, we don't date anymore. But still, I want to hang out with new people. Ben doesn't understand. For him, it's all or nothing, so for a while I choose to make it nothing. Why am I doing this? It's because I'm afraid I'm missing something. There's so much going on out there and so many people to meet, and I want to be involved in it all. Life is beginning to happen to me. I'm excited. I can be anyone.

"Megan, I'm too high. I'm frightened. I'm dizzy. There are voices in my head. Are the cops coming? Help me, Megan, I'm going to faint."

Amy's fainted and I don't know what to do. I'm pretty high myself. Everyone has split because the cops are galloping through the fountain area of the park in the hourly display to break up the getting-high parties.

"David, come and help me. Please get some water for Amy."

David loves Amy. If need be, he'll carry her all the way home—all five foot ten of her. But Amy's condition will improve instantly if she hears that David is going to touch her. No male person touches Amy. They all love her and she ignores them. So I'm stuck with them following us around all day. Amy's waking up. David is beginning to breathe easily.

Amy seems to know what she's doing when it comes to men. She makes them all fall in love with her and then she pretends they don't exist. Then they all try to get me to be their secret ally. Since I broke up with Ben, witnessing Amy's magic hasn't been easy on my ego. There's nothing wrong with me. I'm pretty but I'm not a leggy five-foot-ten raven-haired goddess. I'm five three, average weight, short legs, green eyes and freckles. My best friend is spectacular-looking—deep brown eyes, jet-black hair, thin, with long, long legs. I get lost in her shadow. She's gorgeous, I'm cute. She's also always just a little bit helpless when we get stoned and there's always a willing male around to help the damsel in distress. I can smoke as much as anybody else with no adverse side effects other than the occasional paranoia. When I do get paranoid, there's only Amy to take care of me. I left Ben because I didn't want to "belong" to one person, but since I left him, nobody else has shown any interest.

I'm in love with a freak in the park. He lives on roller skates and calls himself White Cloud. His hair is as long as mine and curlier. He's gorgeous and he knows it. I'm only one of many admirers. Amy says I'm a jerk. (Jerk is an all-purpose word for Amy.)

Back at my house, we're safe from Amy's pursuers and the narcs that I'm sure follow us around. Amy is feeling better. The heebie-jeebies have left and the munchies have taken over, so we park ourselves in the kitchen for some magical munchie cures. First we start with the basics, cookies and milk. Then we top those off with some ice cream and strawberries and some coffee to level us off for the parents. Amy is the best fun to be with if I can forget about the guys. She never seems to care about them and I feel guilty that I'm jealous of her.

"Megan, let's meet after dinner and go to the museum. It's open late tonight and we can smoke a joint and go talk to the mummies."

This is Amy's favorite way to get high, so I go along with it even though I always get lost and scared to death wandering around with all those mummies.

"Amy, they're going to catch on to us at the museum. The guards all know us already so you have to promise not to try to hide there for the night."

"O.K., O.K., no tricks, just a little culture. I have to go home and start dinner before Mother dear arrives, so I'll pick you up at seven-thirty."

"Great. See you later."

We smoked a joint, went to the museum, spooked ourselves and left to go to our favorite coffee shop for ice cream sodas. We went to this particular coffee shop because we knew that all the alcoholics went there after their secret meetings. Amy and I sat in the booth behind them and listened to the stories, laughing hysterically but certain they didn't notice us!

For the most part, we feel good about ourselves. My home life is a wreck and I can't wait to make the great escape. I'm plotting to go far away to college, only I have no money to do it so I make a major decision.

"Amy, I'm going to work next year and save money for college. That way I can go wherever I want."

I'll have to tell the folks my new plans. I know they're not going to agree with me. There will probably be a lot of "discussion," as my father calls it, so I'll have to wait until dinner. That is, if he's home for dinner.

" 'Bye, folks. I'm off to another exciting day in my Catholic institution of higher learning. See you for dinner."

" 'Bye, Megan. Must you wear that hat with the feather? You look like someone out of Shakespeare."

"I'm studying Shakespeare, Dad, and the hat stirs up inspiration."

"I'm sure it stirs up more than that for Sister Aloysius."

"Don't worry about the old sis. I've got her covered. 'Bye again."

Some days I can barely make it out of the house. How will I ever make it to California?

"Hi, Amy. Did you bring the muffins? Great. Let's walk, we have plenty of time."

"O.K., but will you quiz me on chemistry on the way? We can just do the chart. It's easy to read and walk."

"Sure, but why are you nervous? The lowest grade you've gotten this year is 95 percent."

"Well, Megan, if I stay nervous before tests my grades stay up. If I let down my guard, then I screw up and wind up with a 95 percent!"

"You're too much, Amy. Let's talk formulas. Wait a minute! Do you want to get stoned for your test? I've got a joint left."

"You're crazy! If I was stoned for chemistry, I'd be inventing new equations. Megan, we don't have to be stoned *all* the time in order to be cool."

"Well, almost all the time."

Amy is right. We don't have to be stoned all the time, but all day Saturday is a must. As usual, we're spending the day in the park, getting high, roller-skating, playing frisbee. Amy is beginning to withdraw. She says she's bored. I'm trying to keep her entertained because I want to be here and I need her. I'm still trying to get White Cloud to notice me, or at least David's friend Josh, who's always hanging around.

"Amy, here come David and Josh. Please be nice to them. Hi, David. Hi, Josh. What's up for the weekend?"

"Hi, Amy. Hi, Megan. We've decided to give up on these stupid high school dances so we're going down to the Fillmore to hear some music. The Grateful Dead is playing tonight and we have four tickets."

"Sounds great, doesn't it, Amy? I agree with you about the dances. All those yo-yos drunk on beer and throwing up in the bathroom makes me sick. I'd much rather hear some music."

"Terrific! Amy, will you come too?" David pleaded.

"O.K., we'll see you later. Pick us up at my house at seven-thirty."

On the way home I just had to find out why Amy acted the way she did. "Amy, you're such a sport. They act as though they'd lie down and die for you and you barely talk to them. I'm going to have to stop being a part of this. I feel like a turd. They don't even look at me."

"Oh, Megan. Don't be so upset. I'm not interested in those guys."

"That's the point. Why not? I am."

"I'm not because they're nothing special. You know how I feel. There's only going to be one man in my life and he's going to be Prince Charming. So please don't care how those jerks act. You're just as pretty as I am and you know it!"

"Maybe you're right. Maybe we should stop wasting our time. Tonight will be the last time we go out with them. O.K.?"

"O.K."

The Fillmore East is the hottest spot in New York. It's where all the biggest groups give concerts and it's perfect for hippies. The backdrop to the music is an incredible light show—made to order if you're stoned on anything. The concession stand on the second floor is stocked for munchie mania—giant cookies, all flavors of yoghurt (Dutch apple is the best munchie cure), ice cream, soda, chocolate milk, candy. I've flipped out many times just trying to decide how to treat my munchies.

Tonight David brought some hash and we smoked it before we came in. Amy is in another world. She's even laughing at David's jokes. Josh is very quiet and I feel really weird. I'm too high, my heart is racing, the music has permeated my veins and it's making the blood race through my veins. Everything is moving too fast. I'm frightened and nobody knows. They're so stoned and they probably wouldn't understand if I told them. I'll go get some food and maybe I can calm down. Which way out? Where are the stairs? Can't they stop flashing those damn lights for one minute?

Hours pass. Hours and hours. I can't believe that the music is still playing because it has to be the middle of the night. Finally, Amy finds me. I'm sitting on the stairs, crying because I can't stop my blood from boiling and my heart from racing.

"Oh, Megan, why didn't you tell me?"

"I couldn't talk, Amy. Too scared. Too stoned. Please, let's go."

"I'll run and tell David and Josh. They can stay. We'll take a cab home. Stay right here, Megan. It's going to be O.K."

Amy took me home. She sneaked me into her house, into her room, and then called my mother and told her I was staying over. Amy told my parents she wanted to say hi to them so insisted on calling while I was in the shower. "See you tomorrow, Mrs. Moran. Good night."

Amy is a lifesaver. She made coffee and brought me cookies and ran a bubble bath. I started to calm down and swore I'd never smoke hash again. I even considered giving up grass.

"We don't have to give up grass, Megan. Let's just cut down. If we smoke less, we won't get as high."

"O.K., Amy, but you know what happens after I have that first joint. I'm determined to have the second to keep me up there. But I'll try. Maybe we should drink wine when we smoke. Ben taught me to do that. The wine cures the heebie-jeebies."

So we changed our methods somewhat, but continued on with our madness. Amy cut back and I saw less of her. I started hanging around more with the park hippies and Amy didn't approve. I began to see that she didn't have it in her to be a hippie. She is too caught up in all her plans for college, taking all the precollege courses and studying every night. She's taking all this college planning too seriously. She doesn't approve of my decision to wait a year before going away to school. She's not the only one. My parents are also against the idea. I expected it from my parents but not my best friend. Best friends are always supposed to be on the opposite side from your parents, no matter what they really think.

When I finally told my parents and outlined my plans for working a year and then going out to California to school, my mother cried and my father yelled. He accused me of choosing California as the place farthest away from home so I could get away from them (it was very perceptive of him) and so I could become one of those drugged-out Haight-Ashbury bums (another star for his perception). After all this heated screaming, he hit me with the final blow: no money from him for this cockamamie scheme! I knew I wasn't getting any money. That much was clear if I went to Brooklyn

instead of California. There simply isn't any to give. I don't be-
grudge either of them that fact, I just wish they didn't have to
pretend they're holding it back out of disapproval. I pointed out that
I'm staying home and working next year to save for tuition, so I
don't need their money, and they will have a whole year in which to
grieve their loss—or drive me crazy. It may be tough right now, but
I'm doing what I want to do. I'm not yet free but I'm laying the
foundation and that feels very good. If only Amy would see the light
and come West with me. Instead, I know that I'm already losing my
best friend.

I'm losing control with pot. I'm spending time with the park
creeps and winding up in strange apartments, not sure how I've
gotten there. Last night I was somewhere in the East Village, in an
apartment waiting for Sandy, some park dude I've known for two
days, to cop some pot. I thought he was meeting a friend for a
couple of joints but when the drug connection showed up he was
nobody's friend and it turned out that pot was only the icing on the
cake. The real cop was for a suitcase full of pills. I'd never seen so
many pills or so much money. I was high already and silently freaking out, imagining the *Daily News* headlines, CATHOLIC SCHOOLGIRL
FOUND SLAIN IN VILLAGE PAD OVER SUITCASE FULL OF DRUGS. I
prayed for it all to be over and for me to get out alive. When the
dealer left, I begged Sandy to put me in a cab and give me the
money to get uptown. I was losing it and I was sure that he didn't
want to deal with my hysteria.

When I got uptown, it was too early to go home and I was too
flipped out to hide it. I went to Rockers, a local bar, the high school
hangout. I found some friends of Ben's and had some beers with
them. I began to come down and calm down and soon I was having
a good time. Beer isn't so terrible after all. What's wrong with
laughing and having fun? It's better than having the "grass creeps"
and feeling afraid of your own shadow.

I'm going to continue to boycott grapes and protest the war in
Vietnam, but I'm going to stop smoking pot. It's really no fun for
me and it hasn't been fun for a long time—since I broke up with
Ben. He was the only person who truly shared the experience with
me. Amy and I share but when we get high we're both in our own
worlds. Ben was always in my world when we got high together. He
wanted to be in my world more than anything. I miss him. I miss
the good times. It hasn't been much fun lately—too much dope in
my head and no boyfriend to make me feel really special. I'm going
to change things and try to start having fun without pot. Last night
I had a great time at Rockers. I was able to relax and laugh and
dance, so I'm going to cool it with the park scene and make the bar
scene for a while. It seems like a much more social environment and
I want to improve my social life, especially in the male area!

Anyway, I'm frightened of the drug scene. Without Ben or Amy,
I've been mixed up with people I hardly know and who don't really
care what happens to me. After last night in the East Village, I
realize that I'm out of my league. I have no intention of becoming a
dope addict, or of going to jail for hanging around with the wrong
people. Both of those routes seemed like real possibilities if I hadn't
gotten out of that East Village apartment last night. "No more
drugs" isn't a tough slogan for me to adopt. It's going to change my
life-style and might even make me a little less cool, but as long as I
can still get high from drinking, I won't become too uncool! Also, I
miss my old boyfriend and my best friend. I can't get him back but I
can get Amy back. Her only complaint was that she was tired of so
much pot and all those park "jerks." Finally, I agree with her. Now,
I'm going to call her and tell her the good news.

"Hi, Amy, it's Megan."

"Well, well, Megan Moran. I thought you left this planet ages
ago. I'm so surprised to hear from you . . ."

"Amy, try not to give me such a hard time until you hear what
I've got to say. I can't talk about it on the phone. Can you go for a
walk?"

On my way over to Amy's, I tried to sort through all the confusion I was feeling. During the time I was hanging out by myself in
Central Park, I felt lost and detached from the people I care about.

But I did it because I needed to be away from Ben's smothering love (I still need to be away from that), and I needed to be out of Amy's gorgeous shadow for a while. I was becoming so jealous of her and I started thinking of myself as ugly. I don't know why I care so much what men think of me. Maybe I'm trying to prove to myself that there are many other fish in the sea and I did make the right decision when I left Ben. All of this independence and proving things hasn't done anything to improve my life. It's created more confusion. To use Amy's word, I don't need those "jerks" in the park. I need my friends. I need to be a normal teenager for a while.

Amy is so eager to hear my news that she's coming up the block to meet me halfway. "O.K., Megan, spill the beans."

"I've missed you, Amy, and I haven't liked what I've been doing hanging out in the park alone. I had a real drug scare the other night and I've decided to give up the park and drug scene. From now on, I want to hang out at Rockers and drink beer and wine!"

"That's great news, Megan. We'll have much more fun. I've missed you too, especially knowing that there are only a few months before I go away to college. So let's go have a drink and celebrate the new Megan!"

We settled into Rockers sidewalk café and ordered our celebration drinks.

"Amy, don't you agree that drinking is more sophisticated than smoking pot? We can sit in a café like adults. We don't have to go slinking into doorways and behind trees to grab a toke off a joint. And I've noticed that people in the bars smell better than all the park freaks. I feel very grown up and socially acceptable. What a switch!"

"Tell me, Megan, have you written any poetry lately?"

"Just the typical sentimental slobber about the lost love. I think I'm going to give up. Sometimes I feel so foolish trying to write beautiful verse. I've been reading Baudelaire and he's convinced me that I don't have what it takes."

"Nonsense, Megan. You have a natural sensibility. If the love poems are too mushy, stop writing them. Write about yourself, not about men. Write about growing up, discovering."

"Amy do you realize what's going on here? We're getting high on a bottle of wine, but we're also having a real conversation. We're not withdrawing into ourselves or talking silly nonsense. We're growing up, Amy, and maybe now, we're doing it the right way."

As Amy and I walked home that night it all felt perfect. It was a crystal-clear spring evening, stars were shining in New York City, and I was looking out to my future. I couldn't see anything: the future was vast and wide open and, at that moment, I was sure that life was going to be a glorious adventure with endless possibilities.

Once I stopped focusing on copping dope and getting stoned in Central Park, I became a bit more normal. I was more comfortable with my parents because now I felt that I wasn't living a complete lie with them. When I was immersed in the drugs and following around my hippie friends, I really felt like two people. It made me feel very guilty and paranoid and created confusion in my head. "Who am I?" is the big question of the day and I had two different answers because I was two different people. I was becoming afraid of how I was acting. It seemed I would do anything to get high and some guys tried to take advantage of that. I'd already "lost" my virginity a year before, and not to some park hippie. In fact, it was during a short period of time when I'd sworn off grass and was drinking instead. That night, I lost control of myself because of booze, and lost my virginity as a result. After that terrible experience, I decided not to drink anymore and I've been smoking grass until now. I can understand why the phrase "lost my virginity" has been adopted. I did feel a terrible loss and I did want to find it again and put it back. It's been so hard for me trying to forget that night. Amy would never have made such a mistake and I've never told her what happened. I haven't told anybody until now.

It's almost the same old story. I'd been away from Ben for a few months and Amy had an admirer, Steve, who was dying to go out with her. Amy seemed to like Steve more than the others, so I agreed with him to help arrange a double date. Steve promised to get his friend Philip to be my date. Naturally, I had a hot crush on Philip but I knew he was coming along only to help Steve out.

We went to Sea Catch, a big fish restaurant on Third Avenue. It seemed like a strange choice to me since most of the clientele appeared to be over fifty. I don't think the management was overjoyed with our choice of restaurants, either, because we were kept waiting an hour and a half for a table. But the wait was worth it! We settled in at the bar and I had my first whiskey sour. It was delicious! It was sweet and tasted like soda, but it did something sparkly to my head. I had another and another and when we sat down at our table I had another. I have no idea what I ate, if I ate at all. We (or should I say they) finished the meal and we left the restaurant. By this time I was both wildly in love and wildly drunk. I fell down on Third Avenue in front of Sea Catch and it was marvelous! I wanted to sing and dance! Instead, I was put in a cab with everyone else and Amy insisted on getting out first at her house. I went with the guys to Philip's house. I don't know why. I was too drunk to know anything. Steve was mad because Amy wouldn't hold his hand. I laughed.

I truly don't remember what happened next. I don't remember going to bed with Philip. I don't remember having sex. I just remember waking up in his bed and seeing that it was almost four o'clock in the morning, panicking, grabbing my clothes and running for a cab. When I passed through the living room, Steve was sleeping on the couch. Knowing he was there through whatever happened made me feel doubly ashamed. Now there were two people in the world who knew for a fact that I was a slut. I thought I would die. The shame was so great that I really believed I could die from it alone.

Nothing else mattered. I arrived home to find my mother and older brother waiting up for me. The lies just flew out of my mouth as I flew to my room. There was no trouble. My brother helped to cover for me and my mother forgave me. It was easiest for my mother to forgive and ignore. She couldn't bear to know even part of the truth—that I was drunk enough to pass out for four hours.

The next day I hated waking up. I hated myself. I wanted to die. I knew I would never recover and eventually everyone would know what I'd done. I was sure I was pregnant so I went to a pay phone, called Planned Parenthood and told them what happened. I needed to tell someone, so the lady on the phone got the entire story— much more detail than she needed. They sent me to a doctor on Fifth Avenue for a "morning after" shot. It cost thirty dollars. I scraped together every penny I had, then stole five dollars from my mother's shopping money.

I was in a state of terror. Amy called. I wouldn't talk to her. I fabricated a story for my mother about my afternoon plans, then I went to the doctor. It felt like I was going to an illegal abortionist with a coat hanger in his hand. When I arrived at the doctor's door, a famous movie star was leaving the office and I felt sorry for her, that she was in the same predicament as I. But her presence legitimized the doctor in my eyes. He was very handsome and that made me more ashamed. He didn't tell me that I was a bad girl. He told me the shot would make me sick, and it did. He told me that the "morning after" shot was not to be considered a form of birth control because it was dangerous to use too often. He gave me a prescription for birth control pills which I threw in the garbage can on the way home. I wasn't going to need those pills because I was never going to have sex again—never.

I couldn't see Amy. I couldn't let her know. Anyway, I hated her. It was because of her purity and her beauty that I did what I did. I stayed away from her for a week and it was a week of lonely terror. Naturally, Philip never called again. After a week I tried to ease my feelings and pretend it never happened. As the song goes, I picked myself up and "kept on trucking." Amy noticed a change but she didn't push it. I wouldn't let her get close enough.

I vowed never to drink again—and that's how I made my decision to smoke pot exclusively. At that point in time, smoking pot seemed safer. I hadn't yet lost control smoking pot. Now I've come full circle. I feel as though I'm on some search for the perfect high. Grass or booze? Booze or grass? I only want to be happy and have fun and stop feeling ashamed of myself. So for now, I'll try booze again but this time, I'll try to act like a grown-up.

Possibly after my first experience of sex in a drunken blackout, I vowed to stay away from booze and chose pot instead because pot was a distancer. I could retreat into my own little world when high on pot. The only thing social about pot was the act of smoking it— passing the joint around the circle of friends. That's where the socializing ended. Once people got high, they withdrew, became less talkative or else focused on one person or one thing at a time. The more I smoked, the more I withdrew. I passed from the early giggly stage very quickly into the quiet panic stage. This probably happened because I smoked too much and also because I was unsure of myself and afraid of other people.

Now I want to join the human race. I want to be a part of the witty, sparkling conversation that goes along with sharing a bottle of wine or a round of cocktails. I've spent a lot of time watching adults have cocktails and waiting for my chance to come. Stacey, a good friend of mine growing up, lived in one of the fancy brownstones on my block. Her family was wealthy and they knew famous people. For a couple of years we were inseparable (as Amy and I are now) and I spent a lot of time at Stacey's house. Every night Stacey's parents had the "hour of charm." That was the euphemism for cocktail hour, and at Stacey's house it *was* very charming. The adults and children mingled, talked, played games and drank. The children had ginger ale and the adults had martinis. I remember thinking how special it all was; even our soda looked like an adult drink. Not only did I learn about drinking during the "hour of charm," I learned how to play bridge and backgammon. It hurt me so to leave at dinnertime and go to my home devoid of all charm, to possibly face a drunken father. Stacey moved away and I haven't thought about the hour of charm until tonight, sitting in this bar drinking gin and tonics and feeling absolutely charming with Amy.

The only problem with the cocktail hour is that it's too short. One hour is not enough time to get sufficiently high without also getting sick from drinking too fast. When smoking a joint, I can get high in five minutes. When drinking it takes considerably longer. So, although I admire the cocktail hour, I'm going to schedule my drinking dates for after dinner so I have the entire evening to be sociable and charming and get pleasantly high.

Drinking isn't everything. There's school and after-school jobs and evening babysitting—and then there's weekend drinking. It's not my aim. It's just a means to achieve my aim which is to have fun, to fall in love, but really to be the focus of someone else's love. Drinking does something to awaken my sense of my own sexiness or femininity or womanliness. When I drink I'm not clumsy anymore. I can flirt. I can maneuver my body around the dance floor with rhythm and fluid motion. No more jerkiness. A lot more sexiness. Sex has already gotten me into big trouble. My flirting must remain all innocence. The next time I participate in the "unmentionable" it must be from a position of mutual love; maybe then it will become mentionable again. I cannot hurt myself like that anymore.

Amy is changing. She needs more time for painting, she claims, and has less time for me and for weekend partying. I miss her but I also feel freer when she's not around. That's because I need Amy's approval and I never get it, especially regarding my attitudes and relationships with guys. Now that she's not here I don't have to worry about flirting too much and, more importantly, her absence assures me of someone to flirt with. But I miss her terribly. It's as though she represents the "higher" side of life. She's plugged into something that I haven't a clue about. Sometimes I just don't feel good enough.

Finally, I'm eighteen. Totally legal. No doubt about it. It's a great day—cause for a major celebration! Amy's mother has given me a split of champagne and I'm deeply disappointed that it isn't a full bottle. I caught myself and acted very graciously, but why am I so upset? I know I'll be celebrating and drinking all night. This half bottle isn't all I'm going to get.

In fact, I'm getting a "surprise" party. I've known about it for three days but nobody knows that I know. Amy has gone to so much trouble to plan the party I think I should hold up my end and be surprised. I'm nervous. I'm afraid that I don't have enough friends who will show up. I'm nervous for Amy. I wonder if she has enough food and drink. I want to help her with the last-minute details but instead I have to allow myself to be shuffled back and forth by Amy and my parents. My parents are insisting on taking me to dinner tonight. Amy says she has tickets for a concert that starts at nine. She wants me to have dinner with my parents and then pick her up at her house at eight.

My parents order wine. My father is in fine form, telling funny stories, reminiscing about my mother's eighteenth birthday. Mother blushes and then I know it must have been "very romantic." My birthday is turning out well but it's not going to be romantic. I'm boyfriendless. I've been boyfriendless for at least six months and I don't like it. It makes me feel lonely when I drink.

I arrive at the party and prepare myself to act surprised. The loud burst of delight from my friends is shocking enough that, for a moment, I really am surprised. I'm moved. I'm happy and I'm relieved because there are enough people who care that it's my birthday. Mom and Dad disappear with Amy's parents because luckily, we're all beyond the age of chaperones. We'll all behave tonight. There will be too much drinking, but I'm sure that Amy banned dope from the premises. There is plenty of champagne—more than I could possibly drink. I'm pleased.

"Happy birthday, Megan! You've finally reached the age of freedom. I can't wait to catch up."

"Thanks, Joel. Today wasn't any different than any other in terms of feeling free, but it's certainly been a lot of fun! Excuse me—Hi, Sarah, what a surprise!"

"Hi, Megan, baby! Well, New Jersey isn't exactly across the country—and Amy invited me to spend the night. I couldn't miss my favorite person's birthday! This is a great party. Let's boogie!"

We boogied and I had fun—at least until the end of the evening. A little too much champagne and a few too many dances caused my stomach to do too much rocking and rolling. I spent the last hour of my birthday party throwing up in the bathroom. Some guests came in to say goodbye. Others just split. When it was all over I started crying. Why so many tears? Why cry on Amy's shoulder when she gave me the best present she could? I don't know. I feel so ungrateful and unworthy. It must have something to do with too much champagne.

The passing of my eighteenth birthday signifies change for me, but not real freedom. I still have to live with my parents for another year, but I know that freedom is a state of mind and I don't feel trapped anymore. I've made my decision to go to school in California and now I'm working toward that goal. I think that my parents respect me for sticking to it and making it happen, even though theirs have been the loudest voices against it.

Eighteen will be a good year: dreams will not all be realized but they will come closer. It's a whole new world out here. School's out and I'm eighteen! I'm no longer a high school kid but I'm not really an adult either. I still act like a baby because I always want to be the center of attention. If I had any acting talent, I could be a great star simply because I need the attention so badly. Why? What am I lacking? What haven't I been given by my loving but somewhat screwed-up parents, my family and my friends? My boyfriends sense my need, that's why they make their quick exits. And my best friend now sees it quite clearly after my performance at my birthday party. She doesn't understand because such neediness is so foreign to her, but she loves me very much and tries to help me.

I know that smoking pot and drinking are ways to relieve stress and lighten up the day, the night, the life. Drinking is lightening me up. I have fun when I'm drinking. I feel I can let it all out. I feel closer to the truth. Drinking fills me up with warmth, a sense of fullness, of belonging, and, most of all, it helps me become the center of attention. But there's a problem with drinking and that comes late at night. I keep drinking the night away, feeling that I'm dancing on the peak of my high, and always I have one drink too many—the drink that makes me fall off the peak. I try and try to calculate so that I can stay in the happy place, but I always miss and wind up in the sick place or the crying place. Almost everyone else seems to stop before falling off. I'm going to keep trying to get it right because it's the only thing that makes me feel whole and full of myself.

I'm a city kid and when growing up we were too poor to go away in the summer. Sometimes we had a week's vacation in a bungalow somewhere but certainly never more than that. I did my swimming in a makeshift backyard pool, under the sprinklers in Central Park and under the hydrant in the street. I never heard of Cape Cod, Nantucket, Fire Island or the Hamptons, but now that I've been the world's greatest babysitter for six years, I've had offers to go to all those places. A few years ago, I chose Southampton and I've been going every summer since—first as a mother's helper and now as a maid. Of course, Amy and I arranged it so that we both work within a mile from each other. Southampton has taught me the finer things in life. I've learned about setting tables and sleeping on fine linens, and I've seen how the wealthy eat and play and live. This summer, I'm a maid five days a week and a babysitter for the weekend evenings. I do the babysitting work for my former employers in exchange for my own little cottage on their property. Now that I'm no longer an official employee, the Hardings invite me to their parties and to dinner. Tonight, I'm going to the main house for cocktails. This is a first. They haven't ever poured a drink for me.

"Hello, Megan, you're looking very tan this evening, and that's a delightful little dress." I smile at Mrs. Harding Sr., and her condescending remark. My "delightful little dress" is the most expensive article of clothing that I own.

"Oh, Megan, dear, there you are! Come and say hello to your old friends, Carol and Robert Long . . ." Wendy, my employer and the "young Mrs. Harding," whisks me away to see her college roommate and husband. The Longs spent a week with us two summers ago and we became great friends. Their two children added to my duties as playmate, lifeguard and camp counselor, and brought my charges to a total of five, but I didn't mind. The Longs didn't try to make their children disappear all day the way the Hardings do. As a result, Carol and Robert spent as much time with me as with Wendy and Jeff.

"Hello, Carol. Hello, Robert. It's so good to see you both. Are Susie and J.J. here? No, that's right. This is an adult party."

"Megan, we're delighted to see you. Robert, get Megan a gin and tonic and then we want to hear all your plans for college . . ."

I liked the sound of that 'Get Megan a gin and tonic,' as if I were used to gin and tonics at sunset on the decks of waterfront mansions. I couldn't wait for Robert's return so I could experience my first gin and tonic as a guest at my first cocktail party in Southampton.

"Thank you, Robert. It looks delicious."

I don't think I'll ever forget this moment for the rest of my life. Nothing could be so perfect. Not only does it look delicious but it tastes delicious, and it's doing very nice things to my head. This is the way I want my life to be—cocktails at the right places, with the right people, wearing the right clothes and having scintillating conversations. This gin and tonic has released me from my anxiety and I'm finding it easy and enjoyable discussing my college plans with the Longs.

". . . Yes, Carol, it's a small liberal arts college outside of San Francisco. I chose it because the school features a progressive curriculum."

"It sounds as though you've weighed all your choices, Megan, and come up with an excellent school. Are you unhappy about spending a year working before starting school?"

"Oh, no. I'm looking forward to it. As you know, I have to work in order to pay tuition, but I also think that the time off between high school and college will be time for me to mature. I know when I start college I'll be dedicated to it and ready to commit myself to working hard."

What a speech! I'd better get another drink if I'm going to keep talking like this. I wish Robert would ask if I'm ready for a refill. I've been ready for ten minutes. Maybe I'll excuse myself and go get my own . . .

"Would you both please excuse me. There's someone here I must see. It's been wonderful seeing you again and please say hi to the children for me."

Now, to find the bar and some kind gentleman to fetch me a drink. I know it's not ladylike, especially at this party, to order my own. There's Tom Baxter. He'll take care of me.

"Oh, Tom, Hello. How are you?"

"Well hello, little Megan. You grow up more each year."

"That's the way it works, Tom. Would you please stop leering and get me a drink."

"Great idea. I was on my way to the bar for a little refill myself."

"I noticed, Tom. Do they throw you out when you get drunk or just pretend you're not here? Let's stay close to the bar, so we can back this up. O.K., I'm ready for another."

"Don't drink so fast, little Megan. Young ladies are not permitted to make spectacles of themselves the way we boys are."

"I just love the taste of gin and tonics. They taste like a summer's evening. They are going to be my 'summer drink' for the rest of my life."

"I do believe it's time to get you out of here. Allow me to escort you home."

"Only if I can have one more for the road."

"O.K. Stay right here. Don't move and don't talk to anyone. Just smile politely and point, if need be. Oh boy, I've got to get you hidden before 'the young Mrs. Harding' shows up."

Tom took me home. I wasn't as terribly drunk as he said I was. I wanted some more drinks but I didn't have any booze in my little cottage.

"Megan, take a nap and I'll pick you up in a couple of hours and take you to the club dance."

"Oh! How wonderful, Tom! Will you feed me also?"

"Yes, I'll feed you. Just sleep these g&t's off and you'll be good as new at nine-thirty. I'll see you then."

What a sport! Everyone says he's a drunk but he's taking me to a country club dance. I feel like Cinderella tonight—"poor girl succeeds in Southampton society." I just won't let him get too drunk and we'll have a wonderful time. He's a nice person, even if he drinks too much.

"Tom, I've been counting and this is my sixty-eighth gin and tonic. Do you think I'm getting a little tipsy?"

"Megan, you're a character. It may be your sixth or even eighth g&t, but not your sixty-eighth."

"Well, of course. Who said such a silly thing? Let's dance."

Tom isn't such a terrible drunk, but maybe that's because I am. Drunk, I mean. I think I am just a little bit drunk and should be very careful not to fall down during this dance. I wish he would stop twirling me.

"Tom! Stop! I'm going to spin away."

"O.K., baby. Listen, we're leaving this dull party and we're really going to have some fun."

"Where are we going?"

"Just get in the car, kiddo, and say hi to my friends."

"But where? There's not room! There must be ten people in this little thing."

"There are plenty of laps, Megan. There—sit on Chester's lap. He won't notice. He's almost passed out. Hang on, folks! Up, up and away!" We went to the big rock-and-roll bar in town. I feel a little weird being with all Tom's preppy friends in their pink pants and green jackets. And the girls won't talk to me. I'd like to go home now but I'm stuck in this bowl of mush for the rest of the night. I'll just make the best of it. "Waiter, another t&g with a piece of green, please."

"Time for a swim, folks!"

"Oh, God, no. We can't go into the ocean this drunk. We'll all drown."

"Don't be such a baby, Megan. A swim will sober us all up."

"No, I won't go into the ocean. We'll all die! Come home with me and swim in the Hardings' pool."

"Then we'll die for sure. That's much crazier than swimming in the ocean, Megan!"

"No, it's not. They always say 'Our home is your home.' So I'm inviting you all home for a predawn swim."

"What are we waiting for!"

I'm doing this because I don't want to drown. We'll be quiet and the Hardings won't even hear us. I'll explain everything in the morning. I have to be doing the right thing. There's nothing else I could do. I'm saving lives.

We piled into the car again and this time there seemed to be more of us. All I can see is a mass of pink, green and madras. I'm very drunk and I'm glad to be finally going home. A little dip for these folks will be harmless, won't it? Nobody will hear us, and I'm keeping ten drunks out of the dark, treacherous ocean.

"O.K., gang. Out of your clothes and into the pool, let's keep the noise down."

"It's cold, oh! Someone's crawling between my legs. Tom, get away from me!"

"Suzanne, come on in. No sharks here to bite you!"

"Uh-oh . . . Someone put the pool lights on. Here comes trouble."

"Who's down there?" It's Wendy's voice. What should I do?

"It's just Megan and some friends, Wendy. We're having a swim. Come on in."

Tom is warning me, "You shouldn't have said that, Megan."

"Megan, get out of that pool right now!"

"I can't, Wendy. I have no clothes on and there are boys here." I can't stop laughing. We're all laughing. Wendy shut the lights off and went away. She's such an uptight bitch, anyway.

"O.K., guys. I guess the party's over. Everybody out of the pool!"

I finally packed them into their car, stumbled to my cottage and fell into bed. Thank God my clothes are already off because I'm gone . . .

Knock. Knock. Knock. Knock.

"All right, all right. Stop banging. I'm coming."

Oh, no, it's Wendy. I'd better act very sorry.

"Hi, Wendy. Listen—"

"No, you listen to me. You have one hour to pack your bags and leave the premises. You've worn out your welcome. After all we've done for you! I never want to set eyes on you again!" She slammed the door in my face. I didn't get a chance to even try to explain but I didn't have an explanation anyway. Boy, does my head hurt. I'm so sick. What have I done? What am I going to tell my parents? Some debut I made last night into Southampton society. They'll probably remember it for a long time. I have to call Amy. She'll help me.

"Amy, it's Megan. I'm in trouble. Please come and get me. I've been thrown out of the Hardings'."

"Oh, God, Megan. What did you do?"

"Nothing. Just took an unauthorized swim in their pool. Please hurry."

Today I want to die. I am ashamed of myself. I have ruined what was an excellent relationship. I've taken advantage of people who put their trust in me, who shared their home with me. I deserve this banishment because I was wrong last night. I was wrong because, first of all, I was drunk and good judgment isn't a characteristic of a drunk. I thought I was protecting us all from drowning in the ocean. That was my biggest mistake: I shouldn't have started thinking. The way things have turned out, it probably would have been better to have taken my chances with the sharks.

I am the only one being punished for last night. Tom Baxter and his friends walked away unscathed. I'll probably never see them again, but I'm sure they'll continue going to club dances, getting drunk and taking off on some wild escapade. For them it will continue to be fun. I can't imagine any of them being ashamed of themselves. They know they have a rightful place in society here and they can never be denied that.

Amy arrived and helped clean out the cottage and load my suitcases into the car. We drove off in silence, tears streaming down my face. Then Amy let me have it.

"I don't know what's wrong with you, Megan. You court disaster. You never know when you've had enough of anything. Last night I begged you to dump Baxter and let me take you home. You refused to listen. Instead, you insulted me, screaming at me in the ladies' room."

"I did not scream at you, Amy."

"You most certainly did. You were so drunk you just don't remember. But I do. You told me that I was a self-righteous bitch, always doing the right thing and keeping my hands clean—"

"Oh, God, Amy. And after that you drove out here to get me!"

"I know you didn't really mean it. You were drunk. But my feelings are hurt, and even though I'm still your best friend, I need a vacation from you, Megan. I'm glad you're going back to New York tonight. You have to sort your life out and try to understand why you're always pushing the self-destruct button."

"Listen, I'm sorry for what I said, Amy, but please, no lectures right now. I can barely hold my head up it hurts so bad, and I know how terrible I've been. Just take me to your place and let me sleep for a few more hours before the afternoon train. Then I'll be gone."

Amy didn't say another word and I was throwing silent daggers at her for the rest of the ride. She's too damn perfect. I really don't remember insulting her last night but I'm glad I finally let her know how I feel. We should end our friendship right now. All it does for me is make me feel inadequate. But I won't say anything now. I'll wait until I'm getting on the train so I can make a quick escape. Right now I need aspirin and sleep more than anything.

Ever since I've been thirteen or fourteen, I've had dreams of my eighteenth summer. It's always glorified in teen magazine articles and romantic teenage novels. My eighteenth summer finally arrived and I was lucky enough to find myself in an ideal setting, something fitting for a magazine article. I had my own little cottage on a waterfront estate in Southampton, access to society and parties, a summer devoted to swimming, sailing, sunning and partying with a minimal amount of working in between. And my best friend lived down the road. I was on my own in lush surroundings with no parents to hassle me. What more could a girl ask for? Yet I destroyed it. I blew it. I cut off all my chances in that Southampton world. Why? They gave me champagne and gin and tonics and lobster and caviar and strawberries. I cannot believe that I destroyed it all—the highlight of my life—because I insisted on getting roaring drunk and violating other people's property as well as their trust. I don't know why I have to get drunk every time I drink. At the country club last night there were so many "pretty little rich things" in flowery dresses and Pappagallo sandals. They were dancing and laughing and having fun. I laughed at them because they were drinking fruit punch and I was drinking booze. They were the little girls and I was the "sophisticate." Then I became the "falling-down drunk." It was a quick switch. It took about five drinks to get there.

I destroyed my life last night. Now I'm going home to Mommy and Daddy and I can't run into their arms and cry my eyes out. I have to hide this mess. I have to think of a convincing story and I have to lie. I can never tell the truth about this summer. I'm so

EL CAMINO COLLEGE LIBRARY

afraid of facing them. I'm so afraid that they'll see my pain and fear. Oh, God, why is everything turning out wrong for me?

Every time I come home to my parents' house after a summer in Southampton, I go through severe culture shock. The city, and their apartment, is so gray. There's not enough light and there's no inter-mingling of the inside and the outside. No decks, just fire escapes. My parents' apartment is so small; it's just not big enough to be a home. How could we ever have grown up here? Even though this time I'm coming home hanging my head in shame, I still feel above it all. I am angry that this is all they have to offer me.

"Megan, why are you home so early? There's almost a month left before the summer is over." My mother is searching my face for the answer, clearly afraid to hear what it is.

"My maid's job ended early and I decided that I wouldn't start another part-time summer job. It seemed best to come home and start looking for permanent work for the year."

"Are you sure that's all that happened?"

"Of course. It's time for me to start being responsible and stop vacationing at the beach. I've had enough sun and fun. Now I'd love some dinner, a bath and then early to bed. I'm exhausted from the train ride."

"Dinner will be ready in ten minutes. Welcome home, baby." Mom hugged me and for about five seconds I was close to crying and telling all, but I got through it. Telling them wouldn't help anything. They would just have to share my humiliation and my shame. I don't want to lose their love and trust on top of everything else. I'm going to change so that I can deserve it.

The remainder of the summer passed uneventfully. My parents were happy together because my father had been "on the wagon" for about six months. They went out a lot and I joined them for a few dinners and movies. They were glad to have me but I couldn't help thinking they would be having a more romantic time if I weren't there. I tried to leave them alone as much as possible. I loved seeing them so happy. They were transformed. Their whole approach to life became magnanimous and forgiving. I loved them so much for their ability to change and to love despite it all.

I was lost but they didn't notice. I'm glad because, as time passed, I was more determined to keep the truth from them. I found some comfort in witnessing their happiness and I found some peace of mind in spending a quiet month without socializing, without drinking.

The world is no longer as inviting as it seemed a few months ago when, after sharing a bottle of wine with Amy, I felt that life was offering me everything. I've had a rude awakening. It seems that I don't want what is being offered. I'm sabotaging myself because I'm afraid I'm not good enough. I see my severe limitations and I doubt that much will change for me in the next twenty years. I'll wind up like my parents, if I'm lucky enough to find someone to love me. Maybe it won't be so bad after all. All the rest is just an overture. I don't have the grace to lift myself up, to change my life, to join a higher economic and social class. If I were from Brooklyn and had a Brooklyn accent, there would be no choice. I'm from Yorkville without a New York accent and for some strange reason I thought I had a choice. But I'm from a working-class family living in a tenement. My father is sometimes sober, but he's still a drunk. I'm worse than that: I'm a girl and I'm a drunk too.

I know I'm copping out but I just don't think I'm good enough. If I look at what I've done so far with my first year of adulthood, I'm a disaster. Getting high is so important to me. I need to lose myself. I need to always be on another plane from the rest of the world. How can I be a part of the world when I always want to be apart from it? College means work. If I'm going to invest the money, I have to prepare myself to do the work. It's not all partying. I don't like that idea. I don't want to work for it. I just want "it" to happen and I want to have fun.

I also want my life to be meaningful; I just don't know what I want more. I want to make a contribution—but what? I've accepted the fact that I'll never win the Nobel Prize and I'm not going to write the Great American Novel either, so what is there for me? Where is my place? I can barely stand to live within my own skin and I am beginning to think that this feeling is more than just adolescent growing pains.

I'm in the "real world" now. Even though this job will only last for a year, it's a "real" job and I'm a nine-to-fiver. It feels strange working when I'm supposed to be in college. Most of my friends have gone away to school, mainly New York state colleges, and I feel pretty much alone in the city this year. I miss them, especially Amy, but I know I'm doing the right thing. Next year, I'll be in California!

My "real world" job is as a medical assistant to a pediatrician and the office is constantly full of patients—small, screaming ones. Naturally, most of the cases are routine sore throats or school checkups, but already I've witnessed two very serious emergencies, and they both occurred yesterday. First, a young infant with 106-degree temperature was brought in by a hysterical mother. I was put in charge of calming the mother while the doctor worked on the baby. After half an hour, he brought the temperature down to 104, but there were complications. The doctor felt it was safe to take the child to the hospital since the fever had come down. He left with the baby and the mother, whom I had managed to calm down. I have such great respect for Dr. James after watching him care for these children, and when I saw him leave yesterday, cradling the infant in his arms, I was moved to tears.

Once they were gone, I had to keep chaos in the waiting room to a minimum, and that was a big job. After an hour, it was standing room only, wall-to-wall kids, some sick, others full of energy. Some mothers were disagreeable and complained about the wait. But most of them understood what a real emergency means with a child and they knew how they'd want Dr. James with them if it were their sick baby. The doctor finally arrived back at the office with the positive report that the infant was out of danger. I was elated! I am loving this job so much because I am useful and helpful and people and lives are involved every minute of the day. We finally cleared the waiting room by 6 P.M. and I was cleaning up when I heard the screams at the door. Dr. James got there first and found an eight-year-old girl holding a finger that was bleeding profusely. Her mother was hysterical and any effort on my part to calm her made her abusive and more insane. I ignored her and went to work with the doctor on the real patient. Melissa wouldn't let go of her finger. She said it was going to fall off if she let go. Dr. James took her in his arms, rocked her and promised that he would fix it, all the while prying her fingers open. I had the child's arms and as soon as he got the last finger open, I grabbed the good hand and held on for dear life. The child's screams were horrifying—and she was right. The finger seemed to be held on by a small bit of skin. I cringed at the sight but I could bear it. It was essential that I act as an assistant and not respond to the frightening sight. I did it. I moved fast. I did what I was told and somehow the doctor fixed it. When it was all over, he thanked me.

"Megan, you were magnificent today! I couldn't have made it through without you. Your responses were completely professional, which is much more than I expected from a young, inexperienced, untrained teenager. I now have complete faith in you as an assistant and maybe, after this year, you'll think about studying premed in college."

"Thank you, Dr. James. It's an honor working with you and I'm glad I was able to really help today. There was a moment when I saw that little girl's finger when I was afraid I would pass out, but I knew you needed me."

"You know, Megan, I experienced that same moment. I was terribly afraid for her and I wanted to cry at the sight, but instead, I did everything I knew to save that finger. Thank God it worked. Let's split a Coke and then close up for the night. Tomorrow morning comes faster than you think."

I arrived home last night at 8 P.M., exhausted and starving. Mom had my dinner warming in the oven. I ate it while telling Mom and Dad about my day. I was so wound up that, after eating, I took a hot bath and then zonked out in front of the TV. At eleven, Mom helped me into bed. Dr. James was right. This morning came quickly but I can't wait to get to the office and begin another exciting day.

I have very little social life these days because there just isn't room for it, and not many friends are in town anyway. I usually do something on Saturday night—an occasional date, a movie, or a night out at Rockers. Now that I'm no longer a high school teenager, I feel I've outgrown the scene at Rockers, but I don't yet fit in with the after-work crowd. I'm still too young for the singles bar scene, so for the moment I'm in limbo. There's no place where I feel comfortable hanging out and drinking. It's O.K., because my job is forcing me to keep a low profile anyway.

My experience in Southampton this past summer scarred me. I have a terrible secret now and it crops up and reminds me that it's still there, hidden inside me, hurting me. The Hardings' New York apartment is not far from mine and I find myself taking different routes to avoid walking down their block. My mother has asked about them and whether I've heard from them since they returned to New York. I hate lying, but I have to. All that I can hope is that in time I'll be able to forget the whole terrible experience. As a result of this summer, I'm drinking less this year. I don't want to be a sloppy drunk, but when I drink I always wind up drunk. I'm drinking less because I'm going out less, and I feel better about myself. I'm happy in my job and I don't need much more in my life right now to keep me feeling good. I'm a good worker, my instincts are on target and I'm intelligent. It's all showing up in this job and I'm proud of myself. Dr. James keeps pushing premed at me but I know I have no academic strength in the natural sciences; but there are moments when I'm inspired to give it a try.

I feel less like two people these days, maybe I left the "other" Megan in Southampton. I'm hiding that one secret from my parents but I'm not living a lie every weekend—lying about where I'm going, who I'm with and what I'm doing. Frankly, it's a relief even though my social life is quiet.

I'm reading a great deal and I'm writing poetry again. My life has a focus and I'm feeling more positive about it than I've felt in a long time. I look forward to the challenges of college, of learning, of growing up. I'm ready to change. I want to stop behaving like a child and start acting like a responsible adult.

I have such a strong desire to prove myself. I want to be the best. My mother has always pushed for academic excellence in a different way than my father. She wants to tell her friends that her daughter got 100 percent. I've always felt that I had to be an honor student so I wouldn't embarrass my mother. I was in competition with her friends' children. We children never competed directly, but our mothers were having intense grade wars. I got 100 percent as often as possible to help my mother win. I didn't care about winning but I cared about her approval.

Now that I'm working, I want to get 100 percent on my job also. It's hard not getting grades because I need to chart my accomplishments. Luckily, Dr. James tells me often when I've performed particularly well in a specific situation. I need his approval. I want him to like me and accept me, so I do everything I can to do the best job. I'm not doing my best for money or to become successful. I'm doing it for approval. In the work area, it's positive behavior for me. But sometimes my approval-seeking gets me into trouble—and that happens in the social arena.

The incident in Southampton was clearly a result of my approval-seeking. I was the unworthy in the group partying that night and I desperately needed to be liked, so much so that I offered what wasn't mine. As a result, I lost everything and was thrown out of my friends' home as a worthless drunk. That's too much for my eighteen-year-old head to handle. It was approval-seeking but the big mistake was that I was seeking the approval of the wrong people. Why do I so desperately need to be liked, even by people I don't like?

I'm afraid of these feelings. I've had them for a long time—since Amy and I started spending time together around boys. I tried very hard to get at least one of the boys interested in me. It absolutely didn't matter whether or not I was interested in him. My feelings in that regard weren't significant; his carried all the significance. Fueled by large amounts of alcohol, my first sexual experience was a desperate, destructive act. For once, I wanted to feel that a boy wanted me more than Amy. I didn't, even for a minute, feel that way. I felt used and discarded, dirty, ugly, more unloved than ever before. It's been a terrible lesson. I don't know if I've learned enough to keep myself away from trouble—with men, with booze, with people looking for a good time. I can't seem to say no to booze even though I know what disaster too many drinks can cause.

I feel safe away from the idle days of high school and summer vacation. Right now I'm not thinking about spending my nights hanging out in Rockers the way I used to. On the weekends, I want to go out and have fun, but that doesn't only mean hanging out at Rockers looking for guys. I'm worth more than that. I'm going away to college and I'm going to make something of my life. I'm not going to wind up with some construction worker who plans on spending the next thirty years hanging on to a bar, drinking beers and getting fat.

It's been a few months with this new job and quiet social life. It's another Saturday night, I'm home alone and it's beginning to get to me. I don't think much about going out all week, and by Friday night I'm exhausted. But I don't like sitting home alone on Saturday night. It reminds me too much of those sappy songs that are meant to make you cry. My parents have gone to a party and they tried to talk me into going with them but I begged off. Maybe I should have gone. Maybe I would have met a "mature" man. I'm not going to stay home. I'm going out and I'm *not* going to Rockers. I'm going to hit one of those dark jazz bars on the West Side where I can just melt into the darkness and enjoy a few delicious scotches. I'm an adult and I can go out for a drink alone if I choose. I don't need a "date" or a girlfriend. My own company suits me fine.

The Blues Club is exactly where I want to be tonight. It's crowded but there's room for me at the bar, there's music but it's not too loud, there are singles so I don't feel like a leper, but it's not a heavy-hitting scene, so I can relax.

"What can I get you, young lady?"

"I'd like a Dewar's and water, please."

"Coming up."

"This is terrific music. What's the name of the group?"

"They call themselves Hot Jive. Is there anything else I can get you?"

"Oh, yes, can I order food at the bar?"

"Sure, do you want to see a menu?"

"Just tell me the house special."

"It's dynamite chili."

"Sounds great. I'll have one dynamite chili with cheese. And another drink when you get a chance."

He's a very cute bartender and he seems to be taking special care of me. I love this place. It's so dark and I feel wonderfully anonymous. I don't think I'll even use my real name. I'm just passin' through on my way to the Coast.

"Bartender, that chili made me thirsty. I could use a glass of water and another scotch."

"Here you go, babe. The third one's on me for good luck. By the way, my name's Barry. Care to tell me yours?"

"Cynthia."

"Pleased to meet you, Cynthia. Are you enjoying the music?"

"Yes, but it's getting a bit tiresome. I'm going to take off after this drink."

"Would you like to go down to the Village with me and hear

something with a bit more zip? My shift is over in thirty minutes. If you can stand the wait, I'd love to spend more time with you."

"Well—let me think about it while I have this drink."

"Here comes my relief. I have to be cool because we're not supposed to fraternize with the customers, but I'll give you the sign when I'm leaving. If you want to come, just meet me outside. Here's another drink to help you think it over."

Oh, no, a secret rendevous! And my name's Cynthia! I have to go. This is all so evil and romantic and I won't stay long and I'll take a cab home alone. There's the high sign. I'd better saunter out very casually. If only I could whistle.

"Listen, Barry. I'm just coming for an hour—to have a couple of drinks and hear some music. No funny stuff, right?"

. . . "What are you trying to do, Barry?"

"Just get to know you better, mysterious Miss Cynthia."

"Take your hands off me or I'll have this cab turn around right now!"

"I thought we were going to have some fun—"

"We are going to have fun. We're going to listen to some music and have a few drinks—and that's all."

"But, Cynthia, I gave the cabdriver my address. I thought you'd stop playing games and like to listen to some music in my bedroom."

"Pay your fare and get lost, buster. Cabbie, take me back uptown —East Side . . ."

A close call, Megan. A very close call. You can't play around like that or next time you'll be drunk enough to start asking questions after all your clothes are off. Damn you. You're easy, Megan—and some people, like Barry the bartender, pick up on it. I need a drink. I'm going to stop at Rockers before going home. I have to calm down and shake this bad feeling.

"Driver, pull over at the next corner. Thanks, keep the change."

It's the noise, the laughter, the wall-to-wall people at Rockers that I need as much as the calm-down drink. I feel safe in this group. I won't get lost or hurt or wind up alone with some creep as long as I sit at the bar and have Joe the bartender to watch out for me. I went to the West Side tonight for anonymity and excitement and I got

both. I also almost got a large dose of trouble. Was it worth the trip,
I wonder? Just another little adventure to help rip Megan's self-
esteem to shreds. A guy in a bar mistook me for an easy pickup.
Why? Because I was acting the part. I know I didn't consciously
intend to come on sexually but he got the message that I was willing. Yes—I was willing. I was willing to drink some more. Drinking
is my favorite pastime, not sex. I'm practically still a virgin. Obviously, drinking was just a cover for him—a "nice" way of asking me
home to bed. I didn't get the message because I have a one-track
mind. Stay at Rockers, Megan. Reminisce with your old school
chums about who was kissing whom in the eighth grade. I can have
fun here and there's no price to pay.

Things are going to change for me when I get out of this town.
That's a line I hear in a lot of old movies, either from the convict
waiting for parole or from the small-town girl yearning to leave the
family farm in Ohio and come to the big city. I'm in the big city
and using the same line. Supposedly, there's no place better than
New York City for beginning the future. But I have to leave because
it's my home. Even if I come back after college, and I intend to, I'm
investing a lot of faith in the act of leaving home. I have to start
fresh. I have to begin my own life away from all the "knowns" and
then maybe I'll find myself. I feel unhappy about myself here and
now. Since my eighteenth birthday I seem to have taken a down-
ward spin. I feel jinxed. The only positive force is my job. It's so
good that I'm almost tempted not to leave, but then a night like
tonight rolls along and I want to flee immediately. I wouldn't be
content to simply be a "working girl" until I get my big break and
get married. I'm going to become a "career woman" and marriage
isn't in the game plan until I'm at least thirty and established in my
career. I'm sticking with the plan. I need independence. I could
never just be somebody's wife. I want education and intellectual
stimulation. I want to sit drinking wine with my fellow students
discussing philosophy until 4 A.M. In order to do that, I'll have to be
in school learning philosophy. So that's where I'm going.

I feel so unprepared for life. I have no idea what to expect in
California and in college. My parents haven't been much help because they don't have past college experiences to share with me. My

father tries to instill a sense of values and goals in me and I appreciate that, but I need some practical information and I'm not getting any.

I need to get away because I don't want my parents to catch me drunk and I don't want them to see what sometimes happens to me when I drink too much. I'm their smart, pretty little girl and that's who I want to remain. If they knew that last night I went to a bar alone and allowed a stranger to pick me up and almost take me home to his bed, they would be horrified. I'm nineteen and I can take care of myself, but sometimes I don't take very good care. I don't want them to know. It's time to leave. I hope I get through the next few months without a mishap, then I know my life will change once I get to college.

COLLEGE
DRINKING

Mom and Dad have come with me and we've made a vacation out of this trip to college. Dad has a sister and some old friends in California, so we've done the coast from L.A. to San Francisco and it's been fun. We're staying in the Fairmont in San Francisco for a night, and then tomorrow I officially become a college coed. The Fairmont is wonderfully extravagant and I'm very grateful to the parents for making such an effort to give me the grand send-off. "Tonight, Megan my darlin', is our last night together and your mother and I believe champagne is in order! A toast—to our beautiful daughter, our hopes and prayers for a wonderful, successful college career."

"Thank you both so much. This trip has been very special for me. I feel that we've gotten to know one another in a new way. It's hard going off into the 'great unknown' of college life, but it's easier knowing I have your support and love to count on. We've had some rocky years through the sixties and sometimes you may have doubted me, but I want you both to know that I love you very much. So enough with the tears, pass the champagne!"

It was a magical night—a six-course dinner and one of those ridiculous Las Vegas floor shows followed by dancing to the tunes of Lester somebody. The folks were in heaven on the dance floor. I faded and excused myself to bed long before their night was over.

If they have such love for each other, why has their life together been full of so much self-inflicted pain? Why did my father drink so much when he had a wife and family that he loved so dearly? These disturbing thoughts are floating through my head while I'm trying to go to sleep. After seeing them tonight, I can't help thinking that my parents have wasted so much of their lives.

"It's a beautiful campus, Megan, right out of a painting. I have a feeling that you have made an excellent choice in schools, young lady."

Although I've convinced myself that since I'm paying for college I don't need this fatherly approval, it sure feels good to get it anyway. "First we have to find the dorm, then my room, and after we unload it will be time for the opening convocation in the college chapel. After that, there's the president's reception for new students and their parents, and when that's all over we say farewell."

Mother's eyes filled with tears for the tenth time today, "Megan, couldn't you have a farewell dinner with us tonight?"

"Mother, we had a farewell dinner last night. We've been saying goodbye for two days and sooner or later, you really do have to leave."

The president of the college droned on and on. We tried to remain attentive and interested but clearly public speaking was not his forte. I can't understand how he can be a college president and lack that important skill. As my father said, *he* could have done better and at least gotten a few laughs. Finally it was over and we dutifully followed the crowd to the reception. Punch and cookies. What a swell spread!

After going through the reception line and munching a couple of cookies, my parents suggested we leave. After all, we didn't know a soul in the room.

"Right now I'm looking forward to meeting my roommate. I could use just one friend to get through dinner tonight."

"It will be fine, Megan, as soon as you settle in. Walk us to the car, and in ten minutes you'll be a totally free woman!" Dad laughed and put his arm around me as we walked to the parking lot.

I feel panicky—terribly scared and sad to say goodbye—but I can't fall apart now. I've worked too hard for this. Somehow it will all work out. But the tears are coming anyway. "Goodbye. I love you. Don't worry about me. Call me when you get home."

"Don't cry, sweetheart. Start laughing because you'll soon be having a great time. I'll bet anything on it. God bless." Dad is hugging me tightly and I'm holding on for dear life. Mom is crying, laughing, trying to let go. "Call us whenever you want to talk and let us know if you need anything. We love you baby. Bye."

Oh God. They're gone. I want to chase after the car. Now what did I do? It's a fine mess I've gotten into this time!

Nobody in the whole school knows who I am. They don't know where I come from, who my parents are, what kind of background I have, how much money my parents have (or don't have). In this environment I'm a brand-new person. I have no past to mold me, to dictate my present condition. If I wanted to, I could fabricate a complete fantasy life story. It doesn't matter. All that counts here, now, is that I am Megan Moran, I'm nineteen and I'm a freshman. From that point on, I'm whatever and whoever I want to be. I wonder why I'm so concerned with changing my identity. I wonder what it is about the New York Megan that I want to leave behind. Is it my poor, working-class background? Or is it simply the unhappy person I was becoming in New York? Whatever it is, I'm so excited to be a brand-new person here, to be accepted or rejected solely on the basis of who I am here and now. I'm also scared shitless.

Already I feel out of it. My roommate is rich and she has so many clothes—skirts and jeans, turtlenecks, LaCoste shirts and cashmere and shetland sweaters in every color. I have so little and it's not the right stuff. My labels aren't from Saks Fifth Avenue and my sweaters aren't cashmere. I don't have a portable color TV or a stereo, or unlimited funds in my checking account. This is going to be tough. I've been around the very rich before and I wind up feeling like a second-class citizen. I don't want that to happen here. I don't want money to separate me from the rest of my classmates. I have to take the focus off money. My roommate, Susan, isn't throwing it in my face. I'm just overly sensitive about it. All I have to keep remembering is that I can be the best. I don't have to be rich to get the most out of college, to learn and to make friends and to enjoy myself. I may be across the country in California but I'm still the same Megan Moran. I have many more options here but the same hang-ups are in the way. I know I'm going to change as I grow up here. I just have to stop being afraid.

"Midnight trip to Dunkin' Donuts, who's game?" Sally is marching the dorm hall collecting those of us who want a sugar-filled, fattening study break.

"I'm game. I'd walk a mile for a donut!"

"Don't worry, Megan, you don't have to walk. Let's go, group."

Five of us, mostly in nightgowns covered by raincoats, piled into Sally's Fiat and discussed our future dieting plans, after tonight was over.

"I'm really gaining, group. I can barely fit into my jeans and I'm developing very large boobs and a double chin. Who's in psyche 101 and can tell us why we're eating? You all may be laughing now, but I know I'm eating because I'm scared and sometimes lonely."

"Megan, how could you possibly be lonely? When do you ever get a minute alone? You share a room with a roommate and the bathroom with fifteen of us. We all eat together, go to class together, study together. I'm not lonely, I'm claustrophobic. Give me a chocolate-covered custard-filled."

"I'm talking existential loneliness, Polly. It has nothing to do with the number of people around me."

"I know your problem, Megan. You have a crush on your philosophy professor. Here, have a coconut crunch—guaranteed to cure the existential blues."

They're all laughing hysterically while I gulp down my third donut. I know I sound like a true college freshman, spouting my knowledge from my first philosophy course ever. Trouble is, I believe it. I don't like getting fat but I know I need this food to get me through this first semester.

"Listen, guys, when we get back to the dorm, come to my room. I have some Amaretto and it goes great with donuts. We can play the virgin game: we count up all the virgins on our floor and place bets on when they're going to have the sacred experience!"

The Amaretto is tasty but there are too many of us to have enough to get a buzz on. That's so frustrating, but I guess I'm glad because getting drunk on sweet liqueurs makes me terribly sick. I should have passed on the Amaretto because now I really want a couple of snorts of scotch. Two shots of Amaretto does nothing but add a few hundred calories to my overloaded consumption for the day. It's time for me to get to bed. Sometimes this group silliness gets to me.

"Megan, please don't cop out on me. I need you at my party tonight. It's the first freshman party of the year and I'm scared it will be a flop. I'm sorry I invited Steve, but you know I invited him before he dumped you. I bet he won't even show tonight. It's the only decent thing to do."

"Sally, I just feel like such a loser and we're only six weeks into the year. I'm really embarrassed. But if you're sure he's not going to show, I'll come. After all, I could use a good party to help me forget the creep."

"That's the spirit, Megan. Now will you help me clear the furniture out of my room? We'll need every inch of space we can get."

"Who's in charge of the goodies, Sally? What are you serving— tea and watercress sandwiches?"

"Mark and the guys are taking care of the booze. They've decided we should make Harvey Wallbangers; apparently it's a deadly concoction. If you want tea for the ladies then you can set up the teacups in your room."

As the rest of the floor trickled in, the girls started getting psyched for the party and everyone pitched in to get the place ready.

We all went to dinner together and when we came back we had only an hour to wait before the great event began. Naturally, we were all packed into the bathroom doing our eyes and running around to each other's rooms half naked in search of the perfect outfit. Finally, the party was under way and after half an hour it looked as if half the school had arrived. A success! Sally and Liz were beaming!

"Well, girls, you're a definite success. All we need are a few hip professors to send this shindig over the top! Oh, shit, Sally, there's Steve. Damn it, it hurts to see him. What's he doing here?"

"Calm down, Megan. You have to stay cool and show him and everyone else that you don't care two shits if he's here. And don't look now, Megan, but he's brought some dumb sorority cookie. What an asshole! Listen, Megan, show him that you're having fun and you don't care."

"Give me another of those Harvey drinks. You know what, Sally? I'm really glad I didn't sleep with that creep. At least I don't have to feel that he took something from me."

"Right, kiddo. Here, have another Wallbanger and go mingle. Talk to Mark and Sam. I think they both have crushes on you."

It hurts but I'm pretending that I don't care. Part of me knows that I really shouldn't care because how much of an emotional investment does a person make in two weeks? I'm only upset because my ego is bruised and everyone knows I've been dumped. That's not the way I planned to start the year. I want to be one of the winners around here.

"Hey, Mark, will you bring me another Harvey Wall drink. I love them. Maybe you should bring two."

"O.K., Meg; have some of this Southern Comfort while you're waiting. It's a great blues chaser. And listen, sweetie, Sam and I are going to be your dates for the evening."

"Hi, Megan. How are you feeling tonight?" Melanie asks in a concerned voice.

"I don't have a temperature, Melanie. You don't have to play the concerned mother. I'm glad to see he's running around with somebody his own speed."

"Good for you, Megan. Let's go have some fun. I'll race you to the bar!"

"Now you're talking. These Wall bombers are doing wonders for me. Sally, I'll have two more of these and Melanie will have four! Of course they're not all for us."

My façade is beginning to crumble. I don't like being here knowing that I look like a loser. I'll just toss these two drinks back and hope they give me a super buzz, then I'll split. No reason to stay around and pretend I'm not miserable. I'm miserable and after one more shot of Southern Comfort, hopefully I'll be miserable and drunk . . .

"Excuse me, excuse me. I'm trying to get out. I've got to get out. Let me through!"

It's so crowded in there. I'm glad I made it to the hall. Oh, I'm dizzy. I'll lean against the wall. The wall is moving. The wall is upside down. Oh, I'm going to throw up. "Help me. I can't find the bathroom."

"Megan, it's Sally. We're in the bathroom. It's O.K. You're sick but we made it to the bathroom in time. Stop screaming, Megan. It's O.K."

"Help me. Help me. I'm dying. I'm upside down and I can't stand up."

"Liz, get John in here. He's premed. He'll know what to do. Megan, we're taking care of you. Calm down. We'll give you a nice shower and you'll feel better. John, what should we do? She won't stop screaming and she doesn't seem to know me."

"Megan, it's John. Can you hear me?"

"Help me."

"O.K., Megan, we're all helping. Listen, Sally, it looks like alcohol poisoning. She must have drunk large quantities very quickly. She's delirious so we have to keep her conscious for the next couple of hours. If we can't, we'll have to get her to the hospital."

"My head, my head. I can't move. What happened to me?"

"Megan, don't move. Just rest. Here, drink some water and take these aspirin and vitamins."

"Sally, what are you doing in my room? What's happened?"

"I've been here all night, Megan. You got banged up real bad by too many Harvey Wallbangers. Don't you remember what happened?"

"Well, I remember being in the bathroom—and John—Oh, God, not John—"

"Yes, Megan, it was John. He took care of you all night."

"Oh, no. I remember him holding me over the toilet and saying that I had to stay awake. That's all I remember."

"There were many hours after what you remember. You drifted in and out of consciousness, mostly screaming and crying and vomiting. It was scary, Megan. I wanted to take you to the hospital but John knew what to do—so we made it."

"Oh, God, Sally, I don't remember. Oh, God—But I can barely move."

"Just rest, Megan. You're still sick. I'm going to nap in Susan's bed, so I'll be here if you need me. Try to drink as much water as possible and there's also a Coke on your night table. Just sleep for a few more hours and you'll feel much better."

I slept on and off all day. When I finally awoke and was able to make it to the bathroom, it was dark outside and Sally was gone. I hope it's not the middle of the night. I don't want to have to sit up alone all night long. No, wait a minute, here comes Liz.

"Hi, Megan, are you feeling better? I brought you a dinner tray with two desserts. You must be starving."

"Thanks, Liz. What time is it?"

"It's six forty-five and everyone is at dinner. I have instructions from Susan to set up her color TV next to your bed. Your homework for this evening is to watch TV."

"Were you there last night, Liz? Was it really terrible?"

"Yes, I was there. And yes, it was terrible. You were so sick, Megan, and we were worried. It took hours and hours before you stopped vomiting and crying and finally fell asleep. But don't worry, only a few of us saw how sick you were. The rest of the party continued full speed ahead without us."

"Did you sit up all night too?"

"Yes. Sally, Susan and I took turns sitting up with you for two-hour periods each. It wasn't so bad. We each got a few hours' shut-eye. Do you really not remember most of the night?"

"The last thing I remember was John appearing and holding me over the toilet bowl. How am I ever going to face him again? How am I going to face anybody?"

"I'd feel the same way, Megan, but you just have to believe that most people don't know what happened. A number of people did see you collapse in the hall but very few people knew what was going on all night . . . And you can face John again. He took very good care of you. Sally is convinced he saved your life, but you know how she exaggerates. I think you should call John tonight and thank him."

"You're right, Liz. I'm glad he was there, but just talking about it makes me want to disappear. Maybe I'll transfer to another school."

"Here, eat your dinner and we won't talk about it anymore. You can call John tomorrow. I'll call and just report on your condition. Let's watch 'The Waltons'—but only if you promise *not* to cry, Megan."

Sally checked in and she and Liz left shortly after "The Waltons." They were ready for a couple of bubble baths and then a good night's sleep. I felt so guilty about what I'd done to their big party night—causing them to miss all of the party and then keeping them up all night—that it was a relief when they left and I was alone. I needed time to think even though I'd been instructed by my friends not to think. "Watch junk TV and veg out. Tomorrow you'll feel better and then you can start studying and thinking all you want. Tonight, your brain needs a rest and time to unscramble."

Those were their words but I couldn't shut off my thoughts, so I worked myself into a frenzy.

At eleven I shut off the lights and feigned sleep because I knew Susan would walk in from the library any minute. She was home every night at exactly ten past eleven—ten minutes after the library closed—and lights out at eleven-thirty. She'd already established a rigid structure of working, studying, exercising, sleeping. The alarm goes off every morning at six-thirty, and fifteen minutes later Susan is off to the pool to start the day. There isn't much room in her schedule to make friends with her roommate. Even though I know she kept watch over me last night, I know she did it from a sense of "roommate duty," not real caring, so I feel really embarrassed about facing her. I've felt that she's been judging me since our first day together, and by now I must be rated a "hopeless case." I'm sure that she'll have a new room by the second semester and I'll be happy to see her go. Susan is everything that I'm not and that includes some things I'd like to be. For instance, rich, thin, athletic, organized, self-assured. I wouldn't mind having those parts of Susan. I know I'm smarter than she is but she works much harder, so she'll get better grades than me. Who's going to know the "real" truth—that I'm smarter? Nobody.

I kept my eyes closed and my head turned to the wall when her light went on, but I didn't sleep. An hour later, when she was asleep, I left the room and went down to the lounge to find a late movie and a snack. At 3 A.M. I crawled back into bed and when the alarm rang at six-thirty I breathed a sigh of relief that morning had arrived.

Susan bounced out of bed, to the bathroom, into her clothes, and bounced out the door. I plugged in the coffeepot while I had my shower, then sat in bed for two leisurely cups before thinking about facing the world over breakfast in the cafeteria. Since it was still early, I could sneak in to a corner table and bury my head in the newspaper. I know I can't stay in my room any longer. I'm just making it harder to get out there. So here goes: Megan the drunk is on two feet and headed out into the sunshine. Will she make it? Or will she crawl back into her hole?

I can't even make it safely across campus at seven-thirty in the morning. Here comes John, my doctor from Saturday night—the last person I want to face during my first five minutes out of hiding.

"Megan, I'm so glad to see that you're up and about and over your ordeal. I was worried about you but Sally and Liz let me know you were O.K."

"John, I'm sorry I didn't call to thank you. I was going to. I just couldn't, not yet, um what I mean is—"

"I know what you mean, Megan. I've been in a similar situation before—just as drunk but not as sick. Everybody gets drunk, Megan. Put it behind you. Consider it your college initiation and don't worry about facing the rest of the world. They were all too plastered to know what went on in the bathroom Saturday night. Just start feeling better, O.K.?"

"Thanks, John. That helps a lot."

He's right. I'm not such a freak. Everybody has his or her terrible drunk. Mine was pretty traumatic and probably a sicker one than most, but it's still just my first college drunk. I've come through my initiation and now I can go on to bigger and better things. I certainly don't have to stop drinking. I just have to take care to drink properly. I know the two basic rules of good drinking. They are: (1) don't mix drinks and (2) don't drink sweet drinks. I broke both those rules Saturday night and from now on it's either gin and tonic or scotch. No more nonsense. No more sickening grain alcohol punches at the frat parties and no more crazy concoctions like the unmentionable from Saturday night. I've learned my lesson and in the future I'll bring my own.

The cafeteria is mostly empty so I'll be able to find a table alone.

"Hi, Megan, I heard you lost it the other night. Are you feeling better?"

"Yes, thanks, Melanie. If you'll excuse me, I have some studying to do."

"Hi, Megan. How's tricks? Or maybe I shouldn't ask."

Dammit, they all lied to me. Everybody knows and everybody is going to make a point of letting me know that they know. I'm in terrible shape—a loser after six weeks. I want to get out of here but I can't bear to cross that room again.

"Good morning, Megan. Do you feel as bad as you look?"

"Oh, Sally, they all know. Every person I see is asking me about Saturday night. Did you send out an all-points bulletin? Oh, I'm sorry. You're the last person I should be shitty to after all you've done for me. I'm just so ashamed and I feel like a freak."

"There were a lot of people at that party, Megan, so the word spread but, believe me, after today you won't hear another word about it. But you'd better stop crying before somebody spots you."

"Thanks, Sally. I wouldn't be able to make it without you. Tell me about Susan—what does she think?"

"I'll tell you the truth about your roommate. She was horrified and appalled and I'm sure she feels that you might tarnish her image. She's put in for a single room and she'll get it. When she does, we'll all be glad to see her go. So don't worry about what Susan thinks, because Susan only thinks about herself."

I got through the rest of the day without too many inquiries. After lunch, I headed for my room, where I spent the time until dinner. Normally, I spend the afternoon in the library or outside studying, but today I needed more hiding time. Liz came and took me to dinner and that's where I met up with Susan for the first time since Saturday night. We chatted and exchanged pleasantries and she headed for another table. I could clearly tell that the subject of my drunk would never come up between us. I could also tell that Susan wanted very little to do with me. What I didn't know was that she described the scene Saturday night to the dean of women's housing and it got her a single room, beginning tomorrow.

Now that I'm over my heartbreak and my debilitating embarrassment over my drunken episode last month, college life has been terrific. Academically, it's very difficult and I really wasn't prepared for that. I'm so used to breezing through every subject except chemistry. I never had a difficult year from the first grade through the twelfth, and I could get A's with very little effort. College is a different story. I'm beginning to learn the meaning of the word "work" and I'm doing quite a bit of it. I don't expect to get all A's this semester and that's a blow to my ego. I hope that once I learn the ropes I'll be able to maintain high grades. There is so much new to learn that I don't have a clue about, so I'm sure these four years won't be at all boring.

I haven't been to any parties since my "spectacle." The following weekend there was a frat party that I elected to pass up, and even Sally and Liz didn't try to convince me to change my mind. I felt sorry for myself to be missing all the fun but I was so afraid of getting drunk that I was somewhat relieved to spend a quiet night in my room. I've been invited to another big bash this weekend and I'm trying to make a decision about it. Even though in all other areas I've been behaving like a normal college student, part of me is still hiding out. I believe in the old "get back on the horse" theory, but I'm scared. My friends, including Sally and Liz, will all be at the party, so there's a possibility of feeling comfortable and having a good time. Should I go or should I pass? Should I drink or should I abstain? If I go, then I have to drink. I can't imagine being at a party and not drinking, but I won't drink any punches or strange concoctions. I'll bring my own and that way I'll play it safe. Also, I won't get drunk.

These parties scare me. There seem to be so many self-assured, great-looking girls getting picked up by all the great-looking guys. I have to witness all this action and tonight I can't even get high. I'm being very careful to space my drinks and drink very slowly because three is my limit tonight. I've brought my own measured flask of scotch, so there's no chance that I'll suffer a repeat performance from the last party. There's also no chance that I'll have any fun either. I really feel that my reputation is on the line this time. If I get drunk tonight, then everyone will assume that I get drunk at every party. If I stay sober then my drunken episode will be considered a fluke. It's not easy staying sober, especially when I haven't been taken out on the dance floor or had any interesting propositions. I'd better find the gang before I depress myself further. It would be a good idea to talk to at least one person before I leave.

"Sally, I knew you'd be shooting pool. Who are you hustling tonight? Oh, Ted, be careful. If she's still losing, don't add to the stakes because the little snake will wipe you out."

"Megan! I don't need you here. Take a hike! I'm having a lovely time losing to this handsome gentleman."

"O.K., I'll let you destroy another man's ego, not to mention his bank account. Just try to be gentle with him. Good luck, Ted. When you're crying on my shoulder tomorrow, don't say I didn't try to warn you. Oh, by the way, Sally, where's Liz?"

"She and Sam were dancing last time I looked. Go find them and bring them back with you in about half an hour. I should be wiped out by then."

She's incredible! She plays pool as if she were born in a pool hall —and she hustles! Ted thinks I'm teasing, but he's going to lose at least fifty bucks tonight. Sally is a real character. I wish I could play pool like that.

This place is packed and the crowd is beginning to get to me. I think I'll go back to my room. I'm not dancing, I'm not playing pool, I'm not flirting. If I go back to my room then I can safely have a nice strong drink before bed. This is my best idea all night! First I'll find Liz and say goodbye. I don't want anybody worrying about me.

> "Brown sugar, you know you dance so good.
> Brown sugar, just like a young girl should . . ."

"Megan, come on in. The water's great!" Mark is signaling to me to meet him in the middle of the dance floor. Who can resist Mark *and* the Rolling Stones? I'll feel better with at least one dance under my belt.

"Hi, kiddo. This is great! I was on my way out but I can't say no to a guy like you. Oh, there's Liz and Sam. Let's dance in their direction so I can have a word with Liz."

"Hi, Megan. Hi, Mark. Great moves, Megan!"

"Thanks, Sam. Liz, I'm taking off after this dance. I'm tired and I've got a headache. Sally wants to see you guys in about thirty minutes, so tell her I went to bed. Boy, it's a great party. Come on, Mark, let's get into it! See you all later!"

" 'Bye, Megan."

"It was a terrific dance, Mark, but I have to take off. Thanks, I'll see you tomorrow."

"Would you like me to walk you across campus?"

"No, thanks. I know the way. You stay here and practice that Mick Jagger dance routine on some unsuspecting young coed."

"So you think it has potential, Megan?"

"Trust me, you'll knock 'em dead. Good night, kiddo."

I don't think Mark is really interested in me. He likes me and takes care of me in a brotherly way but I don't think there's anything more. I resent his attitude because it makes me feel more like a social invalid. I don't want anybody to think that I have to be taken care of. I'm glad I'm out of that party. I was ready to scream from the pressure of pretending that it was fun, fun, fun. It wasn't fun. Not tonight. Tonight was my test and I passed. I did it but I didn't have to like it. Now I deserve a reward. I'm ready for a bubble bath with a good stiff scotch and water. That should take all the chinks out and send me contented to dreamland.

College is picking up. I've gotten over my "miserables" and now I'm starting to have fun. No more new kid on the block. No more I'm-not-good-enough-to-be-here. My grades have been excellent and I'm enjoying the work. It's the first time in my life that I'm working for myself. I'm paying for this education and if I screw it up, I suffer. I like it too much to even consider screwing up.

I'm happy too. I have real friends. Sally and Liz are at the top of the list, but there are many other casual friends. There's nothing wrong with me! People genuinely like me—and some guys even ask me out! My social life hasn't been rocketing but I've had a number of interesting dates and a few minor crushes; it's just enough to keep me from feeling like an ugly duckling. Sally and Liz keep insisting that Mark is stuck on me, but the only time Mark ever comes to my room is to discuss his current heartthrob. We're friends and that's neat. I haven't had many male friends until now.

I was a "star" in high school and it's been a difficult adjustment to go from "star" to "nobody." At first I had real ego problems but then I realized that every other freshman is on new turf, leaving past glories behind, starting fresh without any history. I almost blew my chances at the Harvey Wallbanger party but I made a great comeback. I haven't been publicly drunk since then, and now I have the very "cool" reputation of only drinking scotch or gin and tonics, depending, of course, on the season. I'm pleased with that. It makes me feel a little bit special and I guess I need to feel that way.

For six months, I hated this place. I was so homesick for New York. It was ridiculous! I waited a year chomping at the bit to leave New York and all the trappings there, and after six weeks here I was pining away for home and family. Luckily, I somehow knew that my homesickness was just a reaction to my newness at college and to my first bad experience here. I wanted to escape, to get out, but if I had gone back I would have wanted to leave home again after ten minutes. I wasn't alone in these feelings of homesickness—it's called "freshman syndrome" around here—and as soon as I felt secure in a few friendships and a few classes, the need to go home passed.

Now I have mixed feelings about going home this summer. I have to work and put together some money and I couldn't save anything if I worked here in California and had to support myself all summer. If I go home, I have no living expenses and all my earnings go into the bank. I've changed so much this year and I don't want to revert to the old Megan—the teenager without any freedom under her parents' thumb and bucking them all the way. If I've changed then maybe they'll see that and respect my new responsibility and freedom. I won't know until I get there. Sometimes I really wish I could write my own script so I could be sure of the right actions and reactions and, especially, the happy ending.

"Well, the college coed is in from the Coast for the summer! We're glad you decided to come home, Megan, even if your decision was based on monetary considerations. It will be great to be able to tell you what to do for the next two months! Just kidding, sweetheart! We know you've been living the life of an adult for the past nine months, so we'll try not to interfere."

"What a break! I've been so worried about coming home, Mom. I thought I'd turn into a high school kid again. When did you guys become so understanding? Or have you always been this way and I just didn't notice?"

"No. We're growing up too, Megan. We're trying to accept the fact that our children are now adults and it's time for us to butt out. We've had a lot of fun being alone this year; our life seems to be switching gears also."

"You'd better stop telling me how happy you've been since I left home or I'll develop a complex and a very large resentment!"

"Oh, Megan, darling, you know I didn't mean it that way. Come on. Let's make ourselves beautiful. We're meeting your father in half an hour at the Manhattan Inn for dinner."

The homecoming was warm and wonderful. Dad wanted to know everything about my classes and when I told him I studied Chaucer, he made me recite the opening lines of *The Canterbury Tales* in Middle English. I then told him about studying Shakespeare's histories and for half an hour, he compared the plays.

"But, Dad, you didn't go to college. How do you know this stuff?"

"Megan, I wasn't able to go to college but I swore that I'd give myself a proper education. With the help of some educated friends, I was given the guidelines of what consisted of a good liberal arts education and I've been going to Moran college for the past twenty years! I may even get my doctorate someday! My real interest lies in history but I also love literature. I'm particularly fond of Shakespeare's history plays because they incorporate my two interests. So, my darlin', I'm sure you'll have a few things to teach me with your college education, but I have a few surprises up my sleeve also!"

"You sure do, Pops. You sure do. But please let me have a few days' rest before you start grilling me again. I just finished my finals for the year and I'm not ready for round two yet."

"Tonight we'll eat, drink and be merry and forget about schoolwork. I'm sorry, love, but I'm just so interested in hearing it all . . . Your mother and I have some news for you. We've planned a trip to Europe this September. After twenty-five years, we're going to have our honeymoon!"

"That's such wonderful news. I'm so glad for you both."

It was a high-spirited dinner and I found myself happy to be home. I left the folks at about eleven and went in search of the "old gang." Amy wasn't home yet because she'd taken a detour to see her new fiancé, but I was sure I'd find plenty of friends at Rockers, hanging on the bar, falling off the same barstools.

Nobody I knew was at Rockers, not even the bartender. I was disappointed but I had a drink and decided I'd comb the neighborhood in search of the new hang-out. I knew my friends hadn't deserted me, they'd simply moved to better quarters. I spent the night stopping in for a drink in every bar on Second Avenue from Eighty-sixth Street to Sixty-sixth Street. No familiar faces. By the time I reached the last bar, I didn't care that there were no friendly faces. I didn't even remember who I was looking for. I took a seat at the bar and decided to stay right there for the rest of the night. It was only two-thirty when the bartender shut me off and sent me home. I was embarrassed and annoyed but I didn't make a scene. After all, I'd been away from New York for a long time and it would take a week or so for me to adjust to the wonderfully long hours of the New York bar scene. I would have to practice in order to get back up to my old capacity.

Naturally, given a short amount of time, I was able to bring my drinking capacity back up to New York's 4 A.M. standards, and the summer passed accordingly. I worked, I drank and I hid my drunkenness from my parents. This wasn't terribly hard because they no longer waited up for me at night.

It was a real transition period for me. My friends from high school seemed to be exactly the same as they were a year ago and I felt that I had really changed. My world had opened up. I'd driven across the entire country and I now had friends in at least ten states. I was no longer living in a ten-block radius like they were. I was so different and they were boring. I only spent time with them when I had to—if I needed some socializing and there was nobody else. I never imagined that I could change so much in one year and that I would really want to close that door. But I did because the one opening up for me had already shown me so much more of life than I'd ever dreamed of sitting in Rockers on Second Avenue. It wasn't just the outside that changed, it was the inside too. I'm becoming a woman. I can feel it and I want a brand-new life to match my brand-new self. This summer is another ending, but this one brings no sadness. I now know what's out there in the world and I want it. Goodbye, New York. Goodbye, Second Avenue.

Sophomore year, off campus, true freedom and adulthood at last! My roommates are two senior women, Tina and Margot, and I'm so glad to be living with upperclassmen instead of a group from my own class. Tina and Margot are fun but they're also subdued, and after last year's twenty-four-hour rowdiness, I want some quiet adult atmosphere. I love our house. It's big and rickety and furnished with Salvation Army chic. It's such a thrill to have our own kitchen, to be sharing cooking, cleaning and shopping duties, to have friends over for dinner. We keep a couple of sixpacks of beer and a gallon of wine on hand at all times. Sitting on the porch for a late afternoon cocktail is one of our great off-campus luxuries. Tina and Margot are both twenty-one so buying liquor is no longer a hassle. Last year was such a drag, always having to search out someone willing to make the trip with the "baby" freshman to the liquor store. I resented that so much and I was embarrassed to be in that position. Now it's less obvious because I have roommates who simply include me on their trips to the liquor store.

Tina is a premed, Margot is history and I'm a literature major. It's a well-rounded liberal arts household and provides for scintillating dinner conversation.

"Tina, who was that gorgeous hunk walking you across campus this afternoon?"

"I'm glad you asked, Margot, because I need your help. He's a new transfer—a history major, so you'll be seeing him in your classes. He's into the French Revolution so I need a crash course this week."

"O.K., Tina, but don't you think it would be a lot easier if you acted reasonably about this guy and introduced him to me? After all, he and I have common interests. You don't speak his language."

"Shut up, you witch! By Friday night you better have taught me his language!"

"Tina, I have to agree with Margot. I've been told that premed students aren't allowed to date anyway—something about upsetting the necessary study hormones—" Uh oh, from the looks of that flying dinner roll, I went too far.

"Megan, you're not supposed to take sides here and you are never supposed to listen to or agree with Margot. If you do, you'll never get out of college. Now, if you'll both excuse me, I'm taking my study hormones to the lab."

Margot and I had a good laugh and then we took our study hormones to the library. The library is the hub of the campus: it's the place for serious study and serious cruising. Margot and I study at opposite ends of the library and then we survey the entire scene during our breaks. We're not the only ones checking out the action while checking out the books. At least 75 percent of the library's inhabitants are playing this game. It makes studying fun; whatever studying I manage to squeeze in between breaks. So far, the results have been positive. My newest crush, Jeb, was spotted during a library cruise and he's already asked me out for a drink. Margot is working on one art major but keeping her eyes open so she doesn't miss someone more spectacular. It's really not a bad life. I would be totally happy if I could be certain that at least one guy was cruising me. I'm not sure that Jeb thought of asking me out before I planted the seed. I want to be, as the classics say, the "beloved," not the "lover."

Things are working out pretty well with Jeb. We're into a relationship mode, spending about two nights a week together at Jeb's place. He lives alone. The only problem is that a drink after the library is turning into many drinks, and some nights I'm going to sleep at 3 A.M. when I have to be up at seven. It doesn't bother Jeb. He loves to drink and I love to drink with him, but it's hard keeping up. When going to sleep he always has a beer by the bed, and first thing in the morning he pops a cold one. The sight and smell of that makes me feel sick, so I make a quick exit. It's tough, hung over with no coffee; I have to bike to the campus coffee shop. Tina is on my case. She thinks Jeb is a loser and she doesn't believe in partying during the week. But Tina is premed and she's always been overly conscientious. Margot doesn't say anything. She's lonely and wants her own man.

I sure don't feel that Jeb is my man. He doesn't say much to me about how he feels. I know he enjoys my company when we're drinking and that's really the extent of it. Every time I've been with him, we've been high or smashed or hung over the next morning. I can't imagine spending an afternoon walking in the woods with Jeb, unless of course, we had a couple of sixpacks. It's convenient right now. It's fun. It's a cure for the midweek blahs. But I know there's nothing between us other than a few drinks, a few laughs and sex, and some mornings when I wake up next to him I really regret it. I wish I were back in my cozy bed with the cat sleeping next to me on the pillow.

Tonight I'm going to suggest cutting back on the weeknight bar prowls and spending the entire weekend together instead. Maybe we could take a camping trip or have a cookout with a bunch of friends. I need to spend some daylight hours with Jeb so I can decide if I like what I see.

On our way to the Sunset Café, I decided to begin my weekend conversation. "Jeb, you know I really enjoy going out with you, but I have to cut back on my weeknight partying. I'm suffering and my studying is suffering, so I have a suggestion. Let's try spending the weekend together instead of a couple of nights a week. That way we could play around in the daytime too."

"No, Megan. That won't work."

"Why not, Jeb? Don't you think you'd enjoy spending a weekend with me?"

"It just won't work. I don't want to discuss it. Here we are. Let's forget this conversation and have a few drinks."

"I'll have a few drinks, but I also want to talk to you. You never want to talk, Jeb, and I'm tired of being shut out. We've been going out for a couple of months now and I feel I have a right to know—"

"You don't have a right to know anything! We go out for a few drinks, we screw and that's it. If you don't like it, then we can forget it right now."

"Damn you! I'm a person. Don't you have any feelings for me?"

"Yes. I like you but I don't want anything to change. No commitment. No weekends."

"Just tell me Jeb, why no weekends?"

"There's someone else who I spend my weekends with."

"You creep! Take me home, you lousy fucking creep!"

So the saga continues . . . "Megan Moran is burned again!" Tina is busy telling me she told me so, and Margot is holding me, telling me I'm much better than that schmuck deserves. She's right and I know it, and this time I'm not heartbroken. I'm mad and I'm going to get even. Margot and Smooch, the cat, are glad to have me home. Margot likes having roommates around when she's feeling lonely and manless, and Smooch likes to sleep with me. I'm glad the affair is over. I was drinking too much and working too little and not having much fun. Part of me knew that I was being used and I guess part of me was using Jeb also. I knew I never really liked him. He was just a little too weird for me.

Already I'm establishing a strange pattern in my relationships. I always choose the most inappropriate person. They are never really available to be boyfriends and I lie and say that's O.K. It isn't O.K. and I don't understand why I set myself up every time. I must be afraid of commitment, even though it's what I say I want. I must also be a masochist. I keep setting myself up for the fall. If only I were strong enough to be happy on my own—to stop wanting a relationship—to enjoy my own company and the company of my friends. It seems that the women I know who enjoy themselves, who don't panic if they're alone on Saturday night, are the ones turning all the silly men away. They are the most sought after, most attractive because they don't need anyone else to fill them up. Strong women. Liberated women. Creative. Intellectual. Independent. My idols—even if I still sleep with a Teddy bear and a cat when I don't have a man to share my bed.

At times I feel I'm learning so much about myself but then I do something crazy and I can't believe that it's really me. I don't trust my motivations. They don't seem to be rooted in any serious convictions. I feel empty inside and here at college I'm trying to fill myself with ideas and knowledge. I hope this is going to do it. I'm here for an education—and a personality.

This year isn't going very well. I can't concentrate on my courses or my studying because I'm too involved in my social life. My birthday is coming up in two days and I've found out about the second surprise party of my life. After what happened at my first one on my eighteenth birthday, I'm really dreading this one. If only I didn't know about it and could bypass this anxiety, but I guess I'm destined never to have a real surprise party

What really bothers me is that James, my new crush, has asked me out for a beer on Friday evening, with an excuse that it be an early date. I know he's the setup, the person recruited to keep me out of the house until all the guests arrive. I want to cancel the "date" but I don't want to make things difficult for Margot and Tina. It was a bad idea for them to get James involved. I just hope I can have a good time and make sure that everybody else does.

"Margot, I really appreciate what you and Tina tried to do, but let's face it, I'm a disaster area. Here we have a house full of friends wishing me well and making a terrific party, and I'm feeling sorry for myself. It's a terrible way to behave."

"Well, Megan, it was a bit tacky for James to invite another woman to meet him at the party. I shouldn't have asked him to be the setup. I'm sorry."

"Oh, really, Margot, that's not it. I'm constantly embarrassing myself, not to mention acting totally ungrateful to you. There are times when I know I'm only crying for attention. But I can't stop it."

"Megan, don't be so hard on yourself. I think the real reason you went all teary was because you drank too much. It can happen to me sometimes if I overindulge."

"Well, weren't you drinking last night, Margot?"

"Sure I was drinking. I just didn't get drunk."

"How do you *not* get drunk?"

"Are you serious, Megan?"

"Yes. I really don't understand how some people drink and don't get drunk."

"It's because they stop drinking *before* they get drunk. I had three beers then I switched to Tab. It's no mysterious formula."

"But, Margot, don't you hate having to switch to Tab, just when you're getting high and having fun?"

"That's just it, Megan. I did have fun last night and you didn't have fun. You drank too much and got yourself all worked up into a crying mess. Maybe now that you understand how too much booze affects you, next time you can do what I do and nip the drunk in the bud. It's a lot more fun and I never get hangovers."

I have to do something to stop my outrageous behavior, but having three drinks for an entire night at a party just seems impossible. Why party? I might as well stay home. Well, that's a possibility. Parties all seem to backfire on me anyway, so I'll just cool the party scene for a while. Oh, damn it! I've done that already! I did it last year after the Harvey Wallbanger party. I'd just better learn how to drink and maybe now is the time to at least try Margot's advice. My way isn't working, maybe hers will.

I finally got out of that deadly political science course with a C, my worst grade ever in my whole life. I had hoped I'd make it through life without ever having to experience getting a C. It's not much fun. It's a dull disappointment, not a terrible feeling of failure. But I've moved beyond the C and now I'm in a poetry-writing course with a famous visiting poet. Spring is here and class begins at eight every morning with a nature-and-birdwatching walk. I'm calming down. I'm focusing in on my life, moment by moment, happy to be writing down feelings and verses and words and colors. I'm pretending to be living the quiet life of a poet and, as a result, I'm not getting caught up in a lot of man nonsense or ego nonsense. There's a real student poet in my class, and he's withdrawn and tortured. He wears sorrow and pain as a mantle and this, along with his poetry, brings him great respect from his classmates, including me. But I hate his poetry. It's about suicide and hate and racism and war, and it's powerful. I want to be the complete opposite of him. I want to wear a poet's mantle of joy and write about beauty and love. We are both good poets but I know I don't have the drive to really stick with it. Peter will be famous someday—hopefully before he kills himself.

On these poetry-writing spring afternoons, I search out secret grassy places under solid old trees where I write my verses. I feel so special having this to do as my schoolwork. Everyone else is chained to the library or lab while I'm getting a suntan. I bring a couple of beers with me on these writing adventures and the afternoon takes on a very mellow glow. I don't think there's anything better than drinking a cold beer on a sunny afternoon contemplating the glory of it all. Whether writing poetry or watching a baseball game, it's probably the finest high there is.

The only problem with drinking in the afternoon is that I need a nap before dinner. If I don't nap for at least an hour then I'm useless for the rest of the night. This can be managed except on days when it's my turn to cook the dinner, and today is one of those days. I've decided to keep drinking through the rest of the evening, especially since I won't get any work done anyway. I did plenty of work this afternoon. I wrote a very pretty poem and I'm happy with it as is. I'll submit it tomorrow and I'll polish it after I get some feedback and criticism. I'm all set for the evening; after dinner I can watch TV and conk out early.

I'll make my specialty, cheese soufflé, for dinner. It will keep Tina off my back for drinking too much wine on a Tuesday night. I think I'll bring home a sixpack to enjoy while I'm cooking. I doubt that anyone is home yet, so Smooch and I can hang out on the porch, listen to some Jerry Jeff Walker music, grate cheese, drink beers and discuss our day. Days like this really make me feel that life is great!

"Here come the troops, Smooch. We'd better get that soufflé in the oven and start rinsing the lettuce. Since you've been such a good kitty, you can have some tuna for supper. Hi, Margot, hi, Tina, special treat for dinner!"

"Yea, Megan! I'm starved and looking forward to a great meal. What is it?"

"Cheese soufflé, salad, rolls. Not bad for a weeknight, huh? We can sit down in half an hour, so have a beer and change the record and tell me the gossip from the library today."

"Megan, why don't you work in the library anymore?"

"Tina, could you imagine John Keats, Lord Byron or Emily Dickinson writing love poems in our library? I need to breathe the sweet air, feel the warm sun and lie in the soft grass in order to be inspired to write."

"Oh, God, please spare us from this flowery nonsense. I hope your poetry is better than that, Megan." Both Tina and Margot exchanged smirks.

"As a matter of fact, it is—and I'm no longer afraid to show it to anyone. Would either or both of you care to read today's poem while I finish slaving in the kitchen?"

"Oh, yes, let us see. I need to be convinced that you're working in this creative writing class." Tina the scientist and skeptic unfortunately has no room for "creative endeavors" in her busy schedule.

"Here it is. Go away and read it and we can discuss it over dinner. Would anyone care to join me in another beer?"

"No, thanks. Just call us when dinner's ready."

They don't understand poetry. Why did I give them that poem? They'll just smile politely and say "Very nice" and I'll really feel stupid. You never learn, do you Megan. After this put-down, you'll have a good reason to get drunk tonight. I'm just fooling myself thinking I can write poetry and my teacher is just encouraging me to get through the course. Tonight I'll get an unbiased reaction and I'll know if they're saying nice things to keep from hurting my feelings.

The soufflé comes out in two minutes and everything else is on the table. "Roommates, it's time to eat, drink and be merry. Hurry, so you can see the soufflé before it flops."

"Looks gorgeous, Megan. You're a woman of many talents. Tina, pass the salad, please."

"Fabulous! Thanks, Megan. I was really hoping that we wouldn't have hot dogs tonight."

They're stalling. They keep filling their mouths so they don't have to talk.

"Tina, will you please give me some more wine? Is everything O.K.?"

"Delicious, Megan. Even the salad is a masterpiece and as soon as I have one more bite, I'll be able to slow down and start talking." Tina is being particularly effusive this evening, and she's even drinking her wine with dinner.

"Tina, while you stuff your face, I want to say something. Megan, you know that I don't know anything about poetry so my opinion isn't worth much technically. It's mainly a gut response, a response rising from the heart. And I want to be the first to say that 'Early Rising' is the most beautiful thing I've ever read!"

"God, Margot, you must be drunk!"

"I mean it, Megan. I was moved to tears."

"Now wait a minute, Margot. I want to have my say also." Here comes Tina, the ax murderer. "I'm so involved in science, Megan, and I place so much emphasis on facts and empirical truths. I don't pay much attention to art and beauty, but this evening you stopped me dead in my tracks. Now I feel as though I'm really missing something. I really believed you were taking the course for an easy credit. I'm sorry for my ignorance. I don't know what it takes to be a poet—but you've got it! More wine! This is a celebration!"

"After I gave you both the poem, I stayed in the kitchen cursing myself, knowing that I'd set myself up for a rejection. I can't believe your reactions! They're so generous and wonderful—and I don't believe you, but thank you both." Then the tears came, and after the tears, the laughter and good humor that is present at a table of friends. It was a special dinner. We all felt it. My poem helped to break through a barrier and feelings were flowing here tonight. We're a good group, we decided, and from now on it's all for one and one for all, and no man is allowed to interfere. Tina and Margot are back on campus, studying. I'm beat but I feel so good I'm going to take another glass of wine up to bed to watch TV. The day has been a success. Going to bed at nine o'clock is a little abnormal but that's O.K., I deserve the night off, the wine and the TV. Today I wrote a beautiful sonnet and made a beautiful soufflé—two significant accomplishments that deserve a reward.

Our warm, sharing soufflé-and-poetry dinner was over a month ago, and we've lost the feelings of affection that sealed that evening. I don't know at what moment the camaraderie ended but as time goes on, I'm feeling more and more that I'm really different from my roommates. They're so serious and rigid in their study schedules whereas I'm much more flexible. Some nights I prefer to work until 3 A.M. and some mornings I choose to get up at six and work for two hours before class. They never do that. They work every night until eleven and that's that. They've been working that way for all four years and I think they've missed out on a lot of little adventures that I've had because I'm flexible. I work better when the spirit moves me. That philosophy is certainly true of writing poetry but it also holds in all my writing. I do all my course reading on a daily basis but I don't plod through all my papers in the same way. I give my ideas time to germinate and then the words just flow onto the paper. I think that Margot and Tina resent this ability because they're always bugging me to spend more time in the library. I'm different and I'm glad. I'm a creative person and that translates into all my subjects. I'm here to be free of all the rules and restrictions I left behind in high school and New York. I'm not interested in making a new set of rules to live by. Work is important, but play is equally important. I haven't yet found the one male on this campus who will embrace me and my philosophy. When I do, I'll have it made. I need some reassurance that I'm not too unique to fit in. I want to fit in but I also want to be able to stand apart sometimes as an observer. I sound like a self-centered little girl when I say it, but I know I'm special. Because of that, my life must be a little bit different from everybody else's.

"Megan, today is our day for shopping. Will you meet me here at four P.M. sharp and we can do it then?" As usual, Tina is scheduling her day over her first cup of coffee.

"Sure, Tina, who cooks tonight?"

"I do and I'm planning on tacos."

"Great! Let's make sure to get plenty of *cerveza!*"

"Megan, it's eight o'clock in the morning. This is no time to discuss *cerveza*. I've got to run. I'll see you at four."

Tina took off on her ten-speed. I got into a bubble bath with my second cup of coffee and my copy of Keats. My class doesn't meet until ten today so I can afford a leisurely morning.

"Bang. Bang. Bang." So much for relaxation.

"Megan, it's Margot. Let me in! I have class in fifteen minutes!"

"Come in, Margot. I thought you left already, but it looks like you overslept."

"And what about you? Every time I see you, you look like the quintessential lady of leisure, and I'm sick of it! You're driving me crazy, Megan! You never seem to be doing anything other than reading and relaxing."

"Listen, Margot, you're late, you're angry and you're saying things that are out of line. I don't want to talk to you now; just wash your face and go to class. We can talk later if you feel more like a human being."

Margot slammed the door and took off. My bubbles were all gone, so I rinsed off and got out of the tub. I wonder where all of Margot's venom comes from? I wonder what I've done to make her so angry?

"Smooch, come here, Smoochie. Have some breakfast. You're my best buddy in this whole house, aren't you? We're lucky that the year is almost over because it doesn't look like I'll be welcome around here much longer. 'Bye, kitty, I'm going to school. Please don't kill any field mice for me today."

Roommates are supposed to fight. It's not much fun, though, when two gang up on one, but I saw it coming and I stood firm. I saw Margot and Tina on campus at different times during the day and neither one said a word to me. When I arrived back home at four, they were both waiting for me and I could tell they weren't writing the shopping list.

"Megan, we have less than a month until we graduate. We're under a lot of pressure and you're not helping. You're barely doing your share around here and you're irritating both of us to the breaking point. You've got to change or we're not going to get through this year in one piece."

"This is terrific. You two are freaking out over graduating and now it's my fault. I haven't done anything wrong—"

"That's right, Megan. And you haven't done anything right, either. We're tired of your attitude, and for the next month this is our house and we're making the rules. If you don't like it, you can find another place to live. Rule number one: No men allowed to sleep over; Rule number two: No company at all after dinner during the week; Rule number three: No drinking during the week; Rule number four: No four A.M. breakfasts with the gang in our kitchen after the Saturday night bash; Rule number five: If you're up past midnight during the week, stay in your room; Rule number six: Dishes are yours every third day. You keep track, we don't; Rule number seven: Housecleaning every Saturday at ten A.M., not eleven and not twelve or whenever else you decide to wake up. That's it. It's time to go shopping."

"You guys are real assholes. I'll follow your rules but I'll have nothing else to do with you."

I went to the store with Tina. It was agony but I was determined not to cry. We didn't say a word. Tina snarled when I grabbed a sixpack of beer, but I stood firm. In retaliation, she bypassed the liquor store and I felt a moment of terror. How am I going to get through this month without drinking? They are being so mean and unfair. I'll get some liquor on my own and I'll hide it in my room. They have no right to tell me what I can or can't do in the privacy of my own room. I pay one third of the expenses here and I'm not going to take orders.

We finally made it home and unpacked the groceries and I split. I went back to campus, grabbed a hamburger at the coffee shop and went looking for a friend in the library. I need to talk to someone. I feel so rejected. I thought we were friends. What happened in these last few weeks that has them telling me to go to hell? If it weren't for Smooch, I wouldn't go home tonight, but I know they won't feed him. But I'm staying out until they go to bed, and if I can find somebody who's game, I'm going to get drunk.

We made it through the end of that year and somehow we parted friends. Margot and Tina got all sloppy and sentimental about ending a chapter in their lives and they didn't want any smudges on the memories. So we hugged and kissed and said goodbye. Now that I'm a senior, I can understand the pressure they were under all year and the presence of a flightly little sophomore with men problems instead of graduation problems must have been terribly annoying. I realize I'm not easy to live with, not even now that I'm a mature senior. I still have men problems, only now they are coupled with graduation problems. My roommates are Sally and Liz, my closest friends since freshman year. Another threesome, but this time more equally matched.

Luckily, college has given me most of what I hoped for. I have learned a great deal academically, and emotionally I've become my own person, I've developed my personality. Sometimes I'm not very pleased with it but at least I've calmed my greatest fears and found that I do have a "personality." Most of the time I'm comfortable with who I am, but still I have nights like some of the miserable milestones of my life—my eighteenth birthday, the freshman party, my sophomore-year surprise party—when I feel completely lost, unloved and hopeless. I still feel as though I'm missing some key ingredient necessary to be a complete and happy person. Maybe we're all missing it and maybe I should stop worrying about it. I can be a real bore when I get into that state and my friends don't want to be around me. So I keep those feelings hidden as much as possible. Sometimes, though, with a little too much to drink, they overtake me and I'm off to the races.

Liz and I are building reputations as gourmet cooks and excellent hostesses. We try to have one dinner party each week, sometimes for an entire class and other times for men we want to get to know a little better; other evenings are devoted to close friends. Sally can't cook and she doesn't like to drink either, so she comes to our dinners but usually leaves early to get back to her studying. On dinner party nights, Liz and I make sure that we don't have any studying to do because we do exactly as the phrase says: we have dinner and then we party. Last night we had two professor friends over. It was a legitimate friendly evening. Neither of us had any romantic illusions about Doug and Fred and the four of us had great fun.

Liz and I devoted the day to the party. We shopped after class, then we cleaned the house and at 3 P.M. we began preparing the boeuf bourguignonne, one of our great successes. The recipe calls for one bottle of burgundy so Liz and I bought half a gallon and sipped the extra burgundy while preparing the meal. Once the beef was cooking, we had time for our baths and toilettes. We brought drinks to the bubble bath, played classical music and thoroughly relaxed before the final preparations were put into motion. The hors d'oeuvre were wonderful—crabmeat and hollandaise on toast points —and they took some time to prepare. I worked on them while Liz prepared the salad and dressing and the rolls and set the table. Luckily, the dessert was cherries jubilee so it didn't need any attention beforehand.

At 7 P.M. we were entirely ready and we made a roaring fire in the fireplace and lit the candles around the living room. Doug and Fred arrived a fashionable ten minute late bearing a wonderful bottle of brandy for their hostesses. The cocktail hour began and Liz and I didn't tell that we'd had a slight head start.

"Megan, Liz, you two are wonderful. The scotch is my brand and these hors d'oeuvre are phenomenal. What we can't figure out is why we deserve such a magnificent dinner. This isn't a bribe since you're not taking classes from us this semester—"

"Well, there's always next semester!"

"Fred, do you think they're out to seduce us?"

"Please, guys, we just want to have a comfortable and delectable evening among friends. We swear there are no ulterior motives. Are you game?"

"Well, Liz, I'd rather be seduced but I'll settle for a great dinner. Let's refill these cocktails and, Fred, work on that fire, will you?" Doug took over the bartending duties while Liz and I put the finishing touches on dinner.

"Should I open both bottle of wine, Megan?"

"Why not?"

After another round of drinks, the dinner gong sounded and the four of us settled down to some serious eating. Everything was perfect and our guests wouldn't stop exclaiming their wonder at it all. We were on seconds—both dinner and wine—when Sally ran through.

"Can't stay, guys, but I'm stealing a plate to take to my room. I only have six hours left to finish this damn paper."

"Have a drink with us, Sally."

"Are you crazy, Fred? A drink is the last thing I need. Good night, folks. Enjoy! It looks like a class act."

It was a class act until dessert time. Liz and I sent the men to relax with a brandy by the fire while we fixed the coffee and prepared the dessert. By this time we were both bombed and we caught a bad case of the giggles in the kitchen. As a result, Liz dropped the ice cream on the floor and I added too much "jubilee"—brandy, that is—to the cherries. When we lit the dessert, it exploded and our screams brought the guests running.

"What's the matter? Are you hurt? Oh, my God, it's a fire!"

"No, wait, Doug! It's just the cherries jubilee. I was a little generous with the brandy. See, it's dying down. There—fire's out. Now, this should *really* taste delicious."

"You ladies should be drinking the brandy, not setting the house on fire."

We all broke up laughing and dessert was served—not as elegantly as originally planned, but still it tasted divine. After dessert, Liz and I put on the Temptations and it didn't take much coaxing to get the guys on their feet.

"I've had more fun tonight than I've had in months!" Fred exclaimed before crashing back down into the couch.

"I'm not surprised. After all, we're with two exquisite and talented women, we've eaten a superb four-star meal and we've consumed a quart of scotch, two bottles of wine and a half bottle of brandy. That combination is enough to make anyone happy!"

"Doug, are you attributing your good time to the amount of liquor consumed?" Liz retorted indignantly. She was a little too drunk for much more conversation. Doug saw that and just drew her into his arms for what he announced was the final dance of the evening. Everything was wonderfully soft around the edges as we all danced to "Just My Imagination." The evening ended happily and hazily. After the guests departed, I barely managed to get Liz into her bed and out of her clothes before she passed out.

This is the time I like best. The guests are gone, the kitchen is clean and I'm alone by the fire with a last cup of coffee, a bite of ice cream and the remainder of the brandy. I'm warm inside. I'm happy. Happy that dinner was a success, happy that I didn't cross the line into unpleasant drunkenness and happy that I'm finally alone with a nightcap. Sally is still awake pounding the keys, but she couldn't be further away from me right now. I want always to live this way—wonderful dinner parties, a roaring fire and always my time alone with a brandy afterward.

"Good morning, Megan. It's eleven o'clock. I thought you'd like me to give you a little push and a little coffee. Anyway, I'm dying to talk about last night's dinner before I leave for class."

"Hold on a minute, Liz. Hand me the coffee and come back in five minutes. Please!"

Liz left me alone with my pounding head for exactly five minutes. Then she returned with more coffee, aspirin, juice and toast and we sat in the sun of my balcony.

"Megan, I'm sorry about passing out before we did the dishes, but at least I made it until the guests left. I must finally be learning to hold my liquor!"

"You were terrific, Liz—except, of course, for the ice cream—"

"Well, what about you and the flaming brandy!"

"Oh, don't make me laugh so hard, my head is killing me."

"Do you have class today, Megan? I'm on my way to campus in ten minutes if you want a lift."

"No, thanks. My class is at two and I think I'll take my bike and go to the pool for some laps to clear my head."

The swimming helped my hangover. It always does. I feel so dry and being completely immersed in the water is soothing as the water actually seems to seep through me. I just wish I didn't always wake up with a hangover. Liz never does and I don't drink all that much more than she does. I guess it's the price I have to pay and as long as the evening is successful all the way around, then it's worth it.

I know that I drink more than most people but that's because I like it more. Liz tries to keep up but she doesn't have the capacity. Last night Doug and Fred certainly drank as much as I, and as long as I'm not getting drunk alone then the more the merrier! Everybody gets drunk at the Saturday night frat parties—everybody, that is, except Sally and Tina before her. All my friends love to drink. It's part of social life. Now that I'm grown up and a sophisticated senior, I don't have to worry about making scenes and throwing up in somebody's car. I do have to worry about not remembering what I've done during part of my Saturday nights, and so far there has only been one bizarre example of my memory lapse which Liz thinks is hilarious and Sally finds horrifying. I brought a young man home from one of the campus parties and he spent the night with me. I woke up at 5 A.M. and found this naked man in bed with me and I almost screamed. I didn't even know his name. I woke him and he tried to get romantic and from what I could piece together (I was naked also) we had already *been* romantic. I slapped him, threw him out of the bed, made him dress in ten seconds flat and threw him out of the house, screaming and crying as I chased him down the stairs to the front door. I couldn't remember his name and I couldn't remember any part of the evening spent with him. Sally woke up and stayed with me until I calmed down. The next morning, Liz filled me in on the previous night and once she filled in the blank hours, it wasn't so frightening. Anyway, Liz claimed that we had a wonderful time and my "date" is the most sought-after man on campus. I tried to laugh it off and Liz helped. Sally remained quietly freaked out for days. I was a lot more upset than I let them see. It was bizarre and somehow horrifying that I'd been to bed with a man and couldn't remember a moment. That occurrence was a few months ago and I've taken measures to prevent a repeat. Sally is my bodyguard and she has strict orders not to let me leave any party with a strange man. When Sally isn't with me then Liz is in charge, but Liz is much less dependable. I usually spend the end of a party evening carrying Liz home—but that makes it tough for me to carry anyone else! Liz is so much more helpless than I am and yet she gets into less trouble. I just don't get it. I seem to always get into terrible trouble when I get drunk, but Liz just quietly passes out in someone's lap. Ah, college life—one adventure follows another!

The party's almost over. One month left until graduation. I'm exhausted and I think I'm ready for it all to be over.

My grades are straight A's this year—a 4.0 average, but there will be no cum laude next to my name. No cum laude because for three years I scorned the thought of honors just as I scorned those of my classmates who went for Phi Beta Kappa. I played my old counterculture silly hippie tapes: "Grades aren't important. It's all just a matter of being here." If I learned one thing in college, it's that those attitudes are bullshit and I never meant them. Just as I never meant it when I said: "Casual sex is O.K.," "I don't want a commitment," "I'm not interested in finding a husband in college," "Who needs money? Poor is honest."

I hope, I've now gotten rid of those silly bullshit theme songs. I've paid the price: I've suffered many one-night stands and nonrelationships. I never had a boyfriend to take home over the holidays and I won't have a damn cum laude after my name on graduation day. That's what hurts the most. I've worked hard all my life for grades. I used to cry whenever I didn't get 100 percent on a test and I cried two years ago when I got my first C. I was a jerk to pretend it didn't matter—to spout some nonsense because it sounded cool, to deny my own real feelings. I'm half a point away from a cum laude and there's nothing I can do about it. I can't get more than a 4.0 for this year. I can make my folks understand. They won't be disappointed. But damn it! At least I've learned that I have to pay for the ideas that I spout, and finally I know they had better be my own. I've been burned by my own immaturity and insecurity.

It certainly hasn't been a total loss. In so many ways, it's been so wonderful, but I'm not all put together yet. I'm still not sure who I am. I still have empty places inside and I still cry too much from loneliness. But it's time to say goodbye and we're doing it with a grand gesture. Sally, Liz and I are having a party for 150 people. It will be one of at least ten parties over graduation weekend and it will be the best! Liz and I have started baking three weeks in advance. We're making twenty-five assorted quiches and another twenty-five assorted sweet breads such as banana, cranberry-nut, apple-cinnamon and carrot. We'll have vats of sangría and a keg of beer and an endless dancing tape. It will be the send-off to beat all send-offs.

The day has arrived! The party will be the crowning social achievement of four years at college. Everyone who is anyone will be here and we're all in the most intense celebration mode of all four years. Tomorrow is graduation and this is our last weekend to party together.

"Liz, are we going to make it? I'm so nervous. How did we have the nerve to invite a hundred and fifty guests for cocktails? Is everything ready? Is there enough? We have half an hour to go and God help us. Where are our parents? They could at least come early and give us some moral support."

"Calm down, Megan. Here, have a drink. Test the sangría to make sure there's the right combination of everything. This party is going to be a blast; everybody is coming, and as long as people show up we have nothing to worry about. We know the quiches and the breads are delicious and we have plenty to drink. Here come your parents now. Let's make your dad tell us a few jokes to lighten us up."

"Hi, folks, we're glad to see you. We've just started a major attack of the preparty jitters."

"Oh, girls, the house looks beautiful! The punch looks delicious and so do all those lovely cakes. Doesn't it look grand, Mike?"

"Absolutely. Throwing a party for a hundred and fifty in grand style is exactly what I expect from my daughter and from her equally talented and beautiful roommates. Where is Sally, by the way?"

"Oh, she's over at the hotel with her fiancé and his parents. I think she's deathly afraid of his parents so we gave her time off to go make sure that they are content and happy and aren't plotting to cancel the wedding."

"And, my dear Liz, where are your parents?"

"They're always late, Mr. Moran. I doubt that they'll make it before the first guests. Uh-oh, Megan, somebody's coming. Oh, good, it's Sally and the reluctant in-laws. Mr. Moran, would you please use your Irish charm to soften those people around the edges? Megan and I want to rescue Sally for five minutes."

"Of course, my dears. I'll take care of them." Dad winked and after the introductions were made he proceeded to charm the frown off Mrs. Miller's face. We grabbed Sally and headed for the kitchen.

"How's it going, Sally? Are they still insisting on a five-year engagement?"

"Megan, do you think that's funny? Well—come to think of it, it is! I'm giving up on them. I'm going to have fun at this party and let Steve fight his parents for me. I'm finished groveling. What am I anyway, a second-class citizen? If I have any luck, your father will take care of Mrs. Miller, Megan, and we'll have him to thank if they agree to an August wedding."

"That's the spirit, Sally. Now get to work. You're the first shift on quiche detail. Here come some guests, Liz. You go and greet them while Sally and I work on the food . . ."

I want this party to last forever. I have never had a better time in my entire life. My parents are in seventh heaven. They're so proud of me—for graduating, for having such good friends, for giving such a successful party. And I'm so proud of them. Right now my father is in the other room surrounded by two of my English professors and two philosophy professors—all of my favorites—and his small group has been laughing and carrying on for an hour. I know that my father is the center of that circle and I've been so elated watching them that I'm keeping myself from going over, from doing anything to break the rhythm. I knew my father would fit in here. In these four years, I've been able to see just how much he knows and what a thinker he is, and I've been waiting for this opportunity to show him off.

In addition to that corner of rowdy gentlemen, there are wall-to-wall, porch-to-porch and lawn-to-lawn people here. The party has stretched the house to its limits and has flowed over outside into the late afternoon sun. Flowing is a perfect word to describe this party. It is flowing; people are moving from room to room, inside and out, the wine is flowing, the music is playing and everybody is staying and having fun. This is one of the last parties for all of us and the feelings are too good to let it end. It is also very special to everyone to have their parents and families with them and having best friends' parents meet one another. It's a connection we haven't had in four years and it's so much fun having it for one weekend.

"Megan, you'd better work your way into the dining room. Your dad and Professor O'Neill have just broken into song. It sounds Irish!" Sally dragged me into the house, where somebody had turned off our endless music tape, and there in the middle of the crowd Moran and O'Neill sang "Danny Boy." There wasn't a dry eye in the house. What a moment! What a father! If only this party could last forever.

"Megan, I'm afraid we're out of food, but there's still plenty left to drink."

"Well, Liz, the party was scheduled to end two hours ago. I don't think we should be concerned if the food has just run out. Isn't this something! They won't leave!"

"I know, Megan. I've had the greatest time, and my parents have made friends with everybody. It really feels as if this party has symbolized all of the good times and good feelings that we've all shared during these four years. I'm so glad we had the guts to pull it off. Let's go find Sally and the three of us can toast each other. This is our moment!"

By 9 P.M., our cocktail party was over. It was just turning dark when the last guests departed and we three roommates collapsed in a heap on the living room couch. The house looked as if a hundred and fifty people had come to call, but there weren't any major disasters. Smooch finally came home. He jumped through the living room window and gave us all a look of disdain for keeping him out so late and away from his dinner.

"Megan, that's one hell of a cat. Do you think he'll really adjust to life in the big city?"

"I don't know, Sally. I'm a little worried since he lives most of the time outside, but if any cat can make the adjustment, Smooch can. I just couldn't bear to leave him behind. He's helped me get through so much—including physics."

"Yes, I think you're right to take him Megan. He'll be happy as long as he's with you."

"If only you were talking about a man, Liz, then this would really be the best night of my life!"

Hung over for graduation is not very smart, but it was unavoidable. Anyway, I'm not alone. Half the class is in pain so I can think about my fellow sufferers as I sweat through three hours in the sun. Some hangovers, like today's, are almost pleasurable. It sounds very masochistic, but if the night before was truly a night to remember, then the hangover helps me to hold on to it. Our party was the only party of my lifetime where I loved every minute—from the very beginning to the very end. Not a moment of unhappiness, anxiety or discomfort, and that's a very rare experience for me. Sitting here today, waiting for my diploma, knowing that my parents are in the crowd beaming with anticipation, is also a wonderful feeling. No hangover can overshadow my happiness today, but I can't wait until the ceremony is over so I can have a cold beer.

DAILY DRINKING

Is there life after college? I've been thinking about writing a piece for the New York *Times* Op-Ed Page using that question as the headline and the first word of my answer would be "Barely." We spent many nights over the past four years joking about making our moves into the "real world." It seems that everyone I knew at college did a perfect imitation of his or her father giving the "real world" lecture. It always began with "You'll look back on these college years as the best years of your life . . ." and we all groaned and howled. But now, three months later, I'm already looking back. Something has definitely been faulty about my entry into the "real world." I've worked all my life—all through high school and all through college—and I was sure that of anyone in my senior class I'd have the least problem. Not true. In three months, the graduation blues have turned into postcollege depression, and I'm still going down. I have very good reasons for this depression. Nobody cares about my literature degree, my excellent liberal arts college, my straight A's. They just want to know if I can type. I have no intention of becoming someone's typist and I'm fed up with the illiterate interviewers in the personnel agencies. I don't think I'll ever break into publishing. It appears as though I'll be working nights cleaning offices forever. Three months ago I was on top of the world. Today I'm on the bottom. Nobody prepared me for this, not even my father with his "real world" lectures. On my good days, I assume this is only a transition period. On my bad days, I can only assume the worst: I'm not good enough or smart enough or ambitious enough or pretty enough or fast enough or rich enough . . .

In the meantime, I'm living in the Village in an apartment that I can't afford with a roommate, Laurie, who can. Laurie is living on the family plan: Daddy pays. He paid her way through college and now through law school and he's very suspicious of me because I'm poor. But Laurie is terrific even though she's a cement heiress, and as long as money isn't the subject we get along very well. I just can't help resenting her.

I have the most bizarre night job, which I took for two reasons: money and hours. Since I'm working nights, I can spend my days pursuing my career. At nights, I dress in a blue uniform and punch in with the other office cleaners—my "colleagues" who mainly carry green cards and don't speak English. At least when I'm on the job, I feel a little bit better than everyone else. I'm almost positive that I'm the only college graduate on staff. An old friend of mine owns the business and it's not such a terrible job if I can get my ego out of the way. That's not true. It is a terrible job. It's only one step up from dishwasher but the money is good. I go to work at five in the evening, leave at ten-thirty and get paid for seven hours. I catch the bus down Fifth Avenue and make it home at eleven on the dot, time to watch "Mary Hartman, Mary Hartman." I pop open a beer and plop down in front of the TV. Another beer and a sandwich during the commercial. When it's over, I take a shower, have some wine, watch a late movie and fall asleep at about one. Sometimes Laurie is home to watch "Mary Hartman" with me, but most often she's in the library until midnight and then goes straight to bed. Laurie doesn't drink. She sees no point in having a headache for class in the morning. I've tried to convince her that headaches don't develop after one drink, but arguing has proven futile. The few times I have gotten her to drink with me, she got drunk on two drinks and sick on three. I've decided I really don't need that nonsense; it's much easier drinking alone, since I've been forced into it! I'm not hiding from anybody. I just happen to be home alone a great deal so it's only natural that I'd have my drink alone.

Since Laurie rarely drinks, she never thinks to buy any booze and that has become a real problem. Laurie is always inviting her buddies over after class or after the library and they're always having a glass of wine or popping a beer and sometimes even having a scotch —in other words, drinking my booze. They don't descend in hordes and drink it all up. They're all sissy one-drink drinkers, but a drink here and a drink there adds up and I wind up out of booze. When I get home from work tonight, I'm going to talk to Laurie about it.

"Laurie, I'm home, are you?"

"Yes, I'm in your room, Megan. 'Mary Hartman' just started."

"Great! I'll be right in." Damn it, my beer and wine are gone. I have nothing to drink. "Laurie, please come out here and explain to me why there's no beer or wine in the refrigerator."

"Oh, sorry, Megan. I forgot to get refills. I had a study group over this afternoon and I guess they finished off the beer . . ."

"And the wine, Laurie. What am I supposed to drink? I've been working all night. You know I look forward to a cold beer when I get home."

"Here, have a Coke instead. That'll quench your thirst. I was going to replace it but I forgot. I'll get some tomorrow. Come on, we're missing 'Mary Hartman.' "

"God damn it! I'm sick of your friends drinking my beer and my wine! I'm broke and you're all still living off your rich fathers, yet I'm supplying you with liquor. I want you to go down to the deli right now and get me a sixpack. And from now on, you buy your own supply for your friends."

"Don't you think you're overreacting just a bit, Megan? It's eleven o'clock at night and I have to go out and get you beer just to make your point? You've made your point. I'll take care of it tomorrow."

"I want a beer *now*, Laurie. Don't make me go myself."

"O.K., but it seems to me that you're a little too dependent on your beer and wine."

"I don't have any interest in hearing your opinions, Laurie. Just go to the deli."

I'm sick of all these spoiled rich kids I've been surrounded with for the last four and a half years. Laurie is so self-centered and spoiled and self-righteous. Not only does she comment on my drinking, the other night she told me I should be out at nine looking for a job because, after all, I only work until 10:30 P.M. and that leaves plenty of time for sleep. She has no right, and after tonight I hope she realizes that.

I guess living with a roommate is risky business and sometimes things get very rocky and uncomfortable. After our confrontation last week, things have improved and Laurie has become conscious of keeping her guests supplied with refreshments. She's not a bad roommate overall. She spends most of her time in school and in the library, so I have the apartment to myself a great deal of the time. Things would be working out very well if she didn't insist on always bringing her friends home. If I don't find a real job soon, I'll go bananas. I'm beginning to feel like, and soon I'll start looking like, all the refugees I work with. There's the phone. I'm glad whoever it is waited until "Mary Hartman" was over.

"Hello."

"Megan, it's Laurie and I have good news. I spoke with my friend Ann tonight who works in publishing and she knows of a job in the publicity department of some publishing company. I can't remember the name. She's close friends with the publicity director and she promised to call first thing in the morning and put in a good word for you. You're supposed to call at ten and then call her friend. Isn't that great?"

"Oh, Laurie, it sounds too good to be true. At the very least, they'll have to give me an interview. Oh, thank you. I'm going to talk my way into this job. I'm not going to take no for an answer.

I'm going to smother them with intelligence and enthusiasm. Laurie, you're wonderful. Did you really sell me to your friend Ann?"

"Absolutely! I told her you were brilliant and you've been learning everything you possibly can about publishing and all you need is your first break!"

"I'll wait up for you and we can celebrate when you get home."

"No, Megan. Go to bed. We'll celebrate tomorrow—after you get the job!"

"Yay!"

I've been awake since seven, counting the minutes until ten. My interview suit is ready, my silk blouse is clean and pressed and I've got my hair in rollers just in case. Thank God for the morning talk shows to help me pass the time. Only ten minutes left before I call Ann Segal and make my first connection to my new job.

Ten o'clock. Now dial the phone, Megan and keep smiling. Don't sound nervous.

"Hello, this is Megan Moran calling Ann Segal. Yes, she's expecting my call. Thank you, I'll hold . . ."

"Hi, Megan, this is Ann. I spoke with Sylvia Davis, the publicity director, this morning and she's waiting for your call. It's an entry-level job so it should be perfect for you. Sylvia is a little crazy but she knows her business, so here's her number and good luck!"

"Thank you so much, Ann. I really appreciate your efforts on my behalf. I'll let you know how it turns out, and I look forward to meeting you sometime with Laurie."

"Hello, my name is Megan Moran and I'm calling Sylvia Davis."

"Just a moment, please . . ."

"Hello, Megan, you certainly come highly recommended and we're looking forward to meeting with you today. I'm going to be out of the office all afternoon but my associate, Hank Richards, would like to interview you at two-thirty. Can you make it?"

"Yes, of course. I'd be happy to meet with Mr. Richards and I look forward to meeting you also, Ms. Davis."

"Well, if my schedule permits, you and I can meet for drinks at five-thirty in the Oak Bar at the Plaza. But Hank will let you know if I'm available after you talk to him."

"That's fine. I'll be at the office at two-thirty. Thank you."

"Laurie, you're an angel. I got the job! I can't believe it but they told me they didn't have to see anyone else. They wanted me, and tonight, over a scotch at the Oak Bar, my career in publishing was launched!"

"Megan, that's fantastic! Let's go out to dinner—my treat! You really deserve this break after cleaning all those offices."

"Oh, no! I'm supposed to start my new job on Monday, and that won't give the maintenance company enough time to replace me. I'll have to work both jobs for at least a week. Well, I can do it. I can do anything now that I'm on my way, and the extra money will help me buy some work clothes. I'm going to call my parents and tell them the good news, then we can go out."

"Great, Megan, I'll fix us some cheese and crackers and a couple of drinks."

"Laurie, why don't you throw caution to the wind tonight and get blitzed with me? After dinner we can go over to Ruth's Piano Bar and sing the blues. The only time to safely sing the blues is when you have nothing to be blue about. We're both in great shape tonight so let's treat ourselves."

We dressed up and had a huge Italian meal and a bottle of vino at Roma's, then walked over to Ruth's to meet two of Laurie's boyfriends and settle in for some serious late night drinking. I adore Ruth's. It's small and dark and almost seedy. There's no nonsense in this bar. The music is great and the drinks are strong, short and to the point. I've never heard a blender going behind the bar at Ruth's and I've never seen anything pastel-colored and foamy being served. That's a sign to me that I'm in the right place. Laurie and Simon and Laurie's other friend, Joel, seem to like Ruth's and they're happy to have a couple of drinks here, but I can tell that they won't settle in for the night. I don't think they really have a feel for the magic of the late night blues bar, and before long they'll be worrying about tomorrow's classes and insisting on getting to bed by one. I'll let them go home and I'll stay by myself. They'll think I'm a little strange but I can tell them how I can't resist the music, and, after all, I don't have class in the morning.

"Megan, it's the witching hour. Do you mind if we take off when we finish these drinks?"

Boy, I'm so tired of students. After four years of being one, I want to start spending time with other types of people. Students are beginning to bore me. I'm glad they've gone home to bed. I feel so guilty being a corrupting influence on these little children. Oh, Megan, you're getting nasty, thinking nasty thoughts about your friends. Time to relax and listen to the music and turn off all that nonsense inside your head.

"Waiter, I'd like another Dewar's, rocks, please—and bring me a Lite beer with it."

The night slipped away. It melted around me to the beat of the piano and bass and Ruthie's soulful voice. My money's gone so it's time to go home now. Three A.M. is a properly indecent hour to crawl into bed. First a taxi, then bed. Keep it straight, Megan, and don't fall asleep in the cab . . .

My new job is fabulous! Sylvia, my boss, seems very crazy but she's teaching me a lot about publishing and publicity. Since my first week on the job, I've been accompanying Sylvia on her luncheon engagements with book reviewers and TV producers. She says my wide-eyed enthusiasm brings a breath of fresh air to what is usually very tedious. I'm in awe of the celebrities and semicelebrities and they seem flattered by a newcomer to the industry who thinks they're hot stuff. Naturally, I don't overdo it. I'm genuinely happy to meet these people and they can tell. Sylvia takes me to the best restaurants in New York—Lutèce, Parioli Romanissimo, Romeo Salta, Le Madrigal, Windows on the World. It's just incredible! We have cocktails before lunch, wine with lunch and "a little something" with dessert. Until now, I'd never had a drink with lunch—other than weekend brunch—and it really hits me fast. It's a wonderful high and by the time lunch is over we're close to drunk when we return to the office around three. It's O.K. because I'm with the boss, and as long as I behave and I'm charming and enthusiastic, she encourages me to have a good time. Often we spend the afternoons drinking a good deal of coffee so that we can get a second wind for a scheduled evening cocktail party or dinner. I love those days the best because I can get high twice before 8 P.M. and then I usually go home and top it all off while I watch TV. It may not sound it but I do work hard and now, after only three months, I'm being given my first book campaign and I'm going to organize my first publicity tour. Sylvia has promised me a promotion to full publicist after six months, provided that all continues to go as well as it's going. My only problem on the job is that the other publicists resent me for being in on all the social aspects of the profession. Of course, they lunch with authors and some reviewers but Sylvia handles all the major print and media people and Sylvia attends all the important industry functions—and Sylvia takes me instead of them. I understand their anger over this situation but it's benefitting me and my career and I certainly don't intend to change it.

Sylvia has just arrived for the day. Her voice can be heard from the elevator before we can even see her. She's always screaming and cursing and it's beginning to grate on my nerves.

"Megan! In my office and close the door. Listen, tomorrow night are the National Book Awards and, naturally, I'm taking you with me. The only problem is, you have nothing to wear, so I want you to take this hundred dollars and go to Saks on your lunch hour today. Buy some elegant black pants, the kind that look like silk, and an elegant multicolored blouse or tunic—something with real pizzazz. I'll look at it this afternoon and we'll see if we can make you look like a real publicity person. Do you happen to own a pair of heels?"

"Yes, Sylvia, but wait a minute. I can't afford this loan right now, I'm still behind on my rent."

"It's not a loan, kiddo. It's a department publicity expense. Now, I want you to find something smashing this afternoon, something that's really *not* you. If you don't do it, *I'll* have to take you shopping."

"Spare me, boss. I'll do my best. In the meantime, can we spend ten minutes on my press release? I think I've finally got it."

"O.K., but first send the secretary in with my mail and messages.

I'll call you back in a few minutes. Oh, and, Megan, get us some coffee and something sweet and deadly. I have the munchies."

I'm glad Sylvia had me close the door for that conversation. If anyone here knew that I was given money for new clothes, I'm afraid they'd use that information against Sylvia. But what a treat for me! I've never had a hundred dollars in my hand just to buy one outfit. I can't wait to get to Saks.

It's almost strange the way Sylvia treats me. I believe she's grooming me for her job someday, but her interest could be misconstrued. Luckily, I know that she adores men, so her attitude toward me is not some sneaky way to make a pass. I'm glad I grew up in New York because I thought of that possibility right off the bat. I doubt that I would have thought of it so quickly if I came from Des Moines.

"Megan, get in here so we can rewrite this press release!"

"Oh, no, Sylvia, you don't really mean I have to rewrite it again. You know I've written it four times already."

"That's right, and each time it's gotten better. It's almost there now but you're still too timid about hitting them with the big punch right off. And you have too much description in here. Rearrange the first two paragraphs and cut the description up into bullets and it will be perfect. O.K.? Do it today so we can get the damn thing printed before the book is published!"

"O.K., Sylvia, I'm sure it won't be too much of a problem. May I ask your secretary to type the final copy for me?"

"Of course, Megan. And don't forget your errand at lunch."

Everyone in the business, including Sylvia, moans and groans about the boring book awards, but I'm so excited being here for the first time. Sylvia is teaching me how to work the room. She's talking to everyone and introducing me. I've been given strict instructions that I'm to mingle on my own after Sylvia has taken me around the room once. I'm so nervous that I doubt I'll remember anyone's name, but my career is being launched by my boss and I'd better not disappoint her. Here goes.

"Hello. My name is Megan Moran. We met about half an hour ago when my boss, Sylvia Davis, had me in tow."

"Of course, Megan. I'm Joe Wallace from the *Book Review.* How are you enjoying the show? Dreadful business, isn't it?"

"Oh, no. I'm in awe, but I must admit this is my first time. I'm new in the business and would you mind if I asked a terribly ignorant question?"

"Shoot."

"How do you choose the books you are going to review in the Sunday book review? Does it depend on the author, the subject, the print run or publisher—or what?"

"Oh, Megan, what a question! Did Sylvia send you over with that bomb?"

"Of course not. I'm really interested and I feel it would help me do my job better if I knew these things."

"I'll buy you a drink, you sweet novice, and I'll tell you this: On Wednesday afternoons all the editors gather with their week's pile of books. At the count of three, we toss them in the air. The ones that land face up are the ones we have reviewed in the next issue. We call that process our 'editorial meeting.' That's top secret information, Megan. Don't breathe a word of it."

"For some reason, Mr. Wallace, I don't quite believe you. I'd like that drink now and I promise, no more questions."

"Well, there you are, Megan. I hope you haven't been listening to a word of what Joe Wallace is telling you. I don't care what he's talking about, it's all lies!"

"Hello, Sylvia, darling, what a charming introduction." Joe and Sylvia kissed and hugged hello and from the looks on their faces, I got the feeling that they had enjoyed more kissing and hugging, and not in public.

"Megan, I hope you're not getting blitzed yet. We're leaving for dinner in half an hour, after Willie"—our prize author, another close friend of Sylvia's—"accepts his award. Joe, would you honor us with your presence at dinner? Willie would be so happy to see you there."

"I'd love to, Sylvia. Where are we dining?"

"Orsini's. Does that suit you?"

"Terrific, I'll see you at the door in twenty minutes. Right now I've got to call my wife and tell her a sob story about the long boring awards now followed by a long boring dinner with a bunch of fat men with cigars!"

"You do that so well, darling. We'll see you in a bit."

"Sylvia, is he your lover?"

"Megan, I don't expect to ever hear that question from you again. Now go freshen up while I round up this crew. By the way, you did very well at Saks yesterday. You look positively smashing this evening—and I'm not the only one who's noticed."

"Oh, thank you. It was the most fun I ever had shopping. I bought the most outrageous outfit I could find."

Dinner was wonderful except that I developed an intense crush on the guest of honor, "Willie the famous" as Sylvia calls him, and after my umpteenth drink I couldn't stop drooling. He was politely gracious to me but I knew that I wasn't knocking his socks off. It depressed me and I clammed up. I made a trip to the powder room and Sylvia followed me.

"Megan, I think you've had enough partying for tonight. When we return to the table, I want you to excuse yourself and go home."

"But, Sylvia, I haven't had dessert yet."

"That's too bad. You're too drunk to remain any longer. I can't trust that you're not going to fall face first into your plate or else make a direct pass at our most important author. Splash your face and emerge from the powder room with a very short excuse for leaving early. Do not sit back down. Say goodbye once to the table as a whole and exit quickly. Do not fall down on your way out. I'll speak to you tomorrow about this."

"I'm sorry, Sylvia. I've tried to be charming and witty and bright. I guess I overdid it."

"Do as I said and go home, Megan."

I cried desperately on the way home in the cab. I'm sure that I'm going to be fired tomorrow and I really didn't do anything bad at all. Everyone else was a bit tipsy too. She's probably just mad because Joe Wallace was trying to score with me all night. Well, the reason that she's mad doesn't matter. I've probably lost my job. Well, who cares? I'm better than she. As far as I can remember, those were my last thoughts before falling asleep in my sexy black outfit on top of my bedspread.

Sometime around 4 A.M., I awoke shivering and got under the covers. When I awoke to the sound of the phone ringing at 8 A.M., I was surprised to find myself fully clothed under the covers. It sure must have been some night!

"Yes, hello."

"Hello, Megan, it's Sylvia. I'm terribly sorry for my behavior last night. I was drunk and that can make me an absolute witch. You were an angel, Megan, for not making a scene. Please accept my apologies and stay in bed this morning. It was a long night and the office can manage without us until noon. See you then."

Oh, God, what a close call! She was drunk too. We all were drunk so all the naughty behavior gets erased. Lucky for me. Now I know what to watch out for: if Sylvia seems sober and very mean, then she's probably very drunk. And as long as she gets drunk along with me, then I don't have to worry about losing my job. I'll have to put up with some verbal abuse but as long as it's followed the next morning by her remorse and half a day off, I can handle it. Right now it's back to bed for this hangover.

The glamorous, successful Sylvia Davis is turning out to be a raving lunatic! Sure, she knows her business and she's given me many wonderful opportunities, but she's so difficult to work for. I've found something out about her: she's desperately lonely. Sylvia spends most weekends alone and she's been trying to get me to go to the movies or concerts with her. I've done it a couple of times but I really don't like her and I'm tired of always having to tell her how right she is, and how terrific she is. I need my weekends off. Sylvia loves to drink, which is great during the week because, even if we don't have drink dates after work, she takes me to wonderful bars "to be seen." Sylvia likes drugs too. She's into cocaine and she smokes joints throughout the day—on her way to work, before lunch, after lunch, after work. She gets annoyed that I'm not interested in pot or cocaine but I'm very happy with my drinks and the other stuff only gets in my way.

This is a great job for partying but it's beginning to be tiring, especially since I don't like the work. I hate being a publicist. I hate being on the phone booking tours all day long. I've learned a lot about the business here but I have to move on and out of publicity before I get trapped—by the job, and by Sylvia. A year is long enough to pay my dues.

After a month or so of discreet inquiries, I've been offered an assistant editor position for the editor in chief of a much more prestigious publishing house. It's exactly what I want so I'm accepting with great pleasure. Unfortunately, Sylvia hasn't accepted my resignation in the same spirit.

"You ungrateful little bitch! I've been grooming you for over a year now and this is how you repay me—by walking out!"

"Calm down, Sylvia, and stop cursing me. I'm giving you two weeks' notice but I'm not taking any verbal abuse."

"You just get the fuck out of here right now. Take your two fucking weeks and shove them. You'll be sorry you did this, Megan. You'll never work in publicity again!"

"That's just the point, Sylvia. That's just the point."

I took off as fast as I could because there was no telling when Sylvia would break into some physical violence and start throwing books at me. What a relief! It shouldn't have taken me this long to see the light. Now that I'm out of there, I can see what a maniac she is. I feel sorry for her because she's so miserable with herself and the world. Maybe it's all those drugs.

I love to drink. That much is very clear, and I loved the drinking that went along with my job. It was all very sophisticated and "literary" and I drank in some great bars, probably most of the great bars in New York. But my drinking was just as much out of hand as Sylvia's. I never wanted to stop. I'd force myself at lunchtime but I couldn't force myself after work, so nine times out of ten our drink dates turned into dinner dates and I rolled home and into bed at eleven, after six hours of an "after-work drink." Many nights I extended the evening on my own, made a late date and rolled into bed at two or three, only to roll right out again at seven or eight, still drunk when the day began. All this high living has been catching up with me and the job just became a vehicle for drinking. No matter how much I love drinking, I still want a career. I want to make my mark in publishing and something told me that hanging around with Sylvia Davis was not the way to the top.

I'm frightened. This last job made me see that my drinking is often out of control. Now that I'm getting out of publicity and I'll be in a job with no expense account, no lunch dates, no parties, now I can stop drinking completely during the working day and I won't have to worry about losing control. The P.R. work was just too much for me; I really felt that I had to drink in that job. Drinking went along with the territory. Now that I'm an assistant editor, I'll be part of a much more subdued area of publishing—quiet and diligent, thoughtful and literary. That's what I want. I don't want to drink at lunch every day and spend my afternoons not remembering what I've done.

"Megan, are you an editor yet? It's been six months in your new job. How's it going?"

"No, I'm not quite an editor, Sal. I spend half my day at the Xerox machine, one quarter relieving the receptionist at the switchboard and the final one quarter from five to seven P.M. wading through the slush pile of manuscripts, praying for a major discovery. The odds are against me and I'm getting bored with this job. I miss the lunches and the parties. Maybe I made a mistake."

"I'm a thousand miles away, Megan, but from what you've told me, I'm sure you didn't make a mistake. Just sit tight and do your job. If nothing changes in a couple of months, then move to another company. But stay in editorial. I think more P.R. work would mean more trouble and less professional satisfaction. Stick with your college roommate's instincts, O.K.?"

"O.K., Sal. Thanks. Stay in touch. I promise I'll write. Love you. 'Bye."

I know Sally is right but I can't help being disappointed in this job. I didn't think I was being hired as a glorified secretary. I thought assistant editor meant something. It seems the only one it means something to is my mother. She still thinks I'm going to be famous someday.

Two months later, it's another publishing house and a better job, but I'm still among the lower ranks. I'm finally learning how to edit and how to "make a book." Part of me is still thrilled by it all and somewhat honored to be among the prestigious publishers. I'm sure that's why they can get people like me to work for this minimal salary. We're all working for the glory of it all! I'm ready for some of my own glory. I want to be recognized and taken under the editor in chief's wing and groomed for the job. I need to start circulating, lunching, meeting authors and agents, and making deals. I'm not meant to stay behind the scenes, especially since I've already had a taste of what's out there. Anyway, I don't like paying for my own drinks after work.

"Megan, it's Robert. An author of mine, Dr. George Sidney, is in town today unexpectedly. You've been working on the book, haven't you?"

"Yes, Robert, and I greatly admire Dr. Sidney's work."

"Good, then would you fill in for me and take him out to lunch? He doesn't expect it since we had no warning, but I want to take very good care of this author and show him he's important to us. All you have to do, Megan, is bring him up to date on the book's production status and act charming and interested."

"No problem, Robert. I have lots of experience lunching with authors."

"I didn't know that. I'll have my secretary make a reservation at the Russian Tea Room, and thank you, Megan."

"Thank you, Robert. I've been getting tired of eating at my desk."

Dr. Sidney loved me and told Robert that I *must* work on all his books! Since then, I've had lunch alone with Robert, lunch with Robert and another author, lunch with Robert and an agent, and lunch with Robert and another publisher. Finally, after his series of tests, the editor in chief has set me off on my own with a promotion and an expense account!

"Sally, I'm an editor! It took a little longer than I'd originally planned, but I've made it, expense account and all."

"Congrats, Megan. I'm sure that it will be smooth sailing from now on. Have you bought any books yet?"

"Sally, I've only been an editor for two days. Give me until the end of the week, please!"

"You waited two days to call me, Megan?"

"Only because I wanted to be sure that they didn't take the promotion away after thinking about it for a day."

"Oh, Megan, you had better start believing in yourself. You're making it because you're worth it—and that's the only reason."

Oh, that lunchtime drink tastes so good. It's been too long since the last one. When Robert was putting me through the "editor's lunch test" I didn't dare drink, but since I've passed, I can drink anything I want. I just won't get too high at lunch and I won't try to seduce any of the house authors. Maybe an agent or two, but no authors!

This afternoon I have to call my parents and tell them the news. I know they'll be so happy now that they can stop worrying for a little while, at least until they decide it's time for the next promotion!

"Hi, Mom, I have some good news. I've been promoted to associate editor!"

"Oh, Megan, that's fabulous! Michael, Michael, Megan's been promoted! Please come up and spend the evening with us. We'll go out and celebrate—Hang on Megan, your father wants to talk . . ."

"So they finally noticed that they have a jewel working for them.

It's wonderful news, Megan. We're delighted. Can you have dinner with us tonight?"

"Sure, Dad, thanks. I'd love to celebrate my promotion. I'll see you after work."

I'm going to stop for a quick one before I see the folks, and I think I'll pick up a bottle of champagne for a toast before we go out. Wait a minute; I was out to lunch and had a couple of drinks, now I'm on my way out to dinner but I need a quick one first, then some champagne, and then dinner. That's a lot of drinking, and a lot of thinking about drinking. Why am I always planning my next drink? It's as if I have to be sure before I make the next move that the drink is waiting—cocktails here, dinner there, nightcap wherever. Often the company is secondary, but not tonight. I'm glad to be having dinner with my parents even though my mother is difficult when it comes to drinking. She counts my father's drinks—that doesn't stop him—and now she's begun counting mine. It stops me because I'm the kid. So I fortify myself beforehand and drink an acceptable amount when I'm with her. I know that later, when I go home, I can relax with a nightcap or two. I just don't understand how my father could enjoy being with my mother when she doesn't drink. Eileen Moran is a wonderful woman but she has one drink a year, and she doesn't even finish it! There's a famous family story about the time mother got drunk. They were young and reckless and she and Daddy were at a party. Before she knew it, Eileen was having her third drink. She got a terrible attack of the giggles and threw up (discreetly, in the bathroom) and Daddy had to take her home. She swore off booze then and there and has stuck to one drink a year ever since.

That story amazes me. First of all, I'm amazed that anybody can get uncontrollably drunk after only three drinks. Three drinks is a marker for me when I drink, it's the point when I can feel the buzz coming on. I love the three-drink feeling, and I love the fourth drink even more. So Mom got drunk. Did she have to swear off drinking forever? Wasn't that going overboard? I love my mother but I've never liked nondrinkers. I don't trust them. Their abstinence makes me uncomfortable. I guess my mother falls into that category.

Tonight I wanted to be treated like a first-grader who got the highest marks in class. I wanted to be their little girl again. I want to run away and give up my new responsibility. I know I can do the job and that's all that counts, so why don't I just leave town? Success is too frightening. I'm only happy with the manageable kind of success —the six-year-old kind.

My parents didn't treat me like a child tonight. I'm an adult and I've achieved adult status in their eyes. My mother even refrained from cautioning me on my drinking so, in her honor, I controlled myself.

Because I was on the verge of juvenile hysterics all evening, I was relieved when dinner was finally over. I departed quickly and now I've landed back in my apartment barely glued together at the seams. I'm frightened. I'm lonely. I'm sad. I want to be held and I want to be understood. Even my parents don't understand me anymore. I suppose the understanding should now be coming from a man—a lover, a husband. A husband for me is a laugh, but I could use a real, caring, love affair. Is it me or is it true that no man in the 1970s wants any commitment of any kind? No commitment to a phone call or even a second date, never mind the unmentionable issue of a "relationship." I feel as though I'm always asking for love. Please fall in love with me. Please stay. Please make me happy. I'm probably asking for a bit too much and this approach hasn't made me all that irresistible. In the meantime, I have the cat, myself and my newborn career. Hopefully, I won't sabotage it before it's a week old.

From rags to riches—not just a date, I'm having a relationship. Only trouble is, he doesn't drink! It's against everything I believe in. Now that I'm running around town every evening with authors and agents, having drink dates in the most chic spots, it seems absurd to come home to Matthew, some scrambled eggs and a cup of tea. Absurd but I like it. I like it that Matthew is so even-tempered, never out of control, and I can trust that when he tells me something, he won't forget it the next day. Matthew makes me feel safe, but he also drives me crazy. I have to get all my drinking done before I see him and after I leave him and I have to maintain a sober composure when I'm with him. I trust him to tell me the truth and to remember from one evening to the next, yet I am constantly lying and forgetting. I don't understand why he's with me. He's got to know I'm high every night, or else I'm a great actress and should switch professions.

"Matthew, I know you don't drink much and you prefer a couple of beers when you do, but don't you think it would be lovely to have a glass of wine with our candlelit dinners?"

"I never thought of it, Megan. That's a good idea. I'll buy some and keep it on hand for our evenings together. I'm embarrassed to admit this, but I don't know anything about wine, about what kind to buy."

"I've come prepared to teach you, Matthew."

Thank God I've gotten him to agree to keep some wine in his apartment. There have been nights when I've been ready to climb the walls for a drink. Last week I left at midnight claiming an early meeting, when I really just couldn't stand it anymore and needed a drink more than Matthew. If Matthew doesn't want to drink, it's his business, but I can't let his habits interfere with my life-style. Drinking is really part of my job, and when the clients go home the couple of extras help me to unwind.

"O.K., Matthew, here's lesson number one. This is a half gallon of an Italian soave. It's dry, crisp, refreshing, and it goes with absolutely anything, or nothing at all. It should be served chilled, so a half gallon should always be on hand in the fridge. Also, this particular brand is cheap but it's much better than California jug wines. I like to drink soave with everything, and I especially love a chilled glass when I'm in the bubble bath."

"I'll keep that in mind, Megan. Now all I need are the proper glasses."

"*Voilà!* Two lovely wineglasses for the new connoisseur—and the lesson isn't over yet. In my hand is a bottle of red wine, also Italian, by the same company as the white. This red is called Valpolicella and it's a delightful, hearty but not heavy red wine, perfect with any pasta with a tomato-based sauce or any meat or veal dish. It's also wonderful to share a bottle of red wine in front of a fire on a cold winter's night. In your case, we'd have to sit in front of the radiator! Well, that's all you need to know for your first class of wines of the world 101! Let's have a toast to end the class and begin the evening."

"You're amazing, Megan. I have a feeling you're going to turn me into a sophisticated New Yorker yet. Now, if I could only increase my capacity for alcohol."

"Practice, Matthew. Practice."

"I'm really enjoying this white wine. Let's have another glass, Megan, and take it into the bedroom with us."

"Not so fast. We'll take our third glass to the bedroom. Just slow down and enjoy the buzz."

Well, he's learning. The wine didn't do much for his sexual abilities, but we'll give that some time. I don't care if I don't have the peak sexual experience of my life with Matthew. I like him because he's sweet and he's so young. I'm only a year older than he but he still has his prep school face along with his prep school clothes. He's dead to the world now. Three glasses of wine and an attempt at making love was all he could handle tonight. I think I'll sit up for a while in the living room and enjoy the silence and solitude with a nightcap.

Six A.M. comes too fast to the poet with a job who watches the night slip away and goes to bed at three. I doubt that three hours' sleep will get me through this day, but I have to give it a shot.

"Good morning and goodbye, Matthew. I have to split and get ready for work. I'll talk to you soon."

"O.K. 'Bye."

He didn't even open his eyes. I wonder if his head is going to feel the way mine does this morning. Probably not. I drank for two hours after Matthew was fast asleep. I hope he doesn't notice that the bottle is almost empty.

What a day this has been! It's much harder in this job to function with three hours' sleep and a hangover because I can't count on my boss feeling the same way. I almost blew it in the editorial meeting. Someone asked me a question and I was sleeping with my eyes open. A wonderful trick except when you get caught. After hearing my name called three times, I was able to fake an answer. Some strange looks were passed across the conference table but I kept my cool and made a comeback. For the final half hour of the meeting, I was awake, alert and talkative. It was a close call and I was greatly relieved when the meeting finally ended. Now the day is over and I can go home to bed. Directly home to bed. Do not pass go. Do not stop at the liquor store. Do not call Matthew.

Well, I'm only human. I stopped at the deli for a sandwich and some ice cream, and at the liquor store for some brandy. A hot bath and a couple of shots of brandy will get me all set for an 8 P.M. bedtime. Otherwise, without the brandy, I'm afraid I wouldn't get to sleep early enough.

What a treat! Brandy and ice cream and a bubble bath. What a life! I feel all unwound now and I'm going to get into bed and turn the TV on. There's a great trashy movie starting at nine and I'm going to indulge in it for just a half an hour. It's still too early for sleep anyway. A little TV and a little more brandy will do the trick.

I'm a bad girl. Bad. Bad. Bad. It's eleven o'clock and past my curfew. Little girls needs their sleepeze. Just a teeny bitty little sip more brandy and I promise I'll go right to sleep. I'll call Matthew and promise him.

"Maaaatthew—hiya, kiddo. It's me."

"Who is this? Megan, is that you? Are you O.K.?"

"Okey dokey. It's Megan, your girlfriend. Am I your girlfriend, Matthew? You've never said so. Am I?"

"Megan, what's wrong? You sound sick."

"Well, you sound sick too, so there. And I am sick. I'm sick of your baby face and sick of your attitude."

Slam. I hung up on the jerk. Wait a minute. How did that happen? I just called to say good night. I'll call back and say I'm sorry.

"Hi. It's me again, Maaatthew."

"I don't want to talk to you now, Megan. I think you must be drunk, aren't you? Go to sleep and I'll call you tomorrow."

"I'm sorry, Matthew, but I'm not drunk. Don't be mad at me—pleee-eze. I was just playing before. Come on over and sleep with me."

"No, Megan, go to bed. Good night."

"Don't you dare hang up on me. I want to talk some more; otherwise I'll have nightmares. Am I your girlfriend, Matthew?"

"Stop crying, Megan, you're making me angry. I'm hanging up right now and don't call back."

He hung up. The bastard. I'm in trouble now. So what? I don't need him anyway. He's a waste of time. He makes me feel like there's something wrong with me . . .

All I wanted to do was say good night. Why did I screw it up? I always screw everything up. But I'll fix it. Tomorrow, I'll fix it . . .

It's been a week and he hasn't answered any of my messages. He's not going to call. I guess he's fed up. Everything in my life is so goddamn predictable. I finally get a boyfriend and after three months I sabotage it. I get drunk and send him away. I like Matthew. He's not as screwed up as me. He made me feel that I was having fun sometimes. But the bastard didn't know how to drink and it was just too degrading always being the one getting drunk and saying the wrong thing. Enough rehashing this silly affair. I have to pull myself together and do my job. My career comes first and I don't want to jeopardize any opportunities by mourning a boyfriend or by being too hung over, as I am today. There's no need to drink every day. I'm going to cut down. Now that Matthew is out of the picture and I don't have to worry about not being good enough, I'm sure I'll be able to cut down. For starters, I won't drink for the rest of this week. I'll wait until Friday before I have my next drink. I'm too busy anyway to get slowed down by booze. I'm a career woman, not a lovesick teenager, and not a drunk. Success is the name of the game and I'm a player who intends to win.

RECOVERY

Before I could win, I had to lose everything. It's been three years now since I crawled into my first A.A. meeting. I'm back at the ocean again. It's October and the mornings are cold but the sun is strong in the afternoon. We swim and run along the beach. I'm never lonely anymore. Never may be too strong a word, but loneliness is now a passing feeling, not a permanent state of mind. Sometimes I'm lonely for a short period of time when I let the old hurt in and I respond in the old way. I don't need to be lonely today because I know how to take care of myself. I see life now as a fascinating journey, not a hostile war zone. I have my God for comfort, my program, which I practice on a daily basis, and people. I let people get close to me today because I no longer have anything to hide. I've given up my shame. We recovering alcoholics all share the same past shames and fears and regrets and sickness. We've faced them and we're released from them. We are moving toward health today and leaving our sickness behind.

To be back at the ocean is significant to me. The ocean is now a healing force in my life. It fills me with joy and gratitude for such beauty, change and life. That's because I'm sober now. When I was drunk and at the ocean, I felt battered by the constant surf. I could find no peace from the noise, the movement, the pounding waves that seemed to beat me down even when I was on dry land. The ocean ripped me apart in August of 1980; it helped bring me to my knees. It made me helpless and was an integral part of the process that led me to put down my last drink.

It's the same ocean today, three years later. I'm different—100 percent different. My life is now free of nameless fears and distortions. My perspective is a sober one; it's open to the vast panorama of life. It's Technicolor. The ocean acts as a measure of how far I've come. I'm healthy today. I'm living, not dying. It's such a reversal that I'm constantly surprised by life's little gifts—things I never noticed before I got sober. I am similar to the person who has a near-fatal heart attack and returns to health. For an instant death was in close proximity but both of us were given life. We now see it as a gift, and that change in our perspective is a rebirth.

When I was lying drunk on the floor of my apartment crying out and making deals with God, begging for some comfort, I always used to cry "I just want to live!" But I didn't want to live. I was on a retreat from life. Booze was my escape. Life was too frightening and I needed booze to soften the focus, remove the sharp edges, cushion me from reality. I never learned how to live and that was at the core of my problem. For a long time alcohol worked. It did what it was supposed to do. It brought the world into soft focus so I could ease my way in and out of life situations without being jarred. Then alcohol took on a life of its own; it took over. I no longer had control over how much I drank or when I drank or whether or not I would get drunk. The world outside of my head became distorted. It became harder to live, not easier. There was no more cushion and, in fact, I had no tools for coping with day-to-day life. I continued to try to escape through booze. I had to drink and I drank daily, but I had no more euphoric highs or even pleasant drunks. It all turned sour. I became depressed and sloppy. The world as I saw it was a vast gray wasteland. A friend of mine says: "Booze worked for me. It worked when I was seventeen for about fifteen minutes. Then came twenty years of all-out war!"

The last five years of my twelve drinking years were certainly all-out war. I received no pleasure from drinking for those last five years. I simply had to drink. The first seven years had some sporadic moments of pleasure but many more unpleasant, sick drunks. Booze would start out working for me at the beginning of the night, when I would act friendly, charming, witty, happy. Two hours later, I'd be either hostile and abusive, sexy and sultry making passes at any man in the vicinity, or weeping uncontrollably for all my great losses. This sorrowful weeping started very early in my drinking career. At seventeen, I was crying for the life I left behind! If only I had known the truth then.

Sometimes I want to drink again, usually to escape from a painful situation or change I'm going through. But I don't drink, and for the first time in my life I go through the changes that are part of growing up. It's never as bad as I thought it would be and it's always better when I come out the other end. Drinking never allowed me to experience the process of living. Sometimes it's hard, but now I'm constantly learning and changing and the joy of living surpasses all the difficulties. All I have to do is not drink and show up for life.

When I went to my first meeting of Alcoholics Anonymous, I didn't know what I wanted except to be released from the awful pain I felt. I didn't want to stop drinking. Booze was all I had in my life to fill me up. Booze was my best friend, my lover, my mother and my father. I went to the meeting to stop hurting and to learn how to drink so that I wasn't constantly going off the deep end. I knew I had to cut down but I also knew that I couldn't survive without booze. I couldn't comfortably go for one day without drinking. At the A.A. meeting, they said I had to stop drinking for one day at a time. They told me I had to get sober, to give up the booze because I couldn't drink safely and sooner or later alcohol was going to kill me. I didn't want to believe these people. They were all happy and smiling and laughing and I was climbing the walls. For weeks before I had tried not to drink too much but I couldn't give it up completely. I couldn't believe that I was an alcoholic at age twenty-seven. So I prolonged my misery for about six weeks and finally, on Thanksgiving 1980, I had my "convincer."

It's so appropriate to me now that I had my last drink on Thanksgiving. It was a day of great pain for me in 1980, but now I feel doubly grateful when the holiday is upon us. I decided on the eve of Thanksgiving 1980 that it was a mistake, I was not an alcoholic. I admitted to having serious problems but they weren't related to alcohol. I called someone in the program and explained this mistake and said I was going to drink and that I felt it was O.K. for me to drink, especially over the holidays. I couldn't imagine getting through the holidays without booze. So I woke up Thanksgiving morning and went to the parade and by 10 A.M., I was drinking Bloody Marys. I drank in the neighborhood bar until it was time to go to my mother's for Thanksgiving dinner. I had at least six Bloody Marys and I didn't feel a thing. Before dinner I tossed down three sneaky scotches in the kitchen, away from my mother's eagle eye. Then I drank as much wine as I could during the meal. No buzz. Nothing, just a slight headache. I didn't stop drinking all day and couldn't wait to get home to finish it off.

I spent the last few hours of the night back in the bar drinking scotch after scotch, as fast as I could. Finally, when I got home I was drunk—and I was out of booze. I raided my sister and managed to get a mugful of rye whiskey to put me to sleep. I'd never drunk rye before, but at this point it didn't matter. I'd been drinking with a vengeance all day and I'd gotten no relief. Luckily, I passed out with the rye, and when I woke up the next morning my body told me it was fed up. It was all over. No more abuse. I couldn't move and my stomach was being ripped to shreds from the inside out. It was my worst hangover ever. I had to remain as still as possible for the entire day in order to keep the pain at a minimum. It was a screaming pain, the kind that made me sorry for everything bad I had ever done, and the kind that made me promise to do anything if only it would be taken away. Twenty-four hours later I was O.K. and back at an A.A. meeting—this time for good.

I can't believe I'm doing this. I shouldn't be here. Just because Father Brennan tells me he is an alcoholic doesn't mean that I should go running to A.A. Father Brennan is a lot older than I am. I'm too young to be an alcoholic and I'm too young to be sitting in this meeting.

Why are they all smiling and laughing and saying hello to me? These can't be the alcoholics. They're too happy. They couldn't possibly know how I feel at this moment. This sure is the end of the line. There's nothing left after this. I blew it. Damn! Why couldn't I have held out until I turned forty? It's going to be a long miserable life without booze. So far, this has been the longest day of my life. I can't imagine going through many more like this.

"For anyone who is new, just sit back and relax. Try to listen and identify with the speaker's feelings. Nobody will call on you and in this program we use first names only. Is there anyone here for the first time who'd like to raise his or her hand and say hello?"

I raised my hand and said my name was Megan. I shouldn't have done it because now they're all looking at me.

The speaker is a man named Martin. I can't believe what he's saying. He's telling all the terrible, shameful things he did while drinking. He's even telling how much he drank and, in this room, he doesn't seem ashamed. When he said that he couldn't wait to get away from whomever he was with for an evening and get home so he could drink in peace, I identified. It hurts a lot to identify with Martin because I don't want to be an alcoholic. I'm here at this meeting to prove I'm not.

Martin finished talking and now they're collecting money, passing the basket just as they do in church, even though they say there are no dues. That's it! This is some weird religious cult. I'd better be on guard. Now everyone is raising hands, talking about not drinking. Someone said, "Just don't drink today. Don't worry about tomorrow," and "If you don't have the first drink, you won't get drunk. It's the first drink that gets you drunk." I never thought about it that way. Maybe these people do know something about not drinking.

I'm so afraid sitting here. I hurt so much. I just want to curl up and die. I can't not drink. I can't. I can't. I can't. "Megan, we're glad you're here. I'm Martin and this is Jim. We're going to take you to another beginner's meeting where some women will take care of you. It's going to be O.K. Don't worry. Just try to relax."

I went with them. I got in their car and wound up in another church basement, deposited in the hands of three women who kept talking to me all night. And when I was ready to talk, they listened.

I didn't understand any of their good cheer. How could they possibly feel good if they were alcoholics and not drinking? I couldn't imagine that I would ever feel good again. I talked to one of the women, Pamela, about my drinking. I told her that only the last two years had been bad, that I'm pretty sure I'm not an alcoholic but I had a breakdown when my father died and that's why I drink too much. Pamela listened and said, "Megan, you may be right. You may not be an alcoholic but you're here tonight because you're in trouble with your drinking. Nobody gets here by accident. If you just try to not drink every day for ninety days and come to a meeting every day, then after ninety days you'll feel better and you'll be able to decide whether or not you're an alcoholic. Don't grapple with the big question now, just stay away from one drink a day at a time, and you'll feel better. Things will get better and you'll be able to see what your problem is."

Pamela gave me her phone number and told me I could call anytime and I should call especially when I wanted to drink. I laughed at that because I want to drink every second. I've been dying for a drink all night.

I stayed at the church until the last meeting was over and they were packing up for the night. I went home sometime after 10 P.M. and I was tired and overloaded with so much information and activity that I just crawled into bed. Ninety-nine percent of me was lobbying to forget all this alcoholic nonsense and a tiny 1 percent kept saying, "Help me, Help me." I fell asleep knowing that I'd done something to help myself and, most importantly, I didn't have a drink for the entire day.

Things didn't look very bright when I woke the next morning. I felt worse than being hung over. Shaking and sweating, I couldn't hold my coffee cup and something told me I was in withdrawal. I called in sick to the office and decided I'd see it through. It was ironic because all the other times when I'd called in sick, it was because I had drunk too much the night before. Today I was calling in sick because I didn't drink the night before. If I'm in withdrawal from booze, the facts are I'm drinking too much. Whether I'm an alcoholic or not, I have to stop drinking for a while. Maybe I should call one of the women from last night. I think I'm going to need help today.

"Jane, hi, this is Megan. I met you last night . . . Well, I'm not very good today. I'm going through withdrawal. Yes, I've taken the day off."

Jane began giving me instructions on how to get through my withdrawal. "O.K., Megan, you can lick this but it's not going to be easy. First, don't drink any more coffee. Make yourself some hot chocolate instead. Your body is craving sugar so you'll have to give it some fairly large doses for the next few days. Take a hot bath while you drink your hot chocolate. Then go out to the grocery store and buy yourself some sweet treats—cookies, ice cream, soda. But also buy something nutritious for your meals—eggs, soup, cheese. You should try to eat three meals a day and that will help a great deal. The food will help fight the desire for alcohol."

"Thank you, Jane, I'll do everything you suggest."

"And another thing, Megan. Call me in an hour when you return from the grocery store."

"But I'll be fine now. There's no need—"

"Listen to me, Megan. You're not fine. You're very sick. I'm going to help you and so are Pamela and Diane. We're going to be on the phone with you every hour today. This way you don't have to go through the hardest day of your life alone."

I hung up thinking that these alcoholics sure are pushy. I'm not going to have a moment's rest today. But as the day progressed, I looked forward to each phone call. It marked the passing of an hour, and each hour felt like an eternity. At five-thirty, Jane picked me up and we met Pamela and Diane for dinner. They comforted me. They helped the hurt and each one of them told me about her first day off booze. Diane told me that she met Pamela on her first day, and the next day Diane called her, ready to jump out the window. "We can laugh about it now, Megan, and someday you'll be able to laugh too. It was about four years ago when Diane walked into her first meeting. It was the same meeting as last night. I was at the door, and I said to myself, 'Here comes a live one.' Diane was a little tipsy for her first meeting. As she tells it, she had to fortify herself for the alcoholics."

Diane started laughing, then interrupted Pamela. "That's right Megan. I'd spent the hour before the meeting drinking martinis around the corner telling my tale of woe. Naturally, the bartender and clientele knew where I was headed and one man escorted me up the street to the meeting for the drunks, as I preferred to call it. I thought you had to be drunk to show up at a meeting. When I didn't see any other drunks, I started to leave, figuring that I was definitely in the wrong place. That's when Pamela grabbed me."

Pamela took over. "That was my first mistake! All night long I had to listen to the reasons why Diane couldn't possibly be an alcoholic. Megan, you reminded me of Diane last night. But Diane's best reason for not being an alcoholic was that she was a woman!"

At this point, all three women howled. I didn't find the remark all that amusing because I thought it was true. Pamela composed herself and continued, "Diane swore that she had just read somewhere, either *Time* or *Woman's Day*, that women couldn't be drunks. I didn't quite know how to refute her direct from the press report. She was so adamant that I was afraid that next she'd produce Walter Cronkite in the flesh to back her up! I managed to get her to listen to the speaker, who, thank God, was a woman. By the end of the evening, she'd calmed down and agreed to try not drinking for a few days."

Jane interrupted, "Megan, I bet you thought you had a rough day today, struggling to make it from hour to hour, on the phone with each of us. Well, you were a peach today compared to Diane on her first day. I was the first person she reached on the phone the next morning. She was hysterical, locked in the bathroom, afraid that if she left it she would jump out the window. I had to leave the office and grab a cab to her apartment. In the meantime, Diane reached Pamela with the same message, and Pamela was on her way. But we weren't enough for Diane. She called the Fire Department; we arrived behind the hook and ladder and reached Diane's apartment just as they broke down the door. After that experience, we decided and Diane agreed that she would be safer drying out in a hospital for a week, so off she went. So, Megan, you had a pretty tough day today but at least you didn't have to call the Fire Department!"

We all cracked up. Even I, in all my misery, found myself laughing. I felt better. These women knew exactly what I was going through because they'd been through it also. They were helping me see that I could make it. One day I might even be as comfortable and happy as they are. Only I can't believe that I'll ever look back and laugh at all this agony.

After dinner we went to a meeting and the speaker was a twenty-nine-year-old woman, sober for four years. So much for my "too young" theory! In addition to identifying with the similarity in ages, I identified with her drinking story. We drank the same way in college, and at the end of her drinking she chose to drink alone for the same reason I did: to stay out of trouble and to keep strangers out of her bed. I went up to her afterward, thanked her and asked for her phone number. Her name was Carol and she was the woman who was to become my sponsor. The 99 percent of me from last night who was holding out for a drink, was weakening. I went home and felt the ratio was now 75 to 25. My little voice calling for help was getting it and I was feeling hopeful for the first time.

It's amazing to me to discover after all these years of living—thirty to be exact—that there's nothing terribly wrong with me other than my alcoholism. Now that I've been sober for three years, my self-esteem and self-confidence have gradually grown and I can see the person I really am—the person I never saw before. I'm pretty, I'm thin, I'm healthy, I'm athletic. After getting sober I went on a diet and lost twenty pounds; that was a major step in my physical self-improvement. Once I was both sober and thin, I could look at myself in the mirror and not shudder. In fact, I began to like what I saw. That change was reflected in the way I presented myself to the world. I started walking with my shoulders back and my head up, something I hadn't done for years. I bought flattering new clothes, fixed my hair and started wearing my contact lenses regularly—one of the greatest benefits of sobriety!

As time has moved on and I've grown healthier and healthier, I've found new outlets. I've been running for one and a half years now and I've stopped smoking. I had hoped that running would help me give up cigarettes and it worked; it was a natural progression. I have very definite plans to run my first marathon in 1985. Two years ago that seemed totally impossible. Four years ago, it would have been a bad joke. But today it is within the realm of possibility and it's now a very real goal for me. I have no doubt that I'll achieve my goal. In sobriety, I've learned how to set goals, how to live within limitations, how to grow beyond those limitations and stretch boundaries and achieve. Today my feet are on the ground; reality is my structure, and in accepting the structure I have found the freedom to extend the boundaries, to reach for the unreachable. I have freedom today that I never even dreamed of—freedom that clearly shows me what a prison alcohol had built for me.

I thought that staying drunk was tough, and recovering from hangovers was tougher, but getting sober certainly was the toughest thing I ever went through. And I'd been through a lot before I started getting sober. The withdrawal was total. It was not simply a two-week physical process, it was psychological and emotional as well. My nerves were shot, my skin crawled. I'd lie in bed at night unable to sleep and it felt as though thousands of ants were crawling all over me. I would scream, throw off the covers and turn on the lights and there were no bugs. I was feeling my nerve endings for the first time in many years and they were going bananas, not knowing how to function without alcohol. It felt as though my whole body was short-circuited; sparks were flying and I was just along for the ride. Some of the time I was so out of it, so foggy from lack of alcohol, that I wasn't aware of the physical chaos. Every time I cleared up just a little bit more, some other part of my body would break down. For the first six weeks, I could hardly sleep. Either the ants took over or my bones ached so badly that I couldn't relax. Hot baths and hot milk with honey helped, but many nights I had to sit up and read and wait for the morning. My fears and anxieties were still full-blown and it was often fear of the night that kept me awake. I would sit up until the sun rose and only when I was sure it was morning would I be able to sleep. My friends in A.A. assured me that nobody ever died from lack of sleep. On some days, I couldn't believe them.

Then, after six weeks, I fell asleep. I fell asleep at eight o'clock at night and woke at eight the next morning. I fell asleep on the subway going to work and coming home from work. I slept through my lunch hour in addition to morning and afternoon catnaps in my office. I fell asleep at meetings and once I fell asleep during dinner. I couldn't stay awake and for weeks I was sleepwalking. I had been praying for sleep and now I had to reverse my prayers, telling God he'd overdone it. I prayed to stay awake during the editorial meetings, the cover conferences, the publishing meetings. It was a great struggle. Sometimes I had to position my head in my hands in such a way that I could nonchalantly prop my eyelids open. It's amusing now, but it was tough going through it.

Recovery was long and slow. My body had no idea how to function without alcohol. Alcohol had been its fuel for many years and my body had adjusted to accommodate the huge amounts I forced it to metabolize. While getting sober, it was clear that my insides had to learn how to function normally. I was trying to become a normal human being again and physically, emotionally and spiritually, it was very hard work.

After three months, I was able to sleep eight to ten hours each night and stay awake for the rest of the day. It was an enormous relief, and sleeping regularly was a great help in stabilizing my mood swings. Once the physical was beginning to come under control, I was able to deal with the mental aspects of my recovery. My nameless fears and free-floating anxiety had lessened but I was still extremely nervous and tense and prone to severe mood swings—from depression to elation and back down again in the space of fifteen minutes, with no stopping in between.

In addition, I was experiencing the most frightening part of recovery: I was beginning to feel! "Oh God, not that!" I prayed, because I had been squashing my feelings for twelve years. Real feelings were alien to me. I didn't know what to make of them, how to respond, where to put them. Feelings kept cropping up all over, making me extremely uncomfortable. Occasionally, I'd become excited over a good feeling. When I felt the joy to be alive for the first time, the awareness of that positive experience was very exciting. But more often than not, I was learning to see and experience the uncomfortable feelings of pain, sorrow, regret, loneliness, confusion, fear of the future. It was all so new and so sharp. I had indeed lost my cushion; there were no more cushions between me and the world, me and myself, my intellect and my psyche, my body and my soul. Bit by bit, piece by piece, I was being glued back together and becoming a real person. I was being filled up with life. It was replacing the alcohol, filling the void that the alcohol left behind. I was learning that life was both a joy and a bitch! I decided to stick around and see what happened.

What's happened and what continues to happen is the beautiful part of my story. I stuck around to see what would happen and sobriety stuck with me. I'm not sure I had much to do with it. For six months, I shook in my boots, afraid of being "struck drunk." I crossed the street to avoid bars and liquor stores and I never went near my old watering holes. I was afraid of getting drunk again and that fear kept me sober. The reason I was so afraid was that I wasn't sure I'd be willing or able to get sober again. Getting sober was so difficult that once I knew what was involved, I didn't think I'd have the guts to go through it again. I also knew that my alcoholism had progressed rapidly and if I drank again I'd be on a very accelerated path to destruction. So I hung on, many days by the skin of my teeth.

There were some very immediate rewards to sobriety. I felt that if the only benefit was waking up without a hangover, then that was enough to keep me sober. Feeling good while waking up was an incredible feeling! I hadn't felt that way in five years. Other very basic pluses were no vomiting, no diarrhea, no stomach cramps. In addition to the physical improvements were some wondrous feats: On my nineteenth day of sobriety, I was able to go grocery shopping on Saturday morning with the rest of the world; on my twenty-seventh day, I vacuumed my apartment. It got better and better.

I stayed away from people, places and things associated with my drinking career and that way I was able to stay away from the next drink. Some days I wanted a drink desperately. I fantasized about drinking champagne in a long-stem glass, wearing a strapless evening gown, in the arms of the man of my dreams. When I fantasized like that, I had to "think the drink through" and remember that the last time I had champagne, I was sitting on packing cartons in my apartment, with my dog for company, drinking from the bottle. The glamour was lost on me. I was very far beyond glamorous drinking, and in my heart I knew that the only way my fantasy of a gorgeous evening dress and the man of my dreams would become a reality would be if the bubbly was Perrier, not champagne. The amazing but true part of the story is that it's happened! And it's only happened because I'm sober. The only guarantee I was given by A.A. was that if I didn't drink, I'd stay sober. Nothing else was guaranteed. I wasn't promised that I'd be able to pay my rent, become a ravishing beauty or find my true love. I was told that once I was sober, anything was possible. I haven't changed my entire appearance and become a ravishing beauty, but I have become more attractive. I like myself on the inside and it shows on the outside. I have found my true love, and it happened when I wasn't even looking. Not every sober alcoholic finds his or her true love, but every sober alcoholic I know in my recovery program does like him or herself better in sobriety—and that always shows!

When I first stopped drinking, I wasn't on the streets. I hadn't lost my job, my apartment or my mind, but I was in serious physical and psychological trouble. I was living in my own Bowery. I hadn't cleaned my apartment for months and I didn't wash the dishes until there were no more left in the cupboard. I didn't always wash myself when I should have. The outside was beginning to stink—figuratively and literally. I was hiding out from the world, in my own bunker, just waiting for it all to be over. I fantasized that there were lines and lines of people outside my door who came professing their love. It gave me comfort to believe there were people out there who cared. In reality, my family and close friends cared very much. I just didn't believe it. They all tried to keep in touch with me but I kept them away so they never knew the extent of my sickness. Since I was hiding out, I was getting sicker and sicker and nobody knew. Naturally, that's the way I wanted it. I was tired of being kept from my drinking. I was determined to be free of all the controls, free to drink and be happy. Happiness never showed up. Drinking just made me sicker and sicker until the day came when I was sick and tired of being sick and tired.

There was so much about getting sober that was very painful. Certainly the physical pain was terrible and staying away from booze was a constant battle for the first few months. Seeing myself for the first time in years without booze was a shock. I felt I had no personality, no content. It was booze that gave me my personality, and then took it all away. Getting sober, all I had was a sick shell. I had to admit that I was an alcoholic and that hurt. It took me a while to believe it and accept it. I felt self-pity and anger. Why me? Why did I have to become an alcoholic? I was ashamed but mostly I was angry because I wanted to get well and drink again. But I learned in Alcoholics Anonymous that alcoholics can't drink safely and that meant I could never drink again. In the program, one of the rules is never say never. We don't drink for today. We don't worry about tomorrow or forever. They were trying to put one over on me and for a long time I wouldn't stop obsessing about not drinking forever. Finally, it was too big for me and creating too much pain and anxiety. I couldn't handle forever but I had to start trying to handle just today. "It's a day at a time, an hour at a time and sometimes a minute at a time that we stay away from the next drink." I heard that said over and over and over—and finally I listened and grasped the meaning. I surrendered to my alcoholism. I gave up the fight. I stopped denying that I was an alcoholic. When I surrendered, I began to feel better. It was less of a struggle. I didn't booze-fight every day and I didn't have to continue to fight with the concept of being an alcoholic or not. I accepted it and began to feel some relief. There's a prayer that we sometimes say following meetings that taught me how to accept my alcoholism and gives me comfort in all my confusion:

> God grant me the serenity
> To accept the things I cannot change;
> The courage to change the things I can,
> And the wisdom to know the difference.

It was through acceptance that I began to experience my freedom. I was sober for about six months before I was able to stop fighting and start accepting, and from that point on I began experiencing so many benefits of sobriety. I started to enjoy life. Everything was new. A walk on a Saturday morning through Central Park was my first sober walk. An A.A. dance introduced me to the joys of partying without booze. I danced sober for the first time in my adult life. I went to the movies sober, I went to a concert sober, I went out to dinner sober . . . I was starting to live sober. There were so many firsts that it showed how my entire life had been structured around booze. Booze was a part of every event, every activity. I discovered that it didn't have to be and I could enjoy myself without it. At the second program dance I attended I met my boyfriend, and that night I learned all about kissing sober. It was much better than kissing drunk because I was nervous, and being nervous heightened the pleasure! Sometime after that night, I had my first experience ever of sex without booze or drugs. I was so frightened that I blacked out most of the experience. It was like losing my virginity; I just had to get it over with. The second time was much easier and a great deal more fun. Every time since has gotten better and better as I've been able to feel complete abandon, ecstasy, pleasure, joy and love. It took me twenty-eight years before I had my first peak sexual experience!

In three years of sobriety, I've done all the things sober that I always thought I had to be drunk to do. I've found that showing up sober is much more rewarding. Sobriety heightens the experience. I used to think that alcohol heightened the experiences but it really dulled everything, put a haze over it and fogged life out. Sometimes I want to be able to fog out again when life gets tough and reality isn't pleasant. Those are the times when I most want to drink. It's because I want to escape. I'm still learning how to deal with life on its terms, not on mine. A little pain, a little hardship, is a necessary part of living and that's something I never understood. Pain was to be avoided at all costs, and that's exactly what I did. Since I avoided the pain, I missed out on a great many of the rewards that people experience when they hang in for the bad times. It's said that without pain there's no pleasure and I've known it to be true. While drunk and hiding out from life, I experienced less and less. My feelings became more and more shut down and I chose to remove myself from life rather than live it. I was afraid of life's difficulties and hard times and I escaped through alcohol. The great irony is that alcohol created much harsher difficulties and, eventually, complete devastation. I had many more bad times than I bargained for. As many people have said before me, "I thought booze was my solution when, in reality, it was the root of all my problems."

T his recovery program is too tough and too demanding on me. Every day I have to go to a meeting and on weekends I have to practically live in meetings, to keep away from my old friends and my old hangouts. Now, this weekend, I'm on my way to my first program dance. This is ridiculous! It's just like being back in high school, only I can't sneak into the bathroom to drink. I'm only going to this dance because I have to. My sponsor is taking me and I can't say no to my sponsor.

I'm three months sober and people tell me I look 100 percent better, but I still feel ugly. Tonight I'm trying hard to make myself look good. I bought a quilted silk Chinese jacket. It's perfect to hide the extra pounds and looks sharp with jeans and boots, the rest of my outfit. A little eye makeup and I've done my best; it's time to take the big plunge. Carol, my sponsor, and her friend Claire, are excited and acting silly, fixing their hair and makeup when I arrive.

"Megan, you're going to have fun tonight. Your first sober dance is tough, we've all been through it, but just stick with us and you'll have a good time." These parting words are from my sponsor and then Claire chimes in.

"You're not supposed to get involved with guys yet, Megan, but this dance will give you an opportunity to check out the program men. Look but don't touch!" With that remark we were off and some of their excitement was beginning to rub off on me.

I was right. The dance is an adult version of the high school mixer. The only difference is that I'm more frightened now than I ever was then. Carol and Claire know everybody and I don't know anybody. They're immediately whisked off to the dance floor and I'm left to make it on my own. Panic strikes. I wander over to buy a soda, then I stand on the sidelines watching the dancers. Thank God for cigarettes. I'm chain-smoking one after another, trying to look occupied. A few people have said hello but nobody has stopped to talk or ask me to dance. What am I doing wrong? Why am I such a wallflower? I never was a wallflower before I stopped drinking. By this time of night at a party, I would have been in the middle of the dance floor making a spectacle of myself. Right now even that sounds better than being a wallflower. Or is it? Carol breezes by to talk to me: "Just relax, Megan. This is your first time so it's the hardest. You have to suffer through tonight so you won't have to do it again. The next dance will be much easier. Just try to look a little bit friendlier and people will stop and talk. You're not on the subway, you don't need all your defenses up."

"But, Carol, I feel like I stick out like a sore thumb. Do I look ugly? What's wrong with me?"

"Nothing's wrong, Megan. You're just scared and you're sending out negative vibes. Your fear is making you look like you want to be left alone. That's all. Other than your subway scowl, you look terrific. Come on, I'll introduce you to some of my friends."

Carol makes it look so easy, and she also seems to be having fun. Now, sitting at her table with a group of people, I feel less conspicuous and more comfortable than I've felt all night. Carol is right. The next time it will be easier. For now, I'll just pray for this night to be over.

The night finally did end and although it wasn't a total success (I never was asked to dance), it wasn't a total failure either (I remembered everything I said and did). It was a beginning of sorts, probably one of the harder beginnings I have to face in sobriety. Tonight I had to socialize without alcohol and I hadn't done that since I was fourteen. My use (and abuse) of alcohol began with my social life. I drank and smoked pot for the first time at a high school dance, and from then on every party or social activity was a reason to get high. Tonight's social activity made me face those facts and, in a sense, I returned to being a fourteen-year-old dealing with my peers without any chemical mood changers, and it was very difficult. Now that it's over and I understand the significance of tonight's struggle, I feel prepared for the next time. I overcame a huge barrier tonight. I wasn't 100 percent successful but I saw it through to the end. I didn't run away and that in itself is an accomplishment.

The next dance was better because I was better. I wanted to enjoy myself. I walked into the room smiling and I greeted people with a happy and open attitude and they responded to me. I danced all night. I talked and mingled and laughed and I partied—sober. It was a wonderful natural high to know finally that I could have fun while staying sober.

I realized that night that I had so much to learn. I had been unaware of life's many nuances while I was drunk, especially in the area of interrelations. I had no idea how to socialize without a drink in my hand. It's frightening but also very exciting to now deal directly with people—face-to-face instead of martini-to-martini. I considered myself such a sophisticate during my drinking days. Without a drink, I'm shy and fourteen years old again, learning day by day what to say, how to act and how to live with the rest of the human race.

I'm also a very fragile person now. I'm recovering from a fatal disease. I've been very sick for a long time and now I'm getting well. I have to take life easy and take care of myself. Now that I've stopped drinking I'm on the road to recovery, but I haven't been instantly cured. My recovery is a process and I'm getting better every day but I must treat myself gently and take very good care. As part of my recovery, I must eat three meals a day because I have to build my strength. While I was drinking, I drank at meals instead of eating and now I must be careful to eat properly so that I avoid getting drink signals when I'm hungry.

Sometimes I feel so fragile and afraid that I want to shout out for everyone to hear, "Treat me gently, I'm a recovering alcoholic." I'm so often tempted to do that at work and I know it's an immature reaction to stress to want to use my alcoholism for sympathy and special treatment. That's an old attitude and an unhealthy one for me today. The easiest way for me to get better is to start living a normal life without expecting special treatment.

The hardest but most rewarding aspect of my recovery is that I am now taking responsibility for myself. For my entire life, I shunned responsibility for my actions, for my well-being, for my own happiness. I handed over the controls to whoever was available. Naturally, at first it was my parents and I hung on to them for as long as I could. When I was twenty-five years old and my father died, I gave my boyfriend and my sister and brothers the responsibility for my recovery from the trauma. I realized from a very early point in my drinking that I could deny responsibility for my actions and this attitude became my modus operandi throughout my life. I wouldn't admit that booze made me irresponsible; I used many other excuses—oversensitive, highly emotional, thin-skinned—but the message was always the same, "I am not responsible. You take care of me." Many people accepted the role of my caretaker, especially my family. Boyfriends were more reluctant to wear the mantle because I was so obvious in my neediness. After three dates, it was clear that I was out to claim the man as my protector. The smart ones fled at the first opportunity, and, as the old country club joke goes, the ones who wanted me were the ones I wouldn't be caught dead with. I truly never had any luck in love during my entire drinking career. I also see that I deliberately chose men who were unavailable in some way, I guess because the healthy part of me didn't really want to give the reins completely to someone else.

My refusal to take responsibility for myself was a rationalization so that I wouldn't be held accountable for my actions. For the first few years this attitude helped to curb any guilt or remorse but as my drinking increased and I was clearly out of control, not being responsible took on some frightening characteristics. It now became a fact. It was no longer an attitude I hid behind to get myself out of a jam. I was out of control because of the booze, and through no more choice on my part I had no responsibility for myself. I was now handing that responsibility over to the guy sitting on the next barstool; often my life was literally in his hands. When drunk and blacked out, I went anywhere with strangers whose first names I didn't even know. The attitude that used to be my out, that provided people to take care of me, now had me trapped in what sometimes was a real game of Russian roulette. Luckily I was too drunk most of the time to realize the danger I was in, because if I had, I might have died from fear alone.

On another level, apart from the booze, not taking responsibility for myself left me at the mercy of forces outside myself. I didn't understand that I should be in control. My quest for happiness had me looking outside of myself, to another person or event, and because of my basic misconception I was always disappointed. Nobody and nothing could bring me happiness. I also used my irresponsibility to make myself a victim of life's cruelties and injustices. I was a sitting duck, a target for people and for "life" to stab. Since I did not mold my own life, I was susceptible to others' decisions and whims. In so many ways, this attitude of mine was utter bullshit, fabricated to give myself an excuse to drink. And unfortunately, in other ways, I believe in my own bleak destiny and truly believed that I had cause to drink. As the saying goes, "If you had to live the life

I'm living, you'd drink too." I had a million made-to-order reasons for drinking. Understandably, number one was that I drank to forget my miserable existence, but reason number two on ad infinitum covered the entire gamut. I drank because it was Friday or Monday or Wednesday, because I won a promotion or lost a promotion, because I fell in love or fell out of love, because it was the first day of spring or the first day of winter, because it was New Year's Eve or Groundhog Day. I drank simply because I needed to drink. Drinking came first and I did anything to make sure I got my drink. Today, my heart still skips a beat when the line "God, I need a drink!" pops out in a book or movie or from the person next to me. I completely understand and identify with that statement, no matter what the reason!

Becoming responsible for my own well-being has changed my life. This process of taking responsibility for myself began at the moment I decided to stop drinking. From the first day of my recovery, I have been responsible. I chose life and I chose to get well. I knew that nobody else could make it better. I was the only person who could stop the progression of my alcoholism and that simple realization changed my life. I can take care of myself. I know my own needs better than anyone else and now I can fill those needs. Deciding to stop drinking was the hardest and best thing I ever did. Since the first day, I've learned to take care of myself on all levels. I've experienced great freedom in no longer being the victim. If I'm sick, I can help myself get well. If I'm unhappy, I can change my attitude. If I'm lonely, I can seek out companions. What's amazing to me is that it took twenty-seven years before I grew up and learned that I was responsible. But it takes what it takes. For many people it takes a lot longer before they put down the drink and pick up their lives. Although I felt that I was at the end of my life, twenty-seven is a fairly young age to trade in misery for health and happiness. If I hadn't gotten killed in a blackout or a car accident, I might have physically endured my alcoholism for a good many years, and now I feel very lucky that I've been spared those extra years of misery and total devastation. In my heart, I don't believe that I had any more time left for drinking. I could have died during my next drunk. I believe that I stopped drinking when I was meant to stop drinking. There was no more scotch left in the world with my name on it. I had my share. It was over and luckily I chose life over death.

I can now look at my life, present and past, and I can make some sense of it. When I examine the past, I can clearly see my disease, my alcoholism, creating a quiet insanity in my life. Alcoholism led me to a very small, dark place and it kept me there. That is why, at age twenty-seven, I felt my life was over. It had become very small and I was very sick and I couldn't see beyond my next drink. I can see so clearly now that I was suffering from a progressive disease and bit by bit my life fell apart. Little pieces were removed year by year and, finally, day by day. I had totally isolated myself—body and spirit—from the rest of the world. I see it now and I understand my growing paranoia, my insanity, my complete dependence on alcohol. I believe that no matter what the circumstances were, I would still be an alcoholic. If I had been loved and married and very wealthy, I would have drunk and eventually I would have come to the same small dark place in my mind. Circumstances might have had something to do with controls on the rate of my progression, but I am an alcoholic and nothing could have changed that fact. In seeing my own disease, I can now understand my father's, and I remember how desperately hard he tried to change and control his drinking. He didn't understand that he had a disease over which he was powerless. No matter what my father did to control his drinking and his environment, I believe he was destined to become a drunk like his parents before him. The facts were somewhat altered. Unlike his father, who died on the Bowery, my father held on to his human dignity. He died sober, at home, but it was booze that killed him in the long run.

I was on the same roller coaster, chasing and drinking away my destiny—and I couldn't see it. I knew that I never wanted to drink like my father; I never wanted to become violent and scare little children. But I did want to drink like him because I loved what it did for me. When the day came that I chose my own brand of scotch, I deliberately chose his. I didn't want his unhappiness or his pain, or his personality changes, but I wanted to drink as much, as often. I certainly wanted his hollow leg.

It is inherent in the disease of alcoholism that the alcoholic cannot and will not see the insanity and destruction that occurs from drinking. I believed that alcohol was all I had to make my life better. I didn't for one moment admit that alcohol was my only problem.

I know hundreds of alcoholics and I've heard hundreds of them tell their drinking stories and never have I heard an alcoholic say that he or she knew that alcohol was at the root of all his or her problems. That is because *denial* is a major component of the disease and alcoholics deny that alcohol is the problem until the very last possible moment. Once an alcoholic gets to that moment when there's no more denial he or she must then choose to stop drinking or to let it take over completely.

For years I practiced complete denial of my alcoholism. Finally, I hit the bottom and had no more time to lie to myself. The truth was there for me to see and I had to admit that I was a drunk. When I did that, I had a choice: continue drinking until there was nothing left to drink, i.e., forever; or stop drinking and start living. I chose to stop drinking only because I had a tiny ray of hope that possibly, one day, I'd stop hurting. I was given one moment of clarity and I believe that if I hadn't chosen life at that moment, I might not have had another chance. That is why I cling to my sobriety. I place it before anything else because without my sobriety, I'm a dead duck.

Now that I can look back and see the progression of the disease, I'm amazed that I couldn't see it while in the throes of my active alcoholism. It was so totally consuming and all-pervasive yet I struggled to hide it and deny it. In three years I've become a completely different person. I've changed and grown faster than I ever thought possible. It's been an exciting and frightening adventure. The life that was dormant for so many years woke up and took off and I've been hanging on, learning how to live it.

In the program, they tell me I have to stay sober for one day at a time. I'm beginning to understand the concept: it's because each day is its own complete struggle. Each day is so difficult that I can't imagine going through another one. My sponsor, Carol, whom I talk to every day and who is the main person helping me to stay sober, keeps saying over and over, "Megan, it's never going to be this bad again. You only have to go through this once." And she's right. It gives me hope to know that I will get better and each day Carol points to some small thing that has improved in my life. She uses these to show me that I'm changing and the struggle is easing up, if only the tiniest bit. This is my fifteenth day of sobriety. It amazes me that I've been this long without a drink. Although I want to scream and cry most of the time, I do have some good moments. They are few and far between, but when they overtake me I feel a glimmer of light and hope and happiness that I've never felt before. I want to reach out and grab that glimmer and so much of the reason why I'm not drinking today is because I want the light to grow larger and stay longer in my life.

In the meantime, there are twenty-three and three quarters hours left in the day that offer very little pleasure or comfort. Probably the worst are the eight hours spent in the office. Today, my trouble started at 9:05 A.M. Charlie, my editor in chief, has decided that something terrible has happened to me and is intent on finding out what it is.

"Megan, you've been looking ill for the past two weeks. You're lethargic, quiet and clearly unhappy. Your work hasn't suffered yet, but if you continue along like this, I'm afraid it will. I want you to take some time off and rest up."

"Listen, Charlie, all I want you to be concerned about is my work. I'm taking care of business and just because I'm not Little Susie Sunshine doesn't mean I need to go for a rest cure. Just ease up and let me take care of myself."

Oh, God, that was such an inappropriate response. He is a person who clearly cares about me and I treat him like shit. He's also my boss and my attitude alone could get me fired. I know I reacted badly because I'm so afraid of anybody finding out what's happening to me. Being an alcoholic would not help my career. But it's the wrong reaction. Here I am for the first time in my life trying to help myself get well, and I'm still hiding, still ashamed. Charlie's offer is a decent one. I do need some time off—some time for sleep, some time to clear up and stop my hands from shaking. I'm acting more like a drunk today than I did when I was drinking. I don't want him to think I'm a drunk and that's why I told him to shove his advice. I should be grateful that Charlie didn't approach me during the days of the deadly hangover. I couldn't have helped myself then and his awareness would have flipped me out. Today, I know he's right and if I had any sense at all I'd appreciate a week off for R&R.

"Joan, please get me Charlie on the phone. And, Joan, cancel my lunch today."

"Megan, I can't cancel today's lunch. You've already rescheduled this agent twice and I'm not going to be the one to do it a third time. Anyway, she just called to confirm and tell you reservations have been made for twelve-thirty at Madrigal. So please suffer through lunch, Megan, and then do whatever you want; take the afternoon off, but your loyal secretary requests you don't cancel."

"O.K., O.K. I just hope I'm together enough at lunch not to be talked into an exercise book for lovers! Get me Charlie, please."

"He's on, Megan."

"Charlie, I'm sorry for being so rude this morning. I do feel lousy and I appreciate your concern. I guess I was upset that it's so noticeable. Please forgive me and scrap your plans for firing this ungrateful little bitch and let me take you up on your offer of a week's R&R. I'll bring home a truckload of manuscripts and stay in bed reading for seven solid days."

"You're forgiven, Megan, you little bitch! Go home and go to bed and forget the truckload of manuscripts. Take a few important things to read just so you don't get bored, but the point of this week off is *rest!* Can you leave this afternoon without any problem? Any auctions coming up that I should know about? O.K. Now please take care of yourself, Megan, and try to feel better. Call me whenever you want."

"Thank you, Charlie. You're wonderful. I'll be back next week with my head screwed on straight."

"Joan, after lunch I *am* going home, but not just for the afternoon, for a week's R&R. I'm beat and I must be coming down with something fatal to be feeling so miserable. Can you hold down the fort and take care of any manuscript in progress that may come through? Also, I'm expecting three cover designs for my spring novel. If they come through and art needs an immediate turnaround, you can messenger them home. I'll call every day to make sure we're both still alive."

"I'm glad you're taking some time off, Megan. I've been worried about you. But don't worry about me, I'll take care of everything here."

The world isn't out to get me after all. I have a boss and secretary who either really care about my health or are having an affair and want me out of the way. I'm so glad to be home, to be able to go through withdrawal in peace! What a ridiculous way to put it! I'll call Carol and give her the news and then I'll try to take a nap until tonight's meeting. The path has been cleared for me to get well. It sure is going to take more than another week, but I know this time off is going to help me immeasurably. I'm grateful for it and it hasn't been such a terrible day after all!

"Good morning, world. This is day sixteen and I'm still sober. No hangover for the fifteenth straight morning. What a wonder! In addition, today is my first day of R&R and I'm ready to do all I can to make myself well."

After my morning news announcement to the rest of the world, I had my coffee, read the paper and called my sponsor, Carol.

"Isn't it wonderful, Carol, that I have a week off. No questions asked. I think my boss assumes I just broke off a love affair—and in a way he's right. But I'm sure he has no idea what's going on. If he did, I'd have lost my job a year ago."

"You're probably right, Megan. I agree that you're very lucky and now, you have something substantial (other than the fact that you're not drinking) to be grateful for. I don't want to hear any bitching this week. Whenever you feel the 'poor me's' coming on, I want you to respond with an attack of gratitude for this week off."

"I'll try, Carol. I've been thinking this morning about how I'm going to devote all my time to taking care of myself and to going to lots of meetings. I'm going to a lunchtime meeting and then again tonight and I'm going to stay and go out with other members for coffee after the meeting. I want to feel better so I'm going to follow all your suggestions."

"Good work, Megan. I think you're on the road to sobriety. I'll see you tonight. 'Bye."

"Goodbye, Carol—and thanks."

This woman, this sponsor of mine, is really saving my life. She's available to me twenty-four hours a day and she really cares that I make it. She listens and talks to me for hours on the telephone, she meets me for dinner three times a week and she shares all the details of her drinking story with me. Why? I asked her why she cares so much about me. She's known me only for ten days and she says that I'm helping her as much as she's helping me. I'm not sure I understand how I could be helping her, but Carol says that the whole basis of the program is for one drunk to help another. If we don't do that, we won't stay sober. I know it's true that I couldn't have stayed sober all these days without Carol, but she has many years of sobriety so how could I be helping her? Carol says don't worry, I'll understand things better in a few months.

I'm planning my days around sleeping, eating and going to meetings. I go to at least three meetings a day, sometimes more. For the first few days, I was in a state of shock at meetings. People reveal intimate and secret details of their lives. They laugh about the times they were drunk and lost for three days; or woke up in bed with a man or woman and had no idea of the person's name; or planned elaborate suicide attempts, really staged more for attention than for results. I couldn't believe it at first and then I realized that when people share their drinking stories, they do it to get rid of secrets, of past shames, of hurt and guilt. They let all of it out in a meeting, sharing with other alcoholics, and it helps to put the past to rest and to start living a fulfilling sober life in the present. It was such a relief for me to tell my sponsor all of my deep, dark secrets—all of the horrors of my drinking that I carried with me, certain that I could never tell any other human being. But last week, I went for a long walk with Carol in Central Park and she told me to trust her and to tell her everything that bothered me from my drinking days. I told her the worst things—about never remembering what I did when I was drunk, about making phone calls in the middle of the night and passing out on the phone, about waking up with strange men in my bed. I opened the dam and let it all out, and I felt better. A great weight was lifted and relief washed over me to finally have it all out in the open. Then the most amazing thing happened. Carol told me her most horrible drinking secrets—and, secret for secret, they were just as bad and almost the same as mine! For years, I thought that I was the one terrible person on this planet who had done such unpardonable acts. Now I know there are at least two of us. And from what I hear at meetings, I'm beginning to believe that all alcoholics have the same secrets and that we all have basically the same stories. We drank, we did things we couldn't control, we drank more to forget the terrible things, we did more terrible things, we drank some more, we hated ourselves, we wanted to die, but we wanted to live just a tiny bit more than we wanted to die. We stopped drinking and started living and our lives changed.

Each day sober is a great accomplishment for me. At sixteen days, the one thing I want more than anything is a drink. But I'm not having one. I'm battling the booze and it's an exhausting fight. By the time the day is finally over, I'm wiped out. All the people in A.A. who got sober before me tell me that every day it gets a little easier, and one morning I'll wake up and I won't have the desire to drink. I don't believe it but I'm hanging on. I try to spend most of my time around recovering alcoholics because they know exactly what I'm going through and they help me to fight my booze battle. I want to drink desperately but I have sixteen days of not drinking put together—more consecutive sober days than I've had in ten years—and I'm not going to give those up for a drink. I know I don't want one drink. I never had one drink in my life and that is a fact. I want at least ten drinks, a whole bottle, maybe two. I want to get drunk and wipe it all out. The only problem with that approach to life, as I know all too well, is that I have to wake up after two or three days of drinking, and everything is much worse than before I started. In A.A., there's a saying: "Try not drinking with us for ninety days. If, after ninety days, you want to drink again, we'll gladly refund you your misery." I'm trying it for ninety days to prove that I'm not an alcoholic. Someone recently pointed out that only an alcoholic would have the terrible trouble staying away from a drink that I'm having. I am surprised that all I can think about is drinking. It seems that every book I open has a description of drinking in it, every magazine is filled with luxurious ads, every TV show and movie has a glamorous cocktail party. I'm taking it very personally. I'm being bombarded by very tempting appeals to me to drink. Intellectually, I understand that they're not personal appeals to me, Megan Moran, to stop all this nonsense and pick up the bottle, but it sure feels like they are. What helps to keep me sober today is that the people in all the drinking situations are much better-looking than I. They're wearing fancy clothes without burn holes, their eyes are clear and their bodies aren't covered with bruises that mysteriously appear almost daily. I know that they don't drink the way I do, and no matter how hard I try to convince myself I know I can never be like them. I'm destined for broken bottles, broken blood vessels and broken dreams. So, on day sixteen, I'm going to bed sober, having won another round.

I can't believe it's ever going to get better. My sponsor tells me over and over, "Each day gets a little bit easier." That is, if I don't drink. Why am I doing this? I know, sooner or later, I'm going to drink again. I'm too young to quit forever and forever is such a long time. All these sober alcoholics talk about the gifts of sobriety, the joys of sober life, and personally, I think it's a crock. I really wonder if this isn't some crazy brainwashing religious cult. They seem to have their own language and they talk about God too much. I could be in trouble here.

I don't have to believe anything they tell me. I don't have to come to these meetings every day. I can give it all up and get free of all this sobriety crap—so why don't I? Part of me feels better, not so alone and less sick than a couple of weeks ago. I am getting better. I just can't believe and trust these people. None of them are hurting. They say they did, but I'm not so sure. I want to drink, I need to drink. I can't stop. I won't stop!

I can stop and I have stopped and I feel so lonely without my bottle, my best friend, my lover, my enemy.

It's a clear cold night and stars are shining. The air is fresh and I breathe it in, happy to be alive and walking down Park Avenue. Have I ever done this before? Have I ever gone for an hour's walk after dinner just to feel the crisp air and watch the city night sky? I feel as crisp and clear as the air. I'm healthy tonight and I'm happy to be sober. Taking walks is so new and exciting to me. With so much to see and do and watch, how could I have chosen to spend most of my time in a bar or in my apartment? That's a silly question to ask an alcoholic, so there's no need to answer it.

Tomorrow I'm going back to the land of books. I'm a new person. My physical withdrawal is over and now I just have to keep my mood swings in check. I'll be fine in the office. I even think it will help me to get better. It's an exciting, challenging job and now I'm ready to get right back in the midst of all that's happening and generate some hot stuff. It amuses me to think that I had decided that life was one gigantic bore! Life wasn't a gigantic bore, I was! All I cared about was one thing—drinking—and that sure limits a person's options.

I'm glad to be going back to work this morning, but I'm a little nervous. I've never dealt with this job straight. I wonder if I'll know how to do what I'm supposed to do. Sure I know the mechanics, but what about the more intricate details of auctions and contract negotiations? That's where the job gets tough for me, having to keep the profit margin straight and only spend what's going to allow us to make money. Well, I sure won't know if I can do it until I try. Time to start moving if I want to arrive early.

I bet there are very few New Yorkers who can understand my joy and sense of triumph to be back riding the IRT this morning. Just the fact that I'm smiling is making them move away from me. How fabulous, after a year and a half, to be able to get on the subway again! No more fear of being swept onto the tracks or tempted to jump. This is a definite sign that I'm changing and I'm getting better.

Oh, good, nobody is here yet. Now I can ease into the day by reading my mail and clearing off my desk before all the activity begins. First, I'll put these flowers for Joan in some water, and I'll start some coffee brewing. This first hour has been relaxing and enjoyable. No messes to clear up, no horrors to fix. Joan is outstanding. I only hope she wasn't given my job while I was away. Here comes Mr. Editor in Chief himself.

"Good morning, Charlie. How are you on this glorious day? I'm so glad to be back."

Charlie gives me a hearty bear hug while returning my hello. "Megan, darling, it's so good to see you. You look terrific—100 percent better! Just like my old Megan, ready to take on the world!"

If only you knew, Charlie. "Well, Charlie, maybe not the whole world today, but I'll start with all of New York City and see where that leads!"

"We have an editorial meeting set for ten this morning. Why

don't I push it back to ten-thirty and you and I can get together at nine-thirty for an hour of catching up. There have been some exciting developments this week, Megan, and I need your opinion on a couple of new book ideas."

"Sounds great, boss. I'll be in at nine-thirty—and I'm going to bring a few ideas of my own."

Here comes Joan looking no worse for wear. My supersecretary appears to have a never-ending supply of energy and enthusiasm. She's also the most organized assistant a person could want. She deserves a more career-oriented spot but I just can't bear to lose her.

"Good morning, Joan. It's good to see you. How's it going?"

"Hi, Megan, welcome back. Everything's just fine and under control. I'll fill you in whenever it's convenient."

"Well, Joan, I'm meeting with Charlie in half an hour. Why don't you bring some coffee into my office and you can fill me in on all the major activity so I'm prepared to talk to Charlie. I know you're on a perpetual diet but I brought some sinful pastry from Dumas to get us going this morning."

"Oh, great! I'm only skinny because I'm always starving. Pastry is just what I need this morning. And, Megan, thank you for the beautiful flowers."

"Well, in addition to the flowers, I'd like to take you to lunch today—someplace really extravagant—if you're free."

"Oh, I'm sorry but I have plans for lunch that I can't get out of. Why don't we go to the Four Seasons for drinks after work? I know how you love to do that—"

"No, Joan, I can't go out for drinks. Let's have lunch whenever you're available this week. And, Joan, don't schedule any business drink dates for me until further notice. I want to take it easy and put in a few normal eight-hour days for a while. All the drink dates and dinners and parties brought me to the edge of job burn-out. From now on, I'm going to try to conduct business between the hours of nine and five, unless it's a command performance."

How I wish I could confide in Joan. She's so stable, so sensible, leads such a happy suburban, married life. She's older than I also, which has made me want to talk to her as to an older sister. But I'm the boss. It would be a big mistake to show my weakness to my secretary. When I was drinking, I wanted to tell her how much trouble I was in, to ask for help. And now, when she suggested drinks after work, I almost lost it. I was torn between saying yes and fuck it to this sober life, and saying no and telling her why I couldn't have any more drink dates. I'm glad I held back because I handled it very well and I need the practice. From now on, I'm going to be in many professional drinking situations, namely lunch, and I have to perfect my manner of saying, "No, thank you, I'm not drinking today."

The morning was fun. My perspective has changed so much in the last week that I was genuinely excited to hear about the new health-and-fitness trade paperback line and the new teen romance series. Charlie asked me to oversee the health-and-fitness books because the line was really an outgrowth of a memo I sent to him six months ago citing the need for a cohesive program. It's so ironic that in the depths of my illness, when I was at the bottom of the scotch bottle, I was writing memos about the need for fitness books. Was I asking for help in a very disguised way? Wait until I tell my fellow alcoholics at the meeting tonight. I'll bring the house down with laughter. Now that I'm getting healthy, it's a perfect new project for me and it's a secret support of my new life-style.

It's now lunchtime and I'm glad that Joan had a date. I need some quiet time to reflect and regroup. I have to keep stopping myself and reminding myself that "easy does it." That's one of the most important A.A. program slogans and I can see why. If I start moving too fast and doing too much at once, I'm going to put myself in a high-stress situation. And the only way I know how to get out of high-stress situations is to drink. Until I'm secure in my sobriety and know how to deal with stress other than drinking it away, I have to practice taking it easy all day long.

So I'm in for lunch, eating at my desk, resting and planning to call my sponsor and another program friend before the afternoon begins. I need to be reminded of who I am and what I am, and I need to be reassured that I'm going to make it through today without a drink. This program is working for me. I feel safe knowing that

Carol, my sponsor, and all the other recovering alcoholics in A.A. are there to help me get through these first few months. I have them to lean on every day and they're teaching me how to live sober. During these occasional moments when I'm not angry that I can't drink, I feel gratitude toward the recovery program and all the people who are helping me to make it. The moments of gratitude are few and far between, but at least they're cropping up now and again.

I wonder if other people in this office have ever been through what I'm going through. How many other recovering alcoholics can I find? Statistics say that one in three people is touched in some way by alcoholism, so even if there aren't recovering alcoholics in my office, there have to be many people touched by the disease. I've learned in the program that my terrible secret is shared by many, so I'm no longer afraid of it. I wonder if any of them, Charlie, Joan or the other editors, have lived with an active alcoholic. I have a sense that if they knew about my current situation they would be very supportive and caring, but in the long run, I believe I'd be treated like some kind of mental invalid. It wouldn't be their fault, but they'd never be able to really understand. Only an alcoholic can understand another alcoholic. So what's the point of my mental exercise when I have no intention of ever revealing that I'm an alcoholic? Sure, I may be forced to reveal it someday but only if it comes down to either drinking or admitting my alcoholism. I also may choose to reveal it to someone with a drinking problem. The program says that it is our duty to carry the message to other alcoholics and if a situation arises in the office where I might be able to help someone, then I'll certainly reveal my alcoholism. Right now though, when I'm sober less than a month, I have no business even thinking about other people. My only concern is for myself. I have to be on my most vigilant guard to protect myself from a drink. I must keep myself away from all circumstances that have anything to do with booze, and, most importantly, I must watch my attitudes and emotions and make sure that they are directed away from a drink. Getting sober is a full-time job. No wonder I'm exhausted and need a ten-minute lunchtime nap.

I really conked out and lunch must be over because my phone's ringing. If lunch is over, why isn't Joan answering the phone?

"Megan Moran."

"Hi, Megan, it's Charlie. I thought you'd be staying in for lunch. Listen, there's a small Literary Guild party tonight, not the usual all-industry affair, that's why you didn't get an invite. From what I gather, only the execs are expected. But, Megan, Helen can't make it and I hate to go to these things alone. I was wondering if you'd like to play executive editor tonight. Even after two thousand of these parties, I guess I'm still a little shy and need a friend to walk through the door with. Will you come with me, Megan? It's the kind of party you can use. I can help you get to know the right people—"

"Charlie, before you go any further—"

"No, wait a minute, Megan. I'm offering you an opportunity because I want you to go places. Don't you understand that?"

"Of course I do, Charlie, and I'm enormously flattered. I feel very lucky to be your protégée and I have learned so much from you. Also, you're a great deal of fun to work with and a most charming escort to all industry social functions. I'd love to go. I'd adore it, but I absolutely can't. I'm still recuperating, Charlie, and I have a doctor's appointment this evening. My instructions from the doctor are to spend very quiet, boring evenings at home until further notice. When he gives me the O.K. for dining, dancing and rubbing elbows with the giants of the publishing industry, you'll be the first to know."

"I didn't know you were under a doctor's care, Megan. It better not be anything too serious. Now I understand why you weren't ecstatic over the invitation. I'll catch you next time. For now, I'll have to ask my next favorite editor."

Oh, Megan, you really blew it this time. Not only did you give up the career opportunity of the year, but you lied to do it. You're not supposed to lie, you're just supposed to say "No, thank you." Well, I'm not that sober yet and boy, did I panic! I don't think I'd be able to not drink at a publishing party with Charlie. So I did the right thing: I got out of it and I didn't offend my boss or really hurt my career. It was the best I could do. I'll call Carol and fill her in.

I am drained. I was so nervous and almost panicked while talking to Charlie. I could see the bar, hear the ice dropping into the glasses and see all those chic people drinking cocktails. Part of me wants to be there, to be chic again and in the mainstream. I'm hopelessly out of it now, struggling just to stay on some sort of even keel, but not quite sure which end is up. Think, Megan, what would happen to you if you went to that party tonight and got drunk. It could have been the end of my career. I most certainly would have said or done something (at least one thing) which I regretted. I can't forget Boston. I can't forget that I'm a drunk—a noisy, messy, ugly, common, garden-variety drunk. I'll try to be grateful that I avoided this party because it's not yet time to test the waters. I can't go to any party until I'm absolutely sure that I won't want to drink. And, at the rate things are going, that won't be for a long time.

"Carol, it's Megan. Hi."

"How are you, Megan? Holding up on your first day back?"

"Just barely. All was going well until I had to lie my way out of a command-performance cocktail party tonight."

"Well, it takes what it takes. I'm sure you did the right thing if it kept you away from a drink. In these early days, it seems so difficult getting out of drinking situations and I understand your need to fabricate a lie. I did the same thing when I was newly sober. After a while it gets easier and easier to extricate yourself from drinking invitations and situations. You'll find that a simple 'No, thank you' is all it really takes."

"Thanks, Carol. I'll talk to you tomorrow. 'Bye."

The afternoon flew by. Joan and I spent it answering letters and doing general correspondence. It was an afternoon of drudge work— no meetings, no authors, no auctions—just what the doctor ordered. I left the office shortly after five to meet another newcomer in A.A. for coffee before our 7 P.M. meeting. My friend Martha has only been sober for one week, so she's feeling just the way I was before I took a week off from work. It should be a pretty intense night. When I arrived at the coffee shop, Martha was already waiting.

"Hi, Martha. I hope you're feeling better than you look."

"Oh, Megan!" With that exclamation, Martha starts crying and I comfort her until the sobs stop and she can tell me why it's so bad at this moment.

"Megan. Have you felt like you want to jump out of your skin?"

"Well, Martha, you're right on schedule because I felt that way last week. I was a mass of live nerve endings. I thought that horrendous feeling would never go away and guess what—it's gone! Martha, it's all a part of the process of recovery, and in these first few weeks we have to go through some serious physical withdrawal."

"Thank God you had it too. I thought I was losing my mind."

"It's hard to get through a day of work when you're feeling this way, Martha. Can you get some time off? I took a week and it worked wonders. If you can't take a week, take at least two sick days —maybe this Thursday and Friday—and that way you can have four days off together. It helped me because I couldn't sleep much at night, so I was able to nap during the day. I went to three or four meetings a day last week and I really think they were my medicine. They helped me to forget about myself, to listen to the speaker and become part of the group. I also spoke up from the floor and let everyone know what bad shape I was in. When I did that, many people in the room came over to me and helped me."

"Oh, Megan, you're right about getting away from work. I don't think I can last until Thursday. It would probably be best if I called in sick tomorrow. I am sick and I'm so exhausted."

We talked for an hour and then went to the meeting. Although I only have one more week's sobriety than Martha, I was able to help her tonight. It's so good to feel that we're in this together: Carol helps me, I help Martha and Martha will help the next person. And then there are so many people in the meetings who help me every day, sometimes just by saying hello, and other times by giving advice when I'm having a problem. There are moments when I really enjoy this process of getting sober. I'm learning so much and I'm changing and growing every day. I know that soon there is going to be a whole person inside Megan Moran. That void left by the booze is gradually being filled with the person. Sometimes I can feel myself coming to life—like Pinocchio in Geppetto's shop. I'm not sure who the real Megan Moran is going to be, but I'm almost certain she'll be stronger and happier than the old Megan.

While the new Megan is being formed, the current, shaky, scared Megan has to sit in meetings every night in order to stay out of the bars and to keep from being alone all night in my apartment. When

I was first told that I had to go to a meeting every night, I was appalled and complained that I just didn't have the time to go to so many meetings. I was so mixed up that I didn't realize how much free time I'd have to fill when I was no longer drinking it away. The nights can go by so slowly if I'm home alone with no bottle to keep me company. So now I spend every night in meetings, and after the meetings I go out for dinner or coffee with other members of the group. We talk about how we're feeling and the people with more sobriety than I have tell me how they stay away from booze.

Tonight's meeting was very special for me. An old friend of the family has been in A.A. for twenty years and tonight he invited me to hear him speak. Usually at New York City meetings there is one recovering alcoholic who leads the meeting by first telling his or her story with booze. This is called a qualification; it is the story that qualifies the person as an alcoholic. What each alcoholic does is describe his or her life with alcohol—from the first drink to the last —and then his life in sobriety. All this is done in twenty to thirty minutes and often includes descriptions of car accidents, fights, hospitalizations, sick drunks, hangovers and, finally, recovery. Every person I've heard speak says almost the same thing about recovery: it was hard and painful in the beginning, but after the pain, very joyous and liberating. That's why I believe it will get better for me. Soon I'll be joyful and liberated, but I won't hold my breath. The other wonderful aspect of hearing another alcoholic's story is that, although the circumstances are always different, the feelings that we alcoholics experienced are the same. I listen to a forty-five-year-old fireman from Queens and when he talks about cradling his bottle in his arms, rocking back and forth and crying, I remember doing the same thing and feeling exactly the same way. Everything else about my drinking life and the fireman's may be completely different but we share an essential feeling: we share that same despairing moment with the bottle. Almost every time I hear another alcoholic speak, there is at least one incident or one feeling that I identify with. I'm not alone anymore, and even when I thought I was alone there was another alcoholic across the city, or maybe even across the hall, crying into her scotch and hating herself for it.

Tonight I heard my family friend Jim speak and naturally I identified with him. I thought to myself: here is a man I've known all my life and tonight is the first time that I'm getting to know the real Jim. Because of what we all share, the alcoholics in these meetings are intimate with each other on a spiritual and emotional level. I don't simply fill up my evenings with meetings, my evenings are being filled up with people. I am learning how to form honest relationships with other people. For now, my focus is only on fellow alcoholics. I can trust them. They can help me. As I get better and grow, I am told that what I learn in meetings can be taken with me to the outside world. Jim's eyes filled with tears the first time he saw me at a meeting. He embraced me and welcomed me, promising me that I was beginning a brand-new life. I must believe him just as I must believe Carol, my sponsor, and all my fellow recovering alcoholics. I have made the leap of faith because if I hadn't leaped I would have fallen. There are moments when these people speak to me that I catch a glimpse of life after booze. I'm holding on and tonight Jim provided the life raft.

I tried to stay sober, but I lost my hold on the life raft and went down one more time. I had to get drunk for Thanksgiving because I couldn't conceive of going through the holidays without drinking. So I drank for Thanksgiving—from 10 A.M. until 2 A.M.—but I didn't get drunk. I got so sick the next day that I wanted to die— and then I realized that instead of dying I wanted to get sober. The booze wouldn't work anymore and I'm sure it was that God I'm having trouble believing in who decided to show me on Thanksgiving Day how it wouldn't work. Not only did the booze not work, but I had a terrible day. I couldn't stand being with my family. I couldn't talk to them and "enjoying the day" was completely out of my grasp. They enjoyed themselves. I was completely isolated in my own disease and my pain. I sat at the Thanksgiving table with two brothers and my sister and their spouses, six nieces and nephews and my mother, and I hated them all. I hated them because I couldn't be a part of the family or the celebration. I couldn't participate because there was no room left in my life. I only had room for booze. I convinced myself that booze would help me enjoy the holidays, but booze hadn't given me any pleasure for years. It only made me sicker and sorrier.

In three days it's Christmas, and I'm sober. I intend to stay sober for Christmas but I'm scared to death. I've told one person in my family—my sister Peg—that I'm not drinking and in A.A. She's very glad and she'll be my silent supporter during Christmas dinner. Although I don't feel ready yet to tell my family the news, I knew I needed some help during Christmas and I'm very happy that I've told Peg. Now all I have to do is fortify myself with meetings before and after Christmas dinner, and I'll make it through. It may not be easy or much fun but that's O.K., my holidays have been disastrous for years. This year I can deal with a few hours of discomfort. Who knows? I may enjoy myself a little.

I've discovered from hearing other alcoholics talking about the holidays that I'm not unique in my feelings of dread about the approach of Christmas. I've always dreaded Christmas and used it as an excuse to get drunk for days. This year I'm dreading it sober. I'll have no booze to protect me. From what? From the truth that I don't have the perfect family? That I always get lousy presents? That nobody loves me? I'm so tired of singing that song. I'm going to start loving me so at least I won't be able to say "nobody" anymore.

My happiness is not "their" responsibility. It isn't up to the rest of the world to make sure that I'm O.K. That's my hardest lesson. I don't know how to be responsible for myself.

"Megan, dear, it's Mother."

"Hello, Mother. How are all your preparations for Christmas coming along?"

"I'm exhausted. I can't go into another store or shop for another gift, and this will be the last Christmas dinner I make for some time. I'm going to give the rest of you a chance from now on."

"Mother, dear, I made Christmas and Easter dinners last year. I'm sorry that you're hassled but we're all helping out."

"That's why I called, Megan. I hope you're planning to bake two pies for dessert. One won't do."

"I always bake two, Mother."

"And, Megan, please get here early to help me with the cooking."

"I'm sorry, Mother, but I have plans in the morning. I won't be able to come early and I'm also not going to be able to stay very late. I'll be leaving shortly after dinner."

"Why do I bother? Why come at all, Megan, if you've got such a tight schedule?"

"Please don't be upset, Mother. We're going to have a lovely day and I'll be there for plenty of time. I'll bring the pies and some Christmas cookies for the kiddies. See you tomorrow, Mom. Try to get some rest. 'Bye."

God, was I cool! She tried to get me going. She wanted me to get wrapped up in her hassles, her bad humor, and I didn't. That's amazing! I'm going to make it through tomorrow after all. And I said, "No, I can't come early." Where did those guts come from? The program. I've been taught that I have to say no to anything or anyone who endangers my sobriety. And if anyone endangers my sobriety, it surely is Mother. My mother who spells love G-U-I-L-T. I feel reassured now that I can do it. My mother isn't going to ruin anything for me anymore because I'm in control of my own life.

"Merry Christmas! Merry Christmas! Merry Christmas! What a lovely tree! Yes, I believe you were up all night decorating it. Hi, Peg, Brendan, Joe, Ann, Tom, Claudia. Hi, kids, here are some more presents!"

"Megan, you look good," my sister-in-law, Claudia, begins to compliment me then decides to take it back, so the word "good" gets swallowed under her breath. No problem. I know that I'm looking good. Brendan breaks in with a hug and "Can we count on you for some dynamite dessert?"

"You bet, Brendan. And you can have the biggest slice of pecan pie."

"If you weren't my sister, I'd fall in love with you, Megan. You should bake a pecan pie for every guy you go out with, and believe me, I'd be at your wedding within six months."

"Don't worry about my wedding, Brendan. I'd appreciate it if marrying me off was not the main topic of conversation at yet another family gathering."

The red light inside my head starts flashing. Hang on, Megan, here comes the tough one.

Brother Joe approaches, glass in hand. "Here's a scotch, me darlin'. Merry Christmas."

"No, thanks, Joe. I'm very thirsty and I'd rather have a soda."

I won't be able to handle too many of these encounters today, but if this is the toughest one, then I'm home free. Here comes Peg, my secret protector today, with a large frosty Coke.

"Megan, do you want a Coke? Come over here and look at my wonderful gift from Tom."

"Thanks, Peg." As we walk away, I can still hear Joe mumbling his surprise. That must have been the first time I ever turned down a drink. "What a beautiful ring, Peg! It really complements your engagement ring. You must have been very surprised. Tom, you're terrific!"

The day progressed quickly. Mother was in the best of spirits. She reserved her cranks for pre- and post-holiday phone calls. Today she was in her glory, surrounded by her children and grandchildren. Everyone was doing all he or she could to bring a lot of good cheer to the gathering because we all felt the absence of our father, the man for whom good cheer took no effort. But we don't grieve anymore. We carry on and Brendan and Joe are now teasing Mom about finding a new husband. We hope she does, mainly because it's been very tough taking care of her. She's constantly taking us on emotional roller coaster rides.

My pies were their usual smash success and soon after dessert I felt it was safe to make my exit. My brothers were getting too high for my comfort and my eyes kept wandering to the wine bottle on the table. Nobody is really noticing that I'm not drinking. I haven't wanted to drink but I haven't been able to stop thinking about booze all day.

"Well, folks, I have to take off. I'm meeting some friends tonight."

"Megan, it's too early for you to leave. What do you mean, you're meeting some friends? Does that translate to you have a date?" Joe teased.

"You can translate however you like," I said, winking. "Just give me a kiss goodbye."

" 'Bye, Megan, Merry Christmas!"

"Thank you, Mom, for a wonderful day. I'll talk to you soon. Good night!"

I made it! Get me to a meeting—*fast!*

"My name is Megan and I'm an alcoholic. I'm twenty-eight days sober and I've just come from Christmas dinner with my family." The tears and the sobs began and I couldn't continue. The woman next to me took me in her arms and comforted me until I could stop crying.

"Oh, thank you. I don't know why I'm so out of control. It's just that I got through it. I never thought I'd make it through Christmas. I'm so relieved and so happy that I didn't have to get drunk today."

"Oh, Megan, congratulations! It's a major achievement and you can cry, laugh, scream and jump up and down if you need to. That's what we're all here for. By the way, my name's Ann."

"Hello, Ann. Merry Christmas. Now that I've finally gotten here, I feel the Christmas spirit coming over me."

"I know what you mean, Megan. I've been watching people trickling in over the past hour, and everyone is breathing a sigh of relief, holding on to each other like survivors. We all made it through!"

The meetings continued all night. It was open house for alcoholics and the place was packed. I calmed down, felt safe and enjoyed myself, finally in a secure place. As midnight approached, I took my weary body home to bed. Alone. If only I didn't have to be alone tonight. I want a man to hold me, to call me his Christmas present. But not this year. Who knows—maybe next year. I'm not going to get all sad and depressed. I've cried enough for tonight. I'm alone but I'm also tired. These sad feelings are so strong because I'm tired and I need sleep right now more than I need love. Anyway, I am loved. Everyone at the meetings loves me. They're there when I need them and right now that's what matters. Under the covers with the night light on, say my prayers, count my blessings, close my eyes and dream of happier times, of Christmases to come—full of peace and joy. For today, I did the best I could.

Maybe there is life after booze after all. There are finally some days when I'm not thinking about a drink or thinking about staying away from a drink. There are moments, and even days, when I can think about the rest of it—living, working, eating, sleeping. A whole month away from a drink is an incredibly long time, especially when the longest I could stay away from a drink was one day. That was only when I was too sick to get it down. Today it's been thirty days —four weeks—one month! I feel proud of myself. I feel clean and healthy. I don't smell like wine anymore. I used to smell it oozing out of my pores. I tried to perfume it away, and when that didn't work I just settled for my own unique fragrance—wine musk. What a terrible joke! I was always envious of those people who drank vodka. I couldn't drink vodka since I almost died in college of Harvey Wallbangers made with vodka. I'm sure that my illness had little to do with the vodka and more with the Galliano and fruit juice, or maybe it was the Southern Comfort that I slugged as a chaser. So for the rest of my drinking life, no Harvey Wallbangers and no vodka. I'd always heard that vodka was a great drink because it had no smell. That didn't much matter to me in my early days of drinking, but when I got to the point where wine was practically seeping through my skin, I cursed and cursed that I couldn't drink vodka and prevent this horrible smelly condition. I've since learned that if you drink enough vodka you smell like vodka, just as I smelled like wine. So the vodka theory proved to be a myth.

Another problem along these lines that drove me crazy was the red wine dilemma. I got tired of white wine periodically and switched to red to put some variety and some color in my life! After drinking a bottle of red wine, my lips would turn purple and no amount of rinsing would fade the purple out. I'd go to sleep with purple lips and wake up with purple lips. Before work I'd have to scrub my mouth with the nail brush. Sometimes I even peeled the skin off to get rid of the stain. On those mornings I didn't need lipstick for a splash of color; the blood took care of that. Eventually I gave up drinking red wine even though I preferred it to white. I knew that if I continued drinking red that I'd have no lips left. It's a relief not to worry about smells and stains anymore.

Now, I really know in my gut that booze didn't help me to feel better ever. It helped me *not* to feel. It was an escape, not a high. Now that I'm away from it for a month and looking at the world through clear lenses, there are moments when I want to run away and hide. I may feel that way but I'm not acting on it. I'm not hiding out anymore. Booze isn't an option and escape isn't an option. It's death for me—a slow, lonely, frightened death. I'm facing the music and some of it is soothing, melodic and beautiful. The harsh notes are fading and becoming fewer. It may even be fun. It certainly is much less frightening than facing life drunk. I'm thirty days sober and I've become a philosopher. All drunks like to consider themselves philosophers, but the sober drunks like myself should know when it's time to cut the bull and get to work.

Work is still a problem for me. It seems that every day I have to confront booze in one form or another. Also, I realize how little self-confidence I have and every day it seems to diminish, not increase. Charlie has noticed the change and he wants to know where my fall list is. I don't know where it is. I can't seem to make up my mind on any books. I was better making decisions drunk after a four-martini lunch. But I know I have to take it easy and have patience. But I don't think I can use that line on Charlie. I'm recovering but they don't know that, and if I don't produce I'm out on my ass. My sponsor keeps telling me that in six months I'll not only be buying the Great American Novel, I'll be writing it. I don't have six months to wait, but I'm determined that if I held on to this job drunk I'm not going to lose it sober. Yesterday, the president of the company made his monthly surprise attack at our editorial meeting. He briefed us on the terrific marketing plans being made for my line of fitness books. I almost choked on my coffee because out of six books scheduled for the publishing launch in twelve months, only one is in the process of being written. I am responsible for delivering material to the marketing department so they can work up their hundred-thousand-dollar compaign! Will I write the books myself? Will I quit before someone else finds out they don't exist? Or will I deliver? These seem like very valid reasons for getting blind drunk. I'll go to a meeting instead and I'll do my job as best I can.

"Keep it all in perspective, Megan. That's all you have to do and you won't drink, you won't lose your job and you'll get the books delivered." Carol is sharing these pearls of wisdom in the kitchen before our 7 P.M. beginners' meeting. I'm crying, as usual, certain that my world is going to blow up. "Perspective" is the word of the week. I feel as if I were back in high school vocabulary building class learning my word for the week. I may not like it, but when I listen to Carol I know that she's right. If I keep it in perspective, nothing is too big to handle. I have to keep my recovery in perspective. I'm not attempting to stop drinking for the rest of my life because that thought blows my mind. I don't drink for today. Just today. I can handle that.

"But, Carol, I'm having trouble translating that perspective into my professional life. I have to look ahead. I have to schedule. I can't close the office door at five o'clock every day and congratulate myself for doing my best. My best isn't good enough right now. These damn tears! Will you please give me a plug for these damn tears!"

"Calm down, Megan. Every alcoholic in search of sobriety who walks into these rooms is in trouble with all facets of his or her life. You've heard many people who come in without jobs, without apartments, without families. You've also heard people who never lost a job, who came in at the height of their career. The point is, it takes what it takes. If you're meant to lose your job, you'll lose it. But I don't think so. You just want to be 100 percent better right now, and you're not, so you scream and cry and carry on. Give up the emotional acrobatics. Go to work tomorrow and do your job. Give yourself a deadline for getting writers and stick to it. And stop crying! Let's go to the meeting. We both could use it."

"Carol, you must be getting tired of me. I'm such a baby."

"Yeah, but not as big a baby as I was!"

As usual, the meeting took care of me. What is it in these rooms that seeps in and gives me a moment's peace and hope and happiness? Some people say it's spiritual, others call it magic. Spiritual magic is a good term to combine both groups. Sometimes I'm really astounded to be sitting in a roomful of drunks who aren't drinking. All of us tried so many times not to drink, but we couldn't do it alone. Together we can do it—and that's the magic. Tonight I'm at one of my regular beginners' meetings and half of the people in the room have under ninety days' sobriety. Ninety days is the suggested beginner's period. For our first ninety days, it's suggested that we go to at least one meeting a day and we count each day of sobriety, often raising our hands at meetings and announcing what day it is. That has helped me so much because now people know I'm a beginner and they talk to me, give me their phone numbers and help me to feel comfortable. It's getting to the point for me, after thirty days, that I know at least one person in every meeting I go to. That's helpful because I need to feel comfortable in meetings and less frightened than I feel during the rest of the day. A lot of people in the room tonight are in my "class." We're getting sober together and we spend a lot of time in meetings, in coffee shops and in the movies together. Almost, but not quite, like camp! We're not children anymore and that's one of the toughest things to learn, even for the forty-five- and fifty-year-old newcomers. I've learned that alcohol stunts one's emotional growth because it's been the substitute for growing up. Run and hide in the bottle is the alcoholics' favorite game. We're not hiding out anymore. We're all survivors in this beginners' meeting. Some have only survived without a drink for one day, or seventeen days, and some for seven years and twenty years. We help each other and if we don't drink today we've won. All we've got is today and all we have to worry about is today. That's quite enough for me. I go through a year's worth of traumas in twenty-four hours. I couldn't handle any more. And yet, I'm amazed that I'm handling what I'm handling. Sure, I came in here tonight hysterical. I'm hysterical almost every night, but I survived another day and Carol's right, that's all I have to do. I feel I can survive almost anything as long as I can come to these meetings and get the help and support that I need from other alcoholics who've been through all I'm going through.

Now it's time to go home—the most dreaded part of my day. I

still have to consciously hold myself back from going straight to the refrigerator for the bottle of wine. The wine is no longer there—there's no liquor in my apartment—but it's taking a long time to break the habit. My apartment depresses me. It's where I almost died. It's where I passed out on the floor and vomited all over the bathroom almost every night. It's still gray and it's still dirty and my moving cartons from two years ago are still packed. I know that I'll fix it as soon as I get better, it just doesn't help me to put the past away and to feel good. Patience and perspective. Soon the walls will be white, the lace curtains will be hung and the floors will be polished. That will be a red-letter day for me because it will symbolize my physical, emotional and spiritual health. For tonight I can be happy that the floor is vacuumed and the sheets are clean and I'm not going to dirty them with vomit.

"Thank you, God, for getting me through another day without booze. Please watch over me while I'm sleeping and watch over all the people I love. Amen."

I've become a child again through my prayers. I haven't prayed every night before going to sleep since I was a child, so I'm using my old format. I don't know how to pray anymore. I'm not sure who God is. I know he's not the big man with the beard who resembles Santa Claus and lives in the sky, but I don't yet have a new image to replace the old one. I try to believe in him because I feel that he protected me when I was drunk, especially when I was roaming the streets at 4 A.M. I also believe that he had something to do with my getting to the program. I never had any intention of getting sober. I found myself at a meeting one day. So now I pray my simple prayer every night because it helps me to feel that I'm not alone and that I'm safe. I also want to believe the simple beliefs of childhood because I cannot yet handle the adult world. I need some remembered comforts to help me get through—both day and night. I don't know what I believe. I just need to believe. I need to have faith and I need hope. Each day gets a little bit easier and my faith and hope grow.

My friends in the program tell me to "act as if." If I "act as if" I believe in God, that's all I need to get by right now. If I "act as if" I feel good, then chances are I'll start feeling better. I'm working the "act as if" theory in every area of my life. I choose what I intellectually know is the appropriate response or behavior and even though I don't "feel" that way, I "act as if." It helps to keep me from thinking too negatively and keeps me from bouts of self-pity and depression. Sometimes I can't stop the depression and negative feelings, but I don't have to prolong those feelings today. I used to drink over any feelings, especially depression, and drinking always made it worse. Now I can get myself out of a depression in a couple of hours. I was always afraid that the bad feelings would never go away. I'm still afraid of that, but the bad feelings *are* going away. I now have proof that if I don't drink I don't have to be miserable.

Today is my ninetieth day without a drink. I'm a new person. I'm sober and alcohol is no longer a part of my life. I've chosen to stay sober because I now believe 100 percent that I'm an alcoholic and to drink is to die—sooner or later.

The phone rings. "Good morning, Megan. Happy ninety days!"

"Thank you, Carol. You know I could never have made it without you. And today I need you more than ever to help me get through my first alcoholic qualification tonight."

"Of course, Megan. I'll meet you at the coffee shop on First Avenue an hour before the meeting. O.K.?"

"Great! Thanks, Carol. See you later."

Yesterday was my birthday and today is my ninety-day anniversary. I'm twenty-eight and my life isn't going to be over before I'm thirty due to the use and abuse of alcohol. It's a cold March at the end of a cold gray winter. I've had plenty of gray days in the past ninety, but today is glorious. I'm on top of the world because I'm part of the world. I'm walking to work but I feel as though I'm gliding. I'm invigorated and glad to be alive.

That's a new feeling for me—glad for life. Just life. Nothing more. Just the simple breathing, feeling, seeing, touching, walking pleasures of being alive. I feel as though a pressure has been removed from my chest, a weight from the top of my head. The gray curtain in front of my eyes is gone. I can see the sky and the sun shining and my eyes and my head aren't aching. This is new and different and I think it's going to work.

Speaking of work, I've arrived in midtown in record time. I was walking at a brisk pace. I pick up the paper and my coffee and ride the elevator to the doors of my prestigious publishing house. What joy to be on the elevator without experiencing paralyzing anxiety and dread at facing another day. I'm looking forward to today—its challenges, its excitement, even its problems—although I'm still easily flustered when the smallest thing goes wrong.

"Good morning, Sue. Any calls yet?"

"Good morning, Megan. No. The phones have been blessedly silent."

I used to be afraid of the receptionist. I imagined she knew about me because I imagined she listened to all my calls. I wouldn't speak to her. I'd slink by her desk hoping she wouldn't notice me. Naturally, she mistook my fear as snobbery and she told Joan, my secretary, that she didn't appreciate being treated as a nonperson by me. I couldn't believe it when Joan told me and of course I couldn't reveal what really had been going on in my head. I muttered something about being distracted by my own thoughts, certainly not meaning to slight Sue. For the past ninety days, I've been making an effort to establish a normal, friendly relationship with the company receptionist. It's been a major project and has taken a lot of effort, but I've done it. It's become a significant accomplishment—proof that I can change old behavior and be released from negative and fearful attitudes. Sue is proof that I'm getting better. It's too bad she'll never know the role that she's played in my sobriety!

Today that feeling of needing to announce my alcoholism through the corridors of the company has pretty much subsided. I realize that I can take care of my own needs. I don't have to wear my disease on my sleeve in order to receive special treatment. The phrase "wears her emotions on her sleeve" was made to order for me. People have always said how easy it is to know how I'm feeling and I've always been proud that my emotions showed. I've loved being "very sensitive" and I've worn it as a badge. I cry at TV commercials. I've called it my Irish inheritance and my creative personality. What it has always been is an attention-getting device. I've always wanted more attention than I've ever received. I drank to be the life of the party—the one who danced on the table tops or jumped naked into the pool. I needed the attention. I still do but I'm learning to pay attention to myself—to take care of my own needs, to love myself. I don't have to be the crybaby or the wounded animal anymore. And it's getting easier not to be those things because I'm not drinking and I haven't had a drink for three months.

My days at work are becoming normal, something they never were. I'm sitting in my office at 8:30 A.M. drinking coffee, reading the paper and preparing myself for the day. No more flying in hung over at 9:45 or 10 A.M. and hiding out until the shakes subside. It's an enormous relief and I'm seeing what energy I really have to devote to a full day's work.

"Good morning, Joan. Are you ready for our auction today? Do you have all the figures for me?"

"Yes, Megan, everything's right here in the file. It looks as if you have some money to spend if you really think we can sell half a million copies. Personally, I loved the book and I've searched out everything else she's ever written."

"Well, if we can get you to endorse Sheila Cooper on national TV then we should get the sales! Thanks, Joan. Please ask Charlie and Paul to come in between nine-thirty and ten so we can prepare our strategy before the bidding begins."

"Right, Megan. Is there anything or anyone else you need as ammunition to convince Paul to hand over the bucks?"

"We're O.K. for now, but this auction remains today's first priority. Put everything else on the back burner and stay close at hand. Let's eat lunch in and spend the time between rounds reading choice tidbits from that six-foot-high pile of manuscripts."

"That's a great idea, Megan. I've been trying to get you to look through that stuff for months. It'll be a great way to keep your auction anxiety level in the medium range for at least a few minutes each hour."

"Very funny, Joan. Please order some coffee and danish for the big guys and myself from the French bakery, not that sickening place next door. And get my mother on the phone. If it's going to be one of those days, I might as well go all the way!"

"Fine, Megan. Do you want some champagne on hand to celebrate at the end of the day?"

"No, thanks, Joan. I don't want to jinx our chances."

We got the book! My head was on the line. Paul still thinks it was a mistake but Charlie and every other editor is behind me 100 percent. So what's $345,000 for a third novel by a writer previously published only by university presses? For starters, it's enough money to lose a job over if the book doesn't fly. But it will fly and Sheila Cooper is going to be very big—a female Updike. So why am I chain-smoking and wearing a hole in the carpet?

"Megan, you were splendid!" Charlie is clearly pleased. "We're all going to the Four Seasons for drinks. You need a couple to calm you down."

"I'd love to go because this really is a celebration. I'm just waiting for Sheila Cooper's agent to call so I can have a word with our new famous author."

"O.K., Megan. Come pick me up in my office when you're ready."

I knew I'd have to face the "celebration drink" sooner or later. I can't bow out tonight but I can call Carol and go fully prepared. After all, what better day for my first challenge? Tonight I'm speaking at my first meeting. That's all I have to remember while everyone is toasting me at the Four Seasons.

"Hi. My name is Megan and I'm an alcoholic. I've just come from having drinks with my boss and the president of my company at the Four Seasons. Tonight was different for me because I said 'No, thank you' to the champagne and drank Perrier. They were slightly taken aback since the champagne was in my honor, but they recovered quickly and soon forgot that I wasn't drinking alcohol. I, on the other hand, was very much aware of the fact that I wasn't drinking booze—and I was aware that that's an unnatural state for an alcoholic. I stayed for half an hour, laughing and celebrating our good fortune. Then I excused myself and hightailed it up here to meet my sponsor before this meeting.

"Today is my ninetieth day sober and this, of course, is my first qualification. I'm extremely nervous but anxious to tell my drinking story from start to finish and let you all know why I belong here. I drank for twelve years. From the time I picked up my first drink, I didn't stop until I crawled into my first meeting . . ."

I shared my experiences with alcohol for the first half of the meeting and then it was opened up and people shared from the floor. What a release! What a purge! I do feel cleansed and, more important, I feel like a "real" member of the fellowship. This is where I belong and I truly feel it tonight. I heard myself say at the end of my qualification that I was grateful to be sober today and a part of this fellowship. If I said it, I must believe it!

"Megan, you were wonderful! You were so articulate that we could really feel what it was like. Thank you for the meeting. And now, let's go out for some real celebrating, not to the Four Seasons for champagne, but to the café with the best chocolate mousse cake in town!" Carol hugged me and grabbed Diane and Pamela, and together with the three people who helped me to get sober, I finally was on my way to celebrate my anniversary!

LIVING SOBER

Have I lost some true friends since I stopped going to my regular bars and hangouts? I felt so terrible giving up that life, and in the first month sober I considered it a loss comparable to death. After I was sober about three weeks, I couldn't bear the thought that life was passing me by in Ryan's Bar. I knew everyone was there laughing and drinking and having a good time. So I did what I was told not to do. I went into Ryan's, sat down at the bar and ordered a club soda. My friend Johnny the bartender didn't ask why I wasn't drinking; he knew. If anybody in the world knows I'm a drunk, it's the bartender at Ryan's. We chatted and as customers arrived Johnny went to serve them and I sat with my club soda. I sat and I sat and I sat. It would have been boring had I not been booze-fighting, but I was staring at those bottles behind the bar and I wanted a drink. Johnny seemed concerned and uneasy. He refilled my club soda and insisted I have a hamburger. By his manner, I knew that even if I had ordered a drink, Johnny would not have served me. Maybe he spent some time himself in A.A., or maybe he had friends, but he knew I was off booze and I needed to stay that way.

The "gang" never arrived and when I asked Johnny about specific people and what was happening with them, he didn't know. I was beginning to think there wasn't a "gang" after all. At the end of the bar was another woman sitting alone.

She was very drunk and her head kept falling on the bar. I'd seen her at Ryan's for years although we had never been friends. I knew she was only a couple of years older than I and as I looked at her drunken struggle, I knew there must have been many nights when I looked like that. Trouble was, I could never see myself. I left some money on the bar and said goodbye. Johnny took my hand and shook it long and hard. He was saying goodbye for good.

Many, many gifts have been given to me in sobriety. Most important, I no longer end my nights on my living room floor and begin my days on my bathroom floor.

The transition from hopelessness to hope was so profound, so utterly complete and overwhelming, even though the accompanying act was as simple as walking into an A.A. meeting. For some people, it's picking up the phone and asking for help; for others it's putting down the last drink knowing that it's all over. In A.A., we call it a "spiritual awakening." There doesn't have to be a flash of light, or a voice in the wilderness (I heard plenty of voices when I was drunk and I knew it wasn't God speaking to me), or even a prayer. There is simply a moment when we see it's all over, and we choose life over death.

I hadn't been to church on a regular basis for years when I went to see Father Brennan. I went to see him because I could physically feel the sensation of my soul dying. It was truly as much a physical sensation as a spiritual one. I was hopeless and the spark inside that breathes life was about to go out. I knew that spark was my spirit and my soul and I went to a priest to have it fixed. No matter how much I hated myself and my life, I was not ready to die at age twenty-seven.

Father Brennan gave me hope because he understood. He understood because he is an alcoholic—and that's the "miracle" that got me sober. In almost every story I hear in A.A., there is a "miracle" that occurs in order to get each alcoholic sober. One person called A.A. and wound up talking to her college roommate, another went for his last drink and the bartender told him he was in A.A. and that he would help. You don't have to be a "holy roller" or a "born-again" Christian to call these miracles. You just have to be a person who was snatched from the hand of death to believe. I'm not a "born-again" anything. I'm an alcoholic who is sober today against all odds, and I didn't have much to do with it. I've been given my life back and for that reason I believe in miracles.

When I look back on my life, my perspective is a wise one. I know what's happened and I can examine the pieces in light of the experience I've gained. I can also look back at my life in terms of themes—success, happiness, growth, etc. But today I feel that the only truthful and accurate way to look at my life is in terms of drinks. There is a very clear path from the first drink to the last and it's in retrospect that I am learning my lessons about life.

I lived from one drink to the next. Drinks are my signposts along the way—from my first boyfriend to my eighteenth birthday, to college graduation, to my first job—drinks were had for every significant event in my life. But drinking wasn't reserved for significant events only—and that became my problem. There were too many drinks in between significant events to mark the most insignificant moments.

To see life in terms of drinks and drinking experiences is a bizarre way to look at the past, except for an alcoholic. While I was living and drinking alcoholically, I couldn't see that my only goal was to get from one drink to another. I thought my goal in life was to be happy. No. My goal was to be drunk. For much of the time, I chose to be miserable because that was *the* perfect reason for drinking. I was always searching for the perfect excuse to drink as much as I could, as fast as I could.

In an insane fashion, the progression of my life and my alcoholism is very orderly. Although my drinking caused a great deal of chaos in my life and the lives of those close to me (few people ever got close enough), after each chaotic experience you could be sure there would be another one. That's the orderly progression. At first, drunken evenings occurred once a month or less, then once a week, then once a day, and finally, two or three times a day. It's simple. Whenever I drank I got drunk. The more I drank, the more I got drunk, and the more I needed to drink. Alcoholism is a progressive disease. It gets worse over time. My disease progressed rapidly. After twelve years of drinking, I couldn't drink anymore because I had drunk too much and done too much damage. It wasn't a choice. I wanted to drink, I just couldn't get one more drink into my body.

It's a gift to be given the opportunity to look back and examine the past—to see my failures and be able to change so that I can stop making old mistakes. It's a very simple path that I'm on today. My only goal is to not drink today. By following that guideline, my life has changed 100 percent and I've had very little to do with the direction it's taking. If I stay out of my own way, my life gets better every day.

Richard Pryor did two minutes on being sober in his act on TV the other night. He exclaimed, "I'm sober!" and then explained to the audience that he had nothing to do anymore. He went home at night with nothing to do. And he was pissed. His shrink asked him how he felt now that he was sober and Pryor told the shrink, "I want to kill you."

I identified completely. Drinking took up a lot of time, and when I was first getting sober I didn't spend any nights at home alone. I spent my nights in meetings and then I went home, tired enough so that I didn't crave a drink. The thought would pass through my mind but I learned not to pay too much attention to it. I got to the point where I wouldn't consider having the drink but I still cried for it. I cried for months. Sometimes now I feel like crying when I indulge myself in booze fantasies. Sometimes I can conjure up the smell of scotch. I recently saw an ad on a bus shelter for a new brand of scotch. I stopped and read it and had a moment of anger that I would never get to taste that scotch.

When I was drinking, I wanted to drink all the drinks in the world. Sometimes now I think about all the drinks I've missed and I mourn them. It's very clear to me that I have a disease and it hasn't gone away even though I'm not drinking. I'm not feeding it but it's still lurking way down inside me, waiting for a chance to spring. It's better for me to admit that my alcoholism is still alive in me today than it is for me to think that I'm cured. Since I'm an alcoholic, it's natural for me to want to drink. I do not have to hide those drink signals for fear of being a bad A.A. We're all alcoholics and we all love booze. The fact that I and everyone else in A.A. doesn't drink today is what is unnatural, because the natural state for an alcoholic is to be drunk. So when I have drink signals, I tell my fellow A.A.'s and they help me to change my thinking, to become more comfortable in my sobriety and not to pick up the next drink.

Living sober is living for the first time for me and it's a much better life than my drunk one. I've grown to cherish my sobriety and my life, and I know one drink will destroy it all. I feel well, strong and happy today and the healthy part of me would never throw it all away for a drink, but my disease has only been arrested, not cured. I must be vigilant about protecting my sobriety. I can't take it for granted and I must grow and enrich my sobriety on a daily basis.

I'm constantly being reminded that I am a drunk. In A.A. they say, "Keep the memory green," which means don't forget your last drunk and don't forget how bad it was. Meetings help to keep the memory green and that's one of the reasons they are essential. Since I feel so good now, it's easy to forget the bad times and forgetting is dangerous for me. I don't spend all my time thinking about the past and talking about being an alcoholic. I have a full sober life today and I spend my time living it. But I give myself at least two moments during the day when I focus on my alcoholism: when I wake in the morning, I pray to God to keep me sober for the day, and when I go to bed at night, I thank him.

When I got to A.A. I thought it was the end of the line, the place where old elephants go to die. I imagined that my first meeting would be full of winos in rags with booze in paper bags. I didn't imagine that the drunks didn't drink in A.A.; I thought they tried to taper off and keep out of trouble.

I was surprised when I walked into my first meeting and couldn't find the drunks. Maybe they bring them out later, I thought. Certainly all these well-dressed, well-groomed smiling people can't be the A.A.'s. I was very confused. Then they started laughing at something the speaker said and the laughter hurt me so much. It had been so long since I had laughed or even heard a room full of laughter. I was in pain. I was hurting and I couldn't imagine that I'd ever laugh again. I came to A.A. to fade away. It was all over for me and there was no place else to go.

I didn't know then that A.A. would teach me to laugh, to love and to live, finally.

The black moods still come and they remind me of how it used to be. They are tempting and they suck me in. I am almost comfortable in a state of black depression and it is an effort to break free and return to reality. Sometimes it takes ten minutes, and other times three hours, but it no longer lasts long enough for me to become lost. When I come through, I am thoroughly drained, and each time I'm more amazed that I lived in these black holes for years. It's so cold, lonely and frightening in there. Life is much less frightening than the escape systems I developed for myself.

When I say I was given my life back when I got sober in A.A., I mean precisely that. Megan Moran was a shell of a person stripped of all self-esteem, all self-love, all sense of worth as a human being. All that was inside of me was booze and my addiction to it. As I got sober, the booze was replaced by the person. Fresh clean blood started flowing through my veins and feelings came back—physically and emotionally.

Megan Moran has turned out to be a person who, once released from the addiction of alcohol, believes in life again, in love again, in hope and faith and joy. A real person with real problems, real happiness, real feelings. My self doesn't come from the inside of a bottle anymore.

❀ ❀ ❀ ❀

The only way for an alcoholic to live sober is for him or her not to drink. Not at all. Not one drink. Not a sip. No booze period.

Social drinkers can have two drinks at a party and remain sober. Alcoholics can't; if they pulled it off at one party, it would only be a temporary condition. I've heard about people who've started drinking again after being in A.A. I've heard the whole story from ones who've gotten back to the program, and I've heard about the ones who couldn't make it back, who died proving they were social drinkers.

When an alcoholic starts drinking again to prove that this time he or she can handle it, it takes an enormous amount of control to pretend to be a social drinker. I've heard from alcoholics who drank two drinks a night for two years or two months and others who could last only two days, and the result was always the same. Once the addiction was fed and the craving set in, it was impossible to control. Those who held off for months or even years were in white-knuckled agony not drinking the way an alcoholic needs to drink. Eventually, alcoholism wins those tests of will. When it wins and the controls are off, the alcoholics will drink nonstop until they can't drink anymore. At that point they'll be lucky to have another opportunity to get sober and stay sober, or they won't.

When an alcoholic has gotten to the point where alcohol is calling all the shots, there's no returning to the world of social drinking. All attempts fail. I don't want to pretend to be a social drinker. I'd be in agony if I had to exist on two drinks a day. I know if I pick up the next drink, I won't stop at two—or even ten.

Living sober means more than not drinking. It means living a life not ruled by alcohol. Sobriety is true freedom for an alcoholic and the quality of a sober life usually exceeds wildest dreams. Happiness, contentment, productivity, success, joy—these can be the benefits of living sober and they're qualities that eluded most drinking alcoholics. An alcoholic sober in A.A. for a few years usually only has praise for sobriety, and will tell you that he or she doesn't want to drink again and lose it all.

Alcoholism is a disease. It has been diagnosed as such by the American Medical Association. The disease is physical, mental and spiritual.

It was most important for me to hear that I had a disease. I never imagined that I was a sick person and not a bad person. It helped so much to know that it was possible to get well and to stop thinking of myself as bad and totally bereft of morals.

Alcoholism can't be cured but it can be treated. The degenerative effects of the disease can be reversed if the alcoholic refrains from ingesting alcohol. This can be accomplished if the alcoholic can admit that he or she has a disease, that he or she is powerless over alcohol, and can stay away from the first drink for one day. A.A. teaches the alcoholic to stay sober, to arrest the disease for a day at a time. I go to A.A. meetings regularly as medicine to treat my disease. I don't think about not drinking for the rest of my life, I just don't drink for one day at a time, and A.A. helps me to get through each day sober.

I'm grateful to be alive today. I'm grateful to A.A. and I'm grateful to so many people who've helped me gain and sustain my sobriety. I cherish my life today and the people in it.

I'm grateful that when all the booze was taken away there really was a Megan Moran. The great revelation for me is that life is worth living without scotch on the rocks. Life isn't always pleasant but it's a constantly flowing, changing process and it's a good deal more interesting than sitting on a barstool staring at an empty face in the mirror.

The last thing in the world I wanted to do was give up booze but when booze controlled me there wasn't room for anything else. Today I don't want to take the life out of me and replace it with alcohol. Alcohol is a killer and I was dying before I got to A.A. I'm sure that if I pick up another drink, alcohol will finish me off. Maybe not tomorrow, but however I go there would be a bottle in my hand. But I'm not staying sober today because I'm afraid of dying; it's because I'm happy to be living this sober life and I want to grow and change and feel it all.

In order to do that, I just have to remember that I am an alcoholic and I can't pick up the first drink.

Alcoholism is a self-diagnosed disease. Nobody could have made me believe that I was an alcoholic and then forced me to get well. I had to accept my alcoholism for myself. At first I thought I was only in big trouble for the last two years of my drinking, when in reality I'd been a daily drinker for five years, and a steady, heavy drinker all my life. It took a little time for me to see the truth.

I was able to admit I was an alcoholic because I couldn't deny what alcohol had done to me; I was completely dependent on it.

Alcoholics come in all shapes, sizes and ages. Some come from alcoholic parents, others come from homes where a bottle of scotch lasted ten years. Some alcoholics drink daily and drink large quantities, as I did. Others are periodic drinkers—a binge every month or so—and still others only drink on weekends, or only drink after dark.

If you think you have a problem with alcohol, please understand that you don't have to drink the same way I did to be an alcoholic. It's not how much or how often you drink that makes you an alcoholic, it's what alcohol does to you. If it changes your personality or your behavior, if it causes temporary memory losses or "blackouts" (where did I park the car last night?), if you're drinking it for effect or to escape, if you feel dependent on it—these are all signs of a possible problem with alcohol. If alcohol is interfering with a normal life-style yet you can't seem to put it down—whether it's one drink an evening or one bottle—then maybe it's a problem. All you have to do is ask for help.